Education in Southern Africa

Available and Forthcoming Titles in the Education Around the World Series

Series Editor: Colin Brock

Education Around the World: A Comparative Introduction,
Colin Brock and Nafsika Alexiadou

Education in East Asia, edited by Pei-tseng Jenny Hsieh

Education in South-East Asia, edited by Lorraine Pe Symaco

Education in West Central Asia, edited by Mah-E-Rukh Ahmed

Forthcoming volumes

Education in Australia, New Zealand and the Pacific, edited by Michael
Crossley, Greg Hancock and Terra Sprague
*Education in the Commonwealth Caribbean and
Netherlands Antilles,* edited by Emel Thomas
Education in East and Central Africa, edited by Charl Wolhuter
Education in Eastern Europe and Eurasia, edited by Nadiya Ivanenko
Education in North America, edited by D. E. Mulcahy, D. G. Mulcahy and
Roger Saul
Education in West Africa, edited by Emefa Amoako

Also available from Bloomsbury

Education as a Global Concern, Colin Brock
*Comparative and International Education: An Introduction to Theory,
Method, and Practice,* David Phillips and Michele Schweisfurth

Education in Southern Africa

Clive Harber

BLOOMSBURY

LONDON • NEW DELHI • NEW YORK • SYDNEY

Bloomsbury Academic
An imprint of Bloomsbury Publishing Plc

50 Bedford Square	1385 Broadway
London	New York
WC1B 3DP	NY 10018
UK	USA

www.bloomsbury.com

Bloomsbury is a registered trade mark of Bloomsbury Publishing PLC

First published 2013

British Library Cataloguing-in-Publication Data
A catalogue record for this book is available from the British Library.

ISBN: HB: 978-1-4411-7149-8
       ePDF: 978-1-6235-6109-3
       ePub: 978-1-6235-6388-2

Library of Congress Cataloging-in-Publication Data
Education in Southern Africa / edited by Clive Harber.
pages cm
Includes bibliographical references and index.
ISBN 978-1-4411-7149-8 (hardback) – ISBN 978-1-62356-388-2 (epub) –
ISBN 978-1-62356-109-3 (epdf) 1. Education–South Africa. 2. Education and state–South Africa. I. Harber, Clive.
LA1536.E35 2013
370.968–dc23
2013011968

Typeset by Newgen Imaging Systems Pvt Ltd, Chennai, India
Printed and bound in Great Britain

Contents

Series Editor's Preface

The volumes in this series will look at education in virtually every territory in the world. The initial volume, *Education Around the World: A Comparative Introduction*, aims to provide an insight to the field of international and comparative education. It looks at its history and development and then examines a number of major themes at scales from local to regional to global. It is important to bear such scales of observation in mind because the remainder of the series is inevitably regionally and nationally based.

The identification of the regions within which to group countries has sometimes been a very simple task, elsewhere less so. Europe, for example, has multiple volumes and more than 50 countries. National statistics vary considerably in their availability and accuracy, and in any case date rapidly. Consequently the editors of each volume point the reader towards access to regional and international datasets, available online, that are regularly updated. A key purpose of the series is to give some visibility to a large number of countries that, for various reasons, rarely, if ever, have coverage in the literature of this field.

This volume, *Education in Southern Africa*, is one of four that together cover the countries of the African continent. The delimitation of these regions has had, necessarily, to be arbitrary to some extent, but for Southern Africa it has been relatively straightforward. This is because all but three of the countries included have a majority British colonial past and in the case of Mozambique, a former Portuguese colony, it was the first non-British territory to join The Commonwealth (in 1995). Namibia was a German colony until 1920 when it was mandated to South Africa, becoming independent in 1990 after being subjected to the *apartheid* regime of that country. The third special case is Madagascar, which has not been placed with the other Indian Ocean islands in another volume because of its massive scale and close proximity to the Southern African mainland. From 1897 until 1960 it was an overseas territory of France.

Sub-Saharan Africa is in general the poorest major region of the world, with all that it means for education. But this southern area, while including some of the poorest, also contains the large, influential and most developed nation on the continent, The Republic of South Africa (RSA). This has significance for the region, not least in terms of education, and especially the number and quality of universities in the RSA. So here we find extremes of diversity between rich and poor, including within the RSA, that are among the greatest in the world. Many innovations in education are evident in this region, some that may lead to the ability of subsistence populations to reach and maintain sustainable development.

As Series Editor I would like to thank Professor Clive Harber for undertaking the task of compiling and editing this book, bringing to it his immense expertise and vast experience of working in Southern Africa.

Colin Brock
Series Editor

The Contributors

Carrie Antal holds a Doctoral degree in International Development Education Policy from Florida State University, USA, where she specialized in teacher training for civic education in democratizing states. Her research and publications explore student-centred and experiential learning as tools for the strengthening of democratic competencies within and outside the school setting in Africa and the Middle East. After several years teaching in France, Madagascar and the United States, Dr Antal worked as an education programme evaluation consultant for national and international development firms. Today she serves as an Education Officer with USAID and is currently based in Rwanda.

Feliciano Chimbutane is Assistant Professor of Linguistics at Universidade Eduardo Mondlane, Mozambique. His research interests include languages in education, with focuses on classroom practice and the relationship between classroom discourse, day-to-day talk and the wider sociopolitical order. His most recent publication is *Rethinking Bilingual Education in Postcolonial Contexts*, published by Multilingual Matters.

Clive Harber is Emeritus Professor of International Education at the University of Birmingham, UK, and Honorary Professor at the University of South Africa, South Africa. From 1995 to 1999 he was Head of the School of Education at the then University of Natal, South Africa. He has carried out research and published widely on education and development in general and education in sub-Saharan Africa in particular. His main interests concern education and political development, particularly in relation to democracy, and education and violence. His most recent publication is *Education, Democracy and Development*, published by Symposium Books and co-authored with Vusi Mncube.

Gregory Hankoni Kamwendo is Professor of Language Education and Dean of the School of Education at the University of KwaZulu-Natal (UKZN), South Africa. Prior to joining UKZN, he taught and researched at the University of Malawi, Malawi, and the University of Botswana, Botswana. He has published on a wide range of topics within Sociolinguistics and Language Education. Some of his works appear in journals such as *Language Policy, Language Problems &*

Language Planning, Current Issues in Language Planning, Journal of Multilingual & Multicultural Development, Language Matters; English Today and *International Journal of the Sociology of Language.*

Mapheleba Lekhetho is a senior lecturer in the Department of Educational Leadership and Management in the College of Education at the University of South Africa (UNISA), South Africa. He has served in various management capacities in the field of education which include being a school principal, senior inspector of schools and Head of Department at the National University of Lesotho. His main research interests include school effectiveness, school improvement and education quality. He and Professor Julia Preece contributed a chapter to the book: *The Burden of Education Exclusion: Understanding and Challenging Early School Leaving in Africa*, published by Sense publishers.

Gilbert Likando is a Senior Lecturer and Director of the Rundu Campus, University of Namibia, Namibia. He holds a BA degree from the University of Nambia, an MA from the University of Salford (UK) and PhD from the Unuvesity of Namibia. He served in various capacities at the University of Namibia. He is the author of various articles and book chapters on the history of education, comparative education and adult literacy. His recently (2011) published book is, *Conceptualizing the Benefits of an Adult Literacy Programme in Namibia: A Case for the Caprivi Region* by Lambert publishers.

Nomanesi Madikizela-Madiya is a lecturer and a doctoral candidate in the College of Education at the University of South Africa, South Africa. She has carried out research and published in higher education, particularly on postgraduate educational research. Her main research interests arc in spatiality in relation to education and environmental and geography education. Her present doctoral project investigates how university space enables and/or constrains education lecturers' work towards the construction of their academic identities.

Edmund Z. Mazibuko is a senior lecturer in the Faculty of Education, Department of Curriculum and Teaching at the University of Swaziland, Swaziland. He holds a BEd degree from the University of Swaziland, Swaziland, an M.Ed from the University of Wales, UK and a PhD from Edith Cowan University in Australia, Australia. His research interests are in teaching and assessment practices with particular interest in secondary school history, assessment of soft skills in the secondary school curriculum and learner engagement in the classroom. Since 2008 he has been the Registrar/Chief Executive Officer at the Examinations Council of Swaziland.

Vusi S. Mncube is Associate Professor and Head of Department of Educational Leadership and Management in the College of Education at UNISA, South Africa. His main academic and research interests concern education for and in democracy. He has carried out research and published on various aspects of school governing bodies in South Africa in relation to education for a more democratic society. He has recently been leading a research team on violence in schools. His most recent work is *Education, Democracy and Development: Does Education Contribute to Democratisation in Developing Countries?* This was co-authored with Clive Harber in 2012.

Shireen Motala held the position of the Director of the Education Policy Unit, Wits University, South Africa, from 1999 to February 2010. In 2010, she was appointed as Director of the Postgraduate Research Centre: Research and Innovation at the University of Johannesburg, South Africa and Associate Professor in the Faculty of Education. Her research interests and expertise are in the areas of education financing and school reform, access and equity and education quality and she is widely published in peer reviewed journals and chapters in books on these areas.

Romain Kléber Ndrianjafy, Chargé d'étude au Secrétariat général du MEN (Ministere de l'éducation nationale), has lengthy experience in the education sector in Madagascar, first working as a high school mathematics instructor before being promoted to various positions of responsibility within the Ministry of National Education, including Director of the National Institute of Pedagogical Training (INFP) from 2004 to 2008, and Secretary General to the Minister of Education from 2008 to 2009. In these capacities, he contributed to the development of numerous education policy documents, including the Education For All Framework for Madagascar in 2005 and 2007, the Basic Education Reform in 2007, and the Reform of Post-Basic Education in 2008.

Nkobi O. Pansiri is Head of the Department of Primary Education at the University of Botswana, Botswana, and a chairperson of the Botswana Educational Research Association. He served in various positions in the Ministry of Education and Skills Development, including as head of Primary Education Inspectorate in the Ministry of Education from 1987 to 2002. He served as chairperson of SADC Technical Committee on Basic Education 1999–2002. He has participated in Commonwealth Education material development and training of headteachers and school inspectors. He has published in both local and international refereed educational journals. His research interest is educational management and policy and education for ethnic minority groups.

Aaron Sigauke lectures in Social Sciences Education at the University of New England, Australia. He has previously been a Teaching Fellow at Aberdeen University, UK and Lecturer at the University of Zimbabwe, Zimbabwe. His research interests are in citizenship education and democracy and education policy, social justice and inclusion. His publications include critical discourse analysis of policy documents, young people and teachers' views on citizenship education and adult literacy programmes in Zimbabwe. He has also contributed to chapters on low-cost resources for science education. He is a member of research organizations on citizenship education, social justice and inclusion in the United Kingdom and Australia.

Richard Tabulawa is Associate Professor of Education at the University of Botswana, Botswana, and is the current Dean of the Faculty of Education there. Between 1996 and 2000 he served as Head of Department. He has published articles in a number of world-class journals, which include *Comparative Education, International Journal of Educational Development, Journal of Curriculum Studies,* among others. He has a forthcoming book entitled *Teaching and Learning in Context: Why Pedagogical Reform Fails in Sub Saharan Africa* being published by CODESRIA. His areas of interest are geography education, pedagogy and education policy analysis, particularly the intersection of education and globalization processes.

Charl Wolhuter obtained a doctorate in Comparative Education at the University of Stellenbosch, South Africa. He was a junior lecturer in History of Education and Comparative Education at the University of Pretoria, South Africa and a senior lecturer in History of Education and Comparative Education at the University of Zululand, South Africa. He is currently Professor in Comparative Education at the Potchefstroom Campus of the North-West University, South Africa. In the winter semester of 2012 has was Visiting Professor of Comparative and International Education at Brock University, Canada. He is the author of various books and articles on the history of education and comparative education.

Introduction

Education in Southern Africa:
Patterns and Issues

Clive Harber
University of Birmingham

Introduction

This book sets out to provide an informative discussion of formal education in southern Africa. While no book of this nature can claim to provide a complete and fully comprehensive discussion of education in a particular region given the limitations of word length and book size, each of the chapters on individual countries does provide a detailed account of the history, structure and nature of education in that particular country. Each author or authors on a country were asked to discuss the historical and political background of the country as a context for education; the current basic structures of education in the country concerned; the main goals and priorities for education in terms of their underlying values and purposes as set out in key government policy documents; equity issues (e.g. social status, gender, race/ethnicity and disability) in relation to access to education, the internal processes of education and educational outcomes; the nature of the curriculum, teaching methods and assessment used in schools; the way in which schools are managed; the organization and nature of teacher education and issues of teacher recruitment and supply, remuneration and professionalism. The size, complexity and regional importance of South Africa necessitated more than one chapter so it was decided that there would be two chapters on that particular country – the first giving a broad overview and the second focusing more specifically on issues of equity in post-apartheid educational reform.

The precise way each author or authors has discussed these topics of course varies from chapter to chapter depending on the particular background and interests of the writer(s). However, the purpose of this introductory chapter is to present an overall picture of education in southern Africa – what do the countries have in common, to what extent are they a community of states, what patterns of education exist across the region and what common issues does education face? Inevitably, to some extent the answers to the last of these questions also reflect the issues that the writer of this chapter himself is interested in or sees as particularly pertinent. However, these are also themes that have emerged from the individual country chapters themselves and reference is made to relevant sections of individual chapters as part of the present overall discussion of education in southern Africa. The chapter begins with an examination of the contextual background of southern Africa – what is the nature of the countries concerned and what are their historical experiences? It then continues with a discussion of the positive nature of developments in education in southern Africa in relation to access and the nature of provision as well as policy towards curriculum and teaching methods before going on to discuss a range of continuing, significant and problematic issues still confronting education in southern Africa: the quality of education, teaching methods, the nature of teacher education, school organization and teacher professionalism, Human Immunodeficiency Virus (HIV)/Acquired Immunodeficiency Syndrome (AIDS) and gender relationships within education.

It is important to note that some form of indigenous education has always taken place in all societies in Africa in the sense of passing on, for example, economic practices, cultural expectations and rituals, food preparation, laws and health practices whether learning by example or from written sources or from stories, songs, folklore, proverbs, dances or myths. Often this was a form of learning integrated into normal daily social practices – the young would observe, listen, copy and practice what they saw around them in their family, village or town and sometimes improve upon it (Omolewa, 2007). However, this differs from the systems of formal education then introduced through missionaries and colonialism in southern Africa with its separate institutions and buildings called a 'school' and with its specialist teachers and a planned curriculum that went beyond traditional knowledge. It is this latter form of education that was inherited at independence by the countries represented in this book and then both expanded and altered in the ways discussed in each of the chapters. Finally, it is important to note that use of the term 'Black', 'white', 'Indian' or 'coloured' in the text, particularly in the chapters on South Africa and Namibia, does not refer to a fixed or biological concept of race, but to the legacy of the social and political system of racial classification under apartheid which still permeates educational debate in parts of southern Africa.

Contextual background

The nine countries of Southern Africa discussed in this book have certain contextual similarities in common as well as differences between them. One key similarity is the level of human development – all are 'developing' countries. While attempts to classify states as 'developed' or 'developing' are fraught with difficulty and controversy, perhaps the most authoritative international statement on issues surrounding human development is the annual publication of the United Nations Development Programme (UNDP) entitled the Human Development Report. The Human Development Index (HDI) is an annual attempt to rank all countries in the world according to three key indicators of development – life expectancy at birth, years of schooling of the population and gross national income per capita. All nine countries discussed in this book feature in the bottom half of the HDI. In the 2011 index of 187 countries, for example, Botswana was ranked 118, Namibia 120, South Africa 123, Swaziland 140, Madagascar 151, Lesotho 160, Malawi 171, Zimbabwe 173 and Mozambique 184 (UNDP, 2011: 128–30).

However, the size of the populations (and hence level of economic activity) varies considerably with South Africa being the largest and most economically dominant country in the region having a population of just under 51 million, followed by Mozambique and Madagascar with populations of just under 23 and just under 22 million respectively, Malawi with a population of 14 million, Zimbabwe with 12.5 million and the (in population terms) smaller countries of Namibia, Botswana and Lesotho at just over 2 million each and Swaziland at just over a million.

Historically all the nine countries discussed in this book have experienced some form of colonialism and subsequent independence, though sometimes this was as the result of a violent struggle (as in Mozambique, Namibia and Zimbabwe and, to a certain extent, South Africa) and sometimes it was the result of a more peaceful transition. Politically, however, there has been considerable variety as a result, though since the early 1990s multiparty democracy has been the dominant form of government and politics in the region. Botswana, which gained its independence from Britain in 1966, having the longest tradition in this regard as it:

> ... stands out as a unique example of an enduring multi-party democracy with a record of sound economic management, that has used its diamond riches for national advancement and maintained an administration free of corruption. (Meredith, 2006: 686)

In 1964 Malawi also gained independence from Britain, though this was followed by a long period of one-party rule under President Hastings Banda which ended in 1994 with the return to multiparty democracy. Namibia achieved independence in 1990 after 100 years of colonization by Germany and South Africa and a war of independence and has operated as a democracy ever since. South Africa, formerly a British colony and then a white/Afrikaaner state, gained its full independence with its first free elections in 1994. After independence from Portugal in 1974 and a subsequent bitter civil war, Mozambique adopted mutliparty democracy in 1994. However, in all these cases, while an opposition exists and free elections take place, there is a dominant political party (or split-off or reformed version of one in both Lesotho and Malawi) which has yet to lose power. From 1992 to 2009, after independence from France in 1960 and periods of military-influenced rule and alignment with the socialist states of eastern Europe, Madagascar also had multiparty democratic rule, though the change of government in 2009 resembled more of a coup d'état than a democratic election.

Zimbabwe became 'independent' from Britain in 1965 after a Universal Declaration of Independence by a white minority government. The following guerrilla war led to full independence after elections in 1980. Subsequently Zimbabwe has operated as only a semi-democratic state at best with evidence of intimidation and fraud by the ruling party at general elections. Unusually in the region, Swaziland remains a functioning monarchy with members of the legislature being elected on an individual rather than party political basis.

So, to what extent does southern Africa constitute an authentic sub-regional bloc of countries within Africa? To what extent do they see themselves as a community? Certainly all the countries in this book are members of the Southern African Development Community (SADC) which was born out of a desire to forge 'developmental regionalism' – the pursuit of greater socio-economic co-operation and integration as well as political co-operation to foster development through attracting foreign investment (Kamwendo, 2009: 5). Its vision,

. . . is one of a common future within a regional community that will ensure economic well-being, improvement in the standard of living and quality of life, freedom and social justice, peace and security for the peoples of Southern Africa. This shared vision is anchored on the common values and principles and the historical and cultural affinities that exist among the peoples of Southern Africa. (www.sadc.int/index/browse/page/52)

In 1997 SADC approved the Protocol on Education and Training which provides the legal framework for co-operation in the field of education and training. While it is not the purpose of this chapter to go into the nature or progress of the protocol in any detail, it is worth noting that one of the underlying principles is that 'Member States should take all possible steps to act together as a community in the gradual implementation of equivalence, harmonisation and standardisation of their education and training systems . . .' (www.sadc.int/ english/key-documents). While doubtless continuing to work towards greater 'equivalence, harmonisation and standardisation', it is nevertheless informative to initially consider educational patterns across the nine countries under discussion here in terms of access, provision, curriculum and teaching methods before discussing some major issues facing education in the region.

Access to education and the nature of provision

One of the key features of education across the region is the rapid growth in access to, and provision of, education since independence, both state and private. Moreover, it is also important to bear in mind the context of colonial and apartheid histories of education, especially, for example, in Namibia, South Africa and Zimbabwe, and that in principle access is now open to all regardless of skin colour or ethnic background.

In Chapter 1 on Botswana, for example, Tabulawa and Pansiri talk of and discuss the 'phenomenal growth of school education provision', including the scrapping of fees at the primary and, to a certain extent, junior secondary levels. Moreover, the government of Botswana has made considerable efforts to improve retention and reduce dropout rates. In Lesotho, Lekhetho notes that free primary education was accomplished in 2006, a bursary scheme for orphaned and vulnerable children in secondary schools was introduced in 2002 and a textbook rental scheme in secondary education in 2004 to reduce the cost of textbooks. As described in Chapter 3, the transformation of the national education landscape in Madagascar began later than in other countries in 2003 when,

> . . . the challenge of inadequate access was addressed through the elimination of primary school fees and the introduction of a program to annually distribute basic school supplies to students. These policies produced a leap in primary enrollment from 67 per cent in 2001 to 97 per cent in 2005 (World Bank, 2005), accompanied by the rehabilitation or construction of two thousand classrooms each year to improve school proximity in rural areas and prevent an unmanageable inflation in class sizes. (MENRS, 2003)

However, there have been declines in enrolment since the semi coup d'état of 2009 and subsequent cuts in donor funding to education. In Chapter 5 on Mozambique Chimbutane notes that when the civil war ended in 1992,

> The government abolished enrolment fees in primary education, provided free textbooks to pupils, constructed more schools with donors and communities' involvement and built teacher training institutes nationwide. As a consequence of these measures, there are now more people attending school in Mozambique, there are more trained primary school teachers, primary completion rates have improved, from 14 per cent in 1999 to 58 per cent in 2010 (MINED 1999, 2011b), and illiteracy has dramatically dropped from 93 per cent at independence to nearly 48 per cent in 2007. (Commissao National do Plano, 1985)

Wolhuter and Likando point out in Chapter 6 that,

> Namibia's post-independence policies have prioritized a rapid build-up of the educated and skilled human resources required to support economic growth and equitable social development.

In South Africa Motala in Chapter 8 discusses the high level of government spending on education, high rates of participation and how the post-apartheid South African government has attempted to achieve equitable access to education for all through measures such as the fee exemption policy and 'No Fee' schools. Finally, as Sigauke notes in Chapter 10 on Zimbabwe, between independence in 1980 and the late 1990s the number of children in primary schools increased threefold and by a factor of 12 in secondary education.

What then is the present overall pattern of educational provision in the region? In terms of educational provision, each country in the world is ranked by the United Nations (UN) according to mean years of schooling and expected years of schooling. Mean years of schooling is the average number of years of education received by people aged 25 and older whereas expected years of schooling is the number of years of schooling that a child of school entrance age can expect to receive if prevailing patterns of age-specific enrolment rates persist throughout the child's life.

As Table 0.1 shows, there is a considerable range of actual years of schooling that has been experienced by people over 25 in the nine countries but in all cases the expectation is that this is rising sharply. Increasing access to schools has indeed been one of the major achievements of governments in southern Africa. The gross enrolment ratio (GER) is the total enrolment in a given level of education regardless of age expressed as a percentage of the official school-age population for the same level of education. Here the primary GER figures for southern Africa are above 100 per cent because of older children and young people attending school when they get the opportunity. What is immediately noticeable are the sharply tapering figures for progression onto secondary and higher education, something much less marked in 'developed' or industrialized countries. As described in the individual country chapters, each country has its own system for training teachers and, from Table 0.1 another positive factor is that, in five out of the six countries where data is available, pupils are taught primarily by trained teachers, which is not always the case in all developing countries (UNDP, 2011).

Table 0.1 Educational provision in southern Africa

Country	Mean Education	Expected Education	P:T Ratio	GER Primary	GER Secondary	GER Tertiary	Trained Teachers %
Botswana	8.9	12.2	25.2	109.4	81.5	7.6	97.4
Lesotho	5.9	9.9	33.8	104.4	45.0	3.6	57.6
Madagascar	5.2	10.7	47.9	160.4	31.5	3.6	NA
Malawi	4.2	8.9	NA	119.3	29.5	NA	NA
Mozambique	1.2	9.2	58.5	115.7	25.5	1.5	75.9
Namibia	7.4	11.6	30.1	112.1	64.7	8.9	95.6
South Africa	8.5	13.1	30.7	101.2	93.9	NA	87.4
Swaziland	7.1	10.6	32.4	107.9	53.3	4.4	94.0
Zimbabwe	7.2	9.9	NA	NA	NA	NA	NA
Average	**6.2**	**10.7**	**36.9**	**116.3**	**53.1**	**4.9**	**84.7**

P:T – Pupil/Teacher Ratio
GER – Gross Enrolment Ratio
Source: UNDP (2011)

In terms of access to education, the overall picture for the nine countries in southern Africa discussed in this book also shows a marked improvement in the position of girls, compared to traditional gender inequalities in access to formal education in Africa (Unterhalter & Oommen, 2008). While most of the chapters comment positively on efforts to improve female access to education, Table 0.2 provides an overall picture by setting out figures for enrolment by gender in each of the nine countries.

In some countries the attempt to ensure gender equity has gone beyond access to the nature of schooling experienced by girls. As Kamwendo points out in relation to Malawi in Chapter 4,

> Malawi has, for example, been taking a number of measures to ensure that its entire education system is gender-friendly and gender-sensitive. This can be noticed in areas such as curriculum development and learning and teaching materials development. For example, school curricula at various levels have been revised to make them gender-sensitive . . . In addition, some donors are assisting in the development and establishment of gender-balanced schools. The goal is also to bring schools closer to communities for the purpose of reducing girls' walking distances to school. There is also a policy that allows pregnant girls to leave school, and then later resume school after giving birth.

Table 0.2 Enrolment in education by gender percentage 2008

Country	GER Primary Boys	GER Primary Girls	GER Secondary Boys	GER Secondary Girls
Botswana	111	109	78	82
Lesotho	108	107	34	45
Madagascar	154	149	31	29
Malawi	119	122	37	27
Mozambique	121	107	24	18
Namibia	113	112	61	71
South Africa	106	103	93	97
Swaziland	112	104	56	50
Zimbabwe	104	103	43	39
Average	**116**	**113**	**51**	**51**

GER – Gross Enrolment Ratio
Source: UNESCO (2011)

Moreover, the education of children with special educational needs has also become much more of a concern in countries in the region. For example, as described in Chapter 4 on Malawi,

> There are three modes through which learners access SNE [Special Needs Education] in Malawi, namely: residential special schools, resource rooms within ordinary schools and itinerant programmes within which SNE teachers travel to schools within their zone or district and provide SNE to learners with disabilities.

In Zimbabwe Sigauke notes in Chapter 10 that,

> During the pre-independence era disabled children were cared for by mission stations and non-governmental organizations. They were segregated in society and therefore given little opportunity in education. Now it is government responsibility to make sure that people with disability receive the same quality of education like their able-bodied counterparts.

In Swaziland efforts are being made to ensure better provision for special educational needs and that schools are safe places for all children as noted by Mazibuko In Chapter 9 since the Ministry of Education and Training,

> . . . is committed to ensuring that children are safe and protected all the time. There are a number of initiatives in place for the protection of children. These include setting up a National Children Coordinating Unit (NCCU) within the MOET and establishing a 'call-in line' for children to report cases of abuse. A Southern African Development Community (SADC) initiative called Schools as Centres of Care and Support (SCCS) is being implemented in schools to ensure that children are safe, healthy, and secure in schools.

Indeed, as Chapters 6 and 7 show, in line with the wider system of political democracy, secondary schools in both Namibia and South Africa are now supposed to be organized along more inclusive and democratic lines generally with a range of key stakeholders, including learners, being involved in school decision-making. Mncube and Madikizela-Madiya's chapter discusses in some detail the extent to which this has been implemented in South Africa.

Curriculum and teaching methods

In all countries the curriculum has been substantially revised since independence to make it more contextually relevant and to try to meet the needs of the local society and with an eye to the global economy. Assessment systems have also been localized and in some countries, such as Botswana, assessment has also been reformed to test a more diverse range of skills and knowledge.

The region has also witnessed attempts to move away from sole reliance on teacher-centred classroom methods towards more diverse, learner-centred pedagogy. As Tabulawa says in relation to Botswana in Chapter 1,

> Learner-centred pedagogy is the officially mandated pedagogy in schools in Botswana. Also, pre-service and in-service teacher education programmes reflect an emphasis on the promotion of this form of teaching/teaching, and substantial resources have been committed to its promotion.

While, as Chapter 3 points out, in Madagascar the new curriculum introduced in 2007,

> ... was designed to engage children as active participants in the learning process, strengthen their critical thinking skills and love of learning, and enable them to become well-rounded, open-minded citizens.

And in Madagascar this has been supported via teacher education,

> Learner-centred, participatory forms of pedagogy are taught theoretically and student-teachers are encouraged to attempt them while in the primary classroom (MENRS, 2005). These reforms built upon an already promising foundation: a UNESCO study ... found that while the majority of CRINFP instruction time (70%) was lecture-based, 20 per cent was dedicated to group work activities, with another 10 per cent dedicated to research and individual learning activities.

While Chapter 6 on Namibia further notes that,

> With the introduction of the new curriculum in 1993 it was decided that the teaching approach would be learner-centred where the classroom practice would reflect and reinforce both values and practices of democracy.

In South Africa Mncube and Madikizela-Madiya note in Chapter 7 that,

> ... the Outcomes-Based curriculum, known as Curriculum 2005 and introduced in 1997, was designed to facilitate more active, participant and democratic forms of learning by focusing more on the desired outcomes of learning than specific content.

While Motala in Chapter 8 adds on South Africa that,

> The new Revised National Curriculum Statements (RNCS) give more emphasis to basic skills, content knowledge and grade progression, and combine a

learner-centred curriculum requiring critical thought and emphasizing the democratic values with an appreciation of the importance of content and support for teachers.

Finally, in Zimbabwe Sigauke adds that,

> a diversity of innovative teaching/learning methodologies have to be used. These include child-centred and discovery approaches which are motivating to young people so that they desire to be in school.

However, while there is much good news about educational developments in southern Africa there are continuing causes for concern as well and some of these key concerns will be discussed in the remaining sections of this chapter.

The quality of education

One such concern is with the quality of education. First, there is the issue that, despite significant increases in access to education overall, access to good quality education still depends to a large extent on the ability to pay for it. This is argued strongly in, for example, Motala's chapter on South Africa and Sigauke's on Zimbabwe. In this way post-colonial education continues to be socially and economically reproductive.

Second, many of the chapters in this book express serious concerns about the poor quality of education experienced by pupils in southern African schools in general. As even a recent book which set out to identify signs of change resilience and the will to succeed in African education, nevertheless, had to admit that,

> On the face of it, the news on educational development in Africa, especially when assessed against indicators such as 'good quality of education for all', appears to be grim. Indeed, for many countries the sheer task of overhauling what are, to a large degree, dysfunctional systems of education is so overwhelming that it is difficult to think in terms of changes and progress. (Johnson, 2008: 7)

Indicative of this are the outcomes of schooling. Verspoor notes in relation to Africa that,

> Less than one third of the children of school leaving age currently acquire the knowledge and skills specified in their national primary education curriculum. (2008: 13)

So what is the position in Southern Africa? In Botswana, Lesotho, Malawi, Namibia, South Africa, Swaziland and to a certain extent in Zimbabwe the good

Table 0.3 Levels and trends in pupil achievement of grade 6 learners

Country	PRS 2000	PRS 2007	PMS 2000	PMS 2007
Botswana	521.1	534.6	512.9	520.5
Lesotho	451.2	467.9	447.2	476.9
Malawi	428.9	433.5	432.9	447.0
Mozambique	516.7	476.0	530.0	483.8
Namibia	446.8	496.9	430.9	471.0
South Africa	492.3	494.9	486.1	494.8
Swaziland	529.6	549.4	516.5	540.8
Zimbabwe	504.7	511.8	NA	519.8
Average	**486.4**	**495.6**	**480.6**	**494.3**

PRS = Pupil Reading Score; PMS = Pupil Mathematics Score

Source: The Southern and Eastern Africa Consortium for Monitoring Educational Quality (www.sacmeq.org)

news is that the situation is improving both in terms of reading and mathematics (see Table 0.3).

Only in Mozambique do the scores deteriorate over time, reflecting the concern with quality that is a key theme of Chimbutane's chapter, though, as Motala argues in Chapter 8, there is considerable concern with the perceived low levels of educational outcomes in South Africa as well. However, while there is definitely evidence of a positive trend, it is also important to note that there is still some way to go internationally. The average Southern and Eastern Africa Consortium for Monitoring Educational Quality (SACMEQ) maths score for the eight countries in 2000 was 480.6 and in 2007 was 494.3, very similar in both cases to that of South Africa. In 2002 the South African Human Sciences Research Council administered the Third International Mathematics and Science Study test to a sample of grade 8 learners in South Africa. The South African learners achieved 264 as opposed to the global international average of 467 (Bloch, 2009: 63/4).

As a number of chapters in this book also suggest, the quality of education in southern Africa is held back by under-resourced schools and classrooms, especially in rural areas. Chapter 2 on Lesotho, for example, notes that,

> . . . many schools with small enrolments in sparsely populated, hard-to-reach mountain areas are terribly under-resourced and educationally unviable. In most cases, teaching is conducted in decrepit, poorly constructed buildings, usually church halls or in the open air. Most teachers in these one- or two-teacher schools are unqualified and yet they do multigrade teaching. These wide disparities in the quality of facilities between schools based on geographic

area predetermine the quality of teachers who teach in them, and the quality of education pupils receive, in the sense that it is usually the unqualified teachers who teach in schools in the hardship areas.

While Chapter 9 on Swaziland argues that,

Some of the challenges facing government at this level include, amongst others; not enough classrooms to cater for the increase in enrolment resulting from the introduction of free primary education; overcrowding is some classes, particularly in grades 1 to 4; not enough primary school teachers for the increase in enrolment; inadequate teaching and learning resources; and these raise questions regarding the quality of education provided in the context of free primary education.

Chapter 4 on Malawi notes that,

Another challenge is that generally Malawian schools are poorly supplied with teaching and learning resources. For example, it is not uncommon to find some pupils learning under trees while others learn in thatched huts. Some classrooms have no desks and pupils have to sit on the floor. Books and other teaching and learning materials are also in inadequate supply. When books are available, they may have to be shared among the pupils. Overcrowded classrooms pose another serious challenge in Malawi.

While Chapter 10 on Zimbabwe notes that,

At the school level classroom congestion and double sessions in urban schools has led to shortages of resources (textbooks, stationary, furniture) in addition to the deterioration of buildings and other facilities that are in need of repair.

However, there are three other factors at work hindering the improvement of educational quality as well. One of these is the teaching methods used in schools, a second is the nature of teacher education and the third is school organization and teacher professionalism and these are dealt with in the following three sections.

Teaching methods

Verspoor (2008) not only notes that learning achievement is so low in Africa that after several years of schooling many students have still not obtained basic literacy and numeracy skills, he also notes the continuing dominance of traditional, rote teaching methods in classrooms and how difficult these are to change. Indeed, despite frequent adherence to the language of learner-centred teaching methods in official documentation, African schools have long been characterized by hierarchical organization, transmission teaching and teacher-centred classrooms. Evidence on this in southern Africa specifically comes from Malawi (Fuller, 1991: 68), Botswana (Prophet & Rowell, 1990; Tabulawa, 1995; Tafa, 2002) and Zimbabwe (Nagel, 1992). In Mozambique one study ranked different pupil activities by the amount of time pupils spend on them. Ranked first was listening to teachers – the probability is that a pupil will get to speak once every second day and even then will be repeating the teacher's sentences, or sentences from the textbook. Second in importance is waiting – for the teacher to begin the lesson, for the teacher to write things on the board, for their classmates to finish exercises, which they have already finished and for their work to be corrected. The third most common activity was copying. The author comments that 'the dominant classroom interaction pattern, then, seems to be that of overwhelmingly passive pupils whose activities are limited to be almost entirely reproductive in nature' (Palme, 1997: 196).

According to the chapters in this book, this pattern remains despite positive efforts to introduce more democratic, learner-centred teaching methods as outlined above. Chapter 7 in this book by Mncube and Madikizela-Madiya notes that a study of schooling in rural South Africa found that while 90 per cent of teachers claimed to be using a variety of active teaching methods, the responses from pupils and the observations of the researchers strongly suggested that the majority of teachers continued to use traditional, teacher-centred methods of monologue and rote learning. Classroom activity was dominated by three modes: reading, writing and correcting. Motala also notes in Chapter 8 of this book in relation to South Africa that,

> In research conducted in 14 schools in the Eastern Cape and Gauteng, the absence of written work in classrooms was striking, rote learning and chorusing of lessons was common, and coverage of the curriculum was very uneven.

In Chapter 5 Feliciano Chimbutane argues in relation to Mozambique that,

> Despite efforts to change the status quo, overall pedagogy remains teacher-centred and teacher discourse remains authoritarian. In general, lessons are organized in a platform format, the teacher is the one who speaks most of the time, uses question-and-answer techniques and evaluates pupils' contributions. Pupils are expected to listen attentively to teachers' discourse, answer their questions, take notes, and follow instructions. In most cases, when pupils raise

questions and challenge teachers' authority, they are taken as *indisciplinados*, that is, as unruly students.

In Chapter 1 on Botswana Tabulawa writes that,

Studies on teaching in Botswana schools report a resilience of teacher-centred approaches (Tabulawa, 1997, 2009). Explanations for this resilience range from technical factors such as poorly trained teachers, selective examinations and limited resources, to substantive issues such as culture and the influence of the enveloping social structure. Also militating against institutionalization of learner-centred methods is the behaviourist model of curriculum development discussed above. The highly specified content leaves no room for teacher initiative. Such a situation reduces the teacher's role to that of a 'technician who dispenses pre-packaged chunks of knowledge without any ethical consideration of what they are doing' (Tabulawa, 2009: 101). It is almost impossible for learner-centred pedagogy to thrive under these circumstances.

In Chapter 4 on Malawi Kamwendo notes that,

. . . teacher-centredness remains predominant in both primary and secondary schools in Malawi (Mizrachi et al., 2010). There is still a need for teachers to embrace active-learning or student-centred pedagogies.

In Chapter 10 on Zimbabwe Sigauke describes the diverse range of teaching methods that are supposed to occur in schools but notes that in reality this only tends to happen in relatively well-to-do schools because of problems with human and material resources and in Chapter 9 on Swaziland Mazibuko states that,

Teacher-centred teaching approaches characterized the old curriculum where teaching methods used were lectures, note giving, handouts and all those techniques that focused on predicting examination questions and focusing on those areas that were likely to come up in the examination. The interest on how schools are performing in public examinations and the role of the media in ranking schools is also putting a lot of pressure on teachers as early as primary school to teach for the test rather than to teach learners for conceptual understanding. Studies conducted since the introduction of the IGCSE and subsequently the SGCSE indicate that though the new curriculum puts emphasis on the development of skills, the teaching methods used by teachers do not reflect this focus as teachers continue to use teaching methods that are not aligned to the assessment objectives in the syllabus (Zondo, 2009; Msibi, 2010). This has resulted in students performing badly in public examinations.

Finally, in Chapter 3 on Madagascar Antal and Ndrianjafy show how historically there has been an emphasis on obedience and deference in education with 'a pedagogical overreliance on lecture and chorused responses to teachers' questions'. Attempts at reform during the first republic (1960–75) were not entirely successful as,

> . . . moving away from didactic, teacher-centred methods of instruction nonetheless remained a challenge in spite of efforts to transform pedagogy at Madagascar's new teacher training institutes.

During the more socialist second republic (1975–91) in Madagascar there was a continued prevalence of teacher-centred pedagogy. Attempts at reforming classroom teaching in the direction of critical thinking, participation decision-making and problem-solving after 2007 have been somewhat stifled and delayed by the change government brought about by the coup d'état of 2009.

One negative aspect of the persistence of authoritarian classroom relationships is the continued existence of corporal punishment in at least some countries of southern Africa. The Southern African Network to End Corporal and Humiliating Punishment of Children at its sixth annual meeting in 2011 noted that corporal punishment was still commonly used in Namibia. In Swaziland there are specific rules about the use of corporal punishment but teachers do not follow the regulations (www.rapcan.org.za). In South Africa, where it has been officially banned, it is still widely used (Nelson Mandela Foundation, 2005). In Botswana, where corporal punishment is legal and still takes place,

> Caning became ingrained in the popular minds as critical to school discipline hence the common refrain that its abolition equals classroom disorder and failure. The result is a cycle of caning transmitted from one generation to another and justified on the basis of experience and sentiment . . . In a class of 35–40 authoritarianism is a means of orchestrating 'mob control'. Instant punishment and military style parades typical of Botswana schools are all about social control. Teachers are saddled with systemic constraints of large and mixed class sizes for which no extra resources were made available. (Tafa, 2002: 23)

While on the effects of corporal punishment in Botswana Humphreys adds that,

> The more obvious effects of corporal punishment included increased student anxiety, fear or resentment in class. Girls, in particular, remained silent, and were mistakenly dubbed as 'lazy' or 'shy' by some teachers, and so did some

boys. Other boys absconded or refused to cooperate in female teachers' classes
... Other studies have also found that excessive physical punishment, generally
of boys, can prompt truancy. (2006)

Teacher education

Part of the problem to the continuation of teacher-centred and authoritarian
classrooms is teacher education. While many of the chapters discuss the
structure of teacher education provision, here the concern is more with the
nature of the teacher education provided. In many countries teacher education
actually tends to help to perpetuate authoritarian practices rather than be a
source of more democratic ones. This is because in practice teacher education
tends to perpetuate traditional, unreflective and teacher-centred pedagogy
rather than challenge it. Some 35 years ago Bartholemew put forward the idea
of the 'myth of the liberal college' – that it is a myth that there is a contradiction
between the liberal, progressive and democratic college or university on the one
hand and the traditional, conservative and authoritarian school on the other
(Bartholemew, 1976). This myth suggests that student-teachers are exposed to
more radical, democratic forms of teaching and learning during their courses in
higher education with a high emphasis on learner participation but are rapidly
re-socialized into more authoritarian understandings and practices during their
teaching practice and their subsequent employment in education. However,
rather than there being a contradiction between the two, in terms of power over
what is taught and learned, how and when, it is argued that in reality teacher
education is often an authoritarian and reproductive preparation for teaching in
schools. There is a contradiction in teacher education between 'do as I say', and
'do as I do'.

The Multi-Site Teacher Education Research Project (MUSTER) was the first
major study of teacher education in developing countries – including Ghana,
Lesotho, Malawi and South Africa since the 1980s. Its findings (Lewin & Stuart,
2003) suggested that teaching in teacher education in fact resembled traditional
high school teaching methods and was lecture-based with most teaching
following a transmission style with question and answer sessions. Overall,
the studies found that the curriculum in teacher education was informed by
a conservative, authoritarian ideology where debate and critical reflection was
not encouraged. This reality was at odds with the principles of participatory,

learner-centred and enquiring pedagogy frequently espoused in curriculum documents of the teacher education institutions. Indeed, there seemed to be a kind of collusion between tutors and trainees, who knew little else from their schooling, to maintain the transmission mode because students found project work 'difficult' and group work 'less useful'.

MUSTER published a number of case studies from Africa. Each of these commented on the seeming predominance of lecturer-centred, transmission teaching, an emphasis on recall and a discouragement of independent learning and reflective practice. There is also a significant gap between the priority given to abstract academic theoretical knowledge in colleges and universities as opposed to the practical skills and application of knowledge also required to succeed in the reality of the classroom.

In teacher education in Malawi,

> Much learning is undertaken in a transmission style where information is projected with few opportunities for students to engage in debate and reflection. Questions were often informational and recall-based and much of the teaching appeared examination-driven, rarely departing from material likely to found in assessment tasks. Few attempts seem to be made to capitalise on trainee insights into teaching and learning based on their experience in schools. (Kunje et al., 2003: xiii)

While in Lesotho,

> Classroom observation confirmed the conservative nature of the programme in that, in practice, most teaching at the College is transmission-oriented, and there is little emphasis on independent learning, critical analysis, creative thought or learning to exercise professional judgement. The interaction between students and tutors during lectures involves a question-answer approach but questions are restrictive and do not allow for full independent thinking for students. (Lefoka & Sebatane, 2003: x)

Kunje et al. make a distinction between teacher education as preparing the 'teacher as technician' and training the teacher as a 'teacher as reflective practitioner',

> The technician is seen as having a restricted role, her job being to deliver the curriculum – which is prescribed at a higher level – as effectively as possible, while the reflective practitioner is expected to play a more extended role, that may include developing the curriculum to suit the context, evaluating and trying to improve her own practice, and mentoring new teachers. (2003: 63)

Again, there are suggestions that this problem remains in southern Africa. In Chapter 5, for example, Felciano Chimbutane writes on teacher education in Mozambique that,

> . . . there is some evidence leading to the conclusion that 'teaching quality and pedagogical methods used to teach student teachers in IFPs are poor, which then transfer to children's learning in classrooms when these IFP graduates are deployed to schools' (Crouch, 2011: 35). This conclusion is further substantiated by a case study of a Teachers' Training College, which showed that this institution was not adequately preparing teacher trainees to meet the specific changes envisaged by the new curriculum for basic education, such as transforming teacher-centred pedagogies to learner-centred teaching styles, introducing interdisciplinary approaches to teaching and learning, and changing teaching practices and pedagogies (Guro & Webber, 2010). These authors found that the lecturers themselves did not understand the meaning of interdisciplinarity and, although they could articulate the meaning of learner-centredness, their own lectures were teacher-centered.

In Madagascar, as Antal and Ndrianjafy put it in Chapter 3, in contrast with the more positive situation in primary teacher education,

> . . . the training of high school teachers, . . . teacher trainers and secondary-level pedagogical counsellors occurs at Normal Schools affilliated with the national university system, through courses that rarely deviate from a traditional lecture format.

School organization and teacher professionalism

However, a more basic issue in relation to educational quality and outcomes is the extent to which schools in developing countries actually function as modern educational organizations and teachers act as professionals. Part of the problem can be below par performance by teachers because of low morale, especially when they do not feel that they are properly rewarded, supported or resourced. This comes out strongly, for example, in Chapter 10 on Zimbabwe where Sigauke notes that,

> Perhaps the worst demoralizing factor at the moment is the salary structure which is very low for teachers and lecturers in teacher training colleges. This has resulted in a 'brain drain', especially of the science and mathematics teachers

as they leave to neighbouring and overseas countries (Ministries of Education, Sport and Culture and Higher and Tertiary Education (2004). While government has made promises to review teacher salaries little has been done to address the situation. Over the last few years teacher unions have mobilized members to boycott teaching over issues of low wages and other bad working conditions worsened by the political and economic crises.

And, as Tabulawa reports on Botswana in Chapter 1,

> . . . teachers' morale and professional concerns need urgent attention. Talk of there being a crisis in Botswana schools should not be taken lightly. Decline (since 2000) in student performance across levels of operation that has been reported can to a large extent be attributed to the teacher factor. A series of teacher industrial actions, the latest being the 2011 public service strike, have adversely affected education quality.

However, there may be another factor at play as well. While many schools in developing countries function as organizations in a professional and effective manner, many others do not. Harber and Davies (1997) used Riggs's theory of 'prismatic society' to argue in some detail that many schools (and other modern organizations) in developing countries have both 'traditional' and 'modern' organizational, social, cultural, economic and behavioural characteristics coexisting side by side within them. Riggs (1964) used the analogy of a fused white light passing through a prism and emerging diffracted as a series of different colours. Within the prism there is a point where the diffraction process starts but remains incomplete. Riggs was suggesting that developing societies contain both elements of traditional, fused type of social organization and elements of the more structurally differentiated or 'modern' societies. The result is an organization that seems like a modern, bureaucratic school but this is often something of a façade as the school functions quite differently in reality in terms of marked features such as, for example, teacher absenteeism, lateness, unprofessionalism, sexual misconduct and corruption as well as cheating in examinations and violent conflict (Harber & Davies, 1997: chs. 3, 4 and 6 – see also Oryema, 2007 on education in Uganda). Davies (1993) studied the national press in Zimbabwe for a six month period and found 53 items that posed serious problems for an effective school organization. The largest category was financial – the embezzlement by heads or senior management of school funds or examination fees. The second largest category was sexual – the rape of pupils or teachers, or schoolgirl pregnancy where the father was a teacher. Favouritism and nepotism came a close third, with claims about preferential treatment with regard to salaries. Alcoholism, running illegal dormitories, examination fraud, absenteeism and excessive corporal punishment also featured.

In South Africa a similar issue of school disorganization exists. The State President of South Africa, Jacob Zuma, called on teachers to be 'in class, on time and teaching and to spend the rest of the day on preparation and marking' (*Mail and Guardian*, 2–8 September 2011), a theme he returned to in his 2012 State of the Nation Address. In the same vein Duncan Hindle, a senior education official in South Africa, has argued that school accountability is lacking when even the basic minimum terms of employment are not being complied with. He describes a situation where,

> ... teachers are absent without good reason, some arrive late or leave early, and others are perhaps at school but not in class. Funerals, council duties and union meetings provide convenient excuses. Fridays become 'early closing' days and on paydays non-attendance is the norm in many schools. Pupils display similar traits. ... (*Mail and Guardian*, 2–8 September 2011)

A research report of 2007 noted that educator attendance varies widely between schools but is known to result in significant loss of learner time. Apart from arriving at school late and leaving early, reasons for educator absence include strikes and stay aways, examinations and sporting events and municipal activities. The report also noted that loss of learning time will undoubtedly adversely affect achievement, outcomes and progression (Motala et al., 2007: 58–9).

In their research in schools in three provinces of South Africa, Hammett and Staeheli (2011) noted that,

> On multiple occasions during our work at a township school in Cape Town we witnessed educators either arriving late or leaving early from class or even remaining in the staffroom for the duration of the teaching period (despite being timetabled to teach). ... On a number of occasions at other schools, it appeared that educators were drunk. At many schools, educators used learners to run personal errands – primarily to fetch food or drinks from the school tuck shop or neighbouring street traders. (275)

This is confirmed by Mncube and Madikizela-Madiya in Chapter 7 of this book who cite Bloch to the effect that,

> Schools are often not well organised, timetabling is poor, institutional process is arbitrary and ineffective. At a teaching level, haphazard planning and time

management are often reflected in a poor ability to plan and timetable teaching plans for the curriculum over the year. (2009: 82–3)

In Chapter 8 Motala further comments on this issue that,

Other research notes that there is very little actual teaching and learning taking place: lessons often start late, much time is spent maintaining order, teachers do most of the talking, and learners are passive and contribute little (Dieltiens & Motala 2011). This confirms earlier research which found that many teachers come late to school, leave early and spend only some 46 per cent of their time teaching during a 35-hour week, with most of the rest of their time at school spent on administrative tasks . . . Lack of meaningful access has to do, too, with poor time management, a misutilization of teachers, and a shortage of expertise in specific subjects; with teacher disillusionment and learner demotivation; with a culture of disrespect; and with bullying, sexual harassment and corporal punishment, and perhaps the lack, the lack of awareness, or the ineffectiveness, of alternative forms of discipline.

There are also issues of this nature in Malawi. Kamwendo in Chapter 4 provides the following examples,

The public examination system has to an extent lost the support and trust of the very public it is supposed to serve. Leakage of public examination questions has been one such situations. MANEB has on a number of occasions been faced with the embarrassment of finding examination papers being sold by vendors on the streets. Some school heads, teachers, examination invigilators, security personnel/law enforcers, students, parents and other stakeholders have been involved in a public examination-related irregularities and/or scams. Some of the culprits have been prosecuted and sentenced in courts of law . . . the media contains stories or allegations of teachers who sexually harass their, usually female, learners (see, for example, Maluwa-Banda 2003). Some teachers engage in excessive and irresponsible drinking habits. Some teachers are frequently absent from duties on no good grounds. For instance, some teachers run away from duties and engage in private jobs that would earn them income to supplement their low salaries.

Also, in relation to Swaziland Mazibuko notes in Chapter 9 that,

Teacher professionalism is at a low level and there is an increase in teacher misconduct seen in the rise in cases of teacher–pupil relationships in schools.

Increasing abuse of school resources and funds, even examination fees.

Problems of teacher absenteeism and lack of punctuality are also noted as continuing issues in the chapters in this book on Mozambique and Namibia which note that, 'High absenteeism rates among teachers suggests, similar to that among pupils, a deficient culture of teaching on the part of the teachers' (Chapter 6).

HIV/AIDS

However, there are two further issues highlighted by contributors to this book that both impact on the quality of education in southern Africa and which are exacerbated by the problems of educational quality discussed so far – HIV/AIDS and gender relationships within education, the latter being discussed below.

HIV/AIDS is a serious problem facing education systems in southern Africa causing shortages of skilled and trained personnel such as teachers and administrators and having an impact on pupil attendance, both because of illness and because of extended family duties in the absence of mothers and fathers who have died from AIDS related diseases. Sigauke notes in Chapter 10 in relation to Zimbabwe that,

> The HIV/AIDS pandemic has affected a number of children who have had to withdraw from school as they become orphans and cannot raise the finances needed for school fees, examination fees and levies. In terms of gender this has again affected girls more than boys as circumstances force them to remain at home doing most of the domestic duties in a family affected by the disease.

As Kamwendo further puts it in Chapter 4 in relation to Malawi,

> An education system that is already suffering from an acute shortage of trained and experienced teachers gets a serious blow when the little it has (in terms of number of teachers) is taken away through HIV/AIDS deaths. Deaths of parents is another challenge, given that some learners are left without any parents to look after them. Some of these children drop out of school and engage in wage-giving activities for economic survival while others go into socially unfavourable activities such as crime and prostitution. Some of the children, due to the deaths of their parents, are forced to step into positions of responsibilities and take care of their siblings. Some girls may have to play a motherly role to their siblings, and this may lead to lack of concentration in school. It is not uncommon for such girls to be absent from schools so that they are able to attend to siblings' illnesses. HIV/AIDS has also led to more funerals than was previously the case before

the rise of the pandemic. Such numerous funerals disrupt school activities as parents, teachers and learners have to attend them. Furthermore, those teachers who are living with HIV/AIDS are often sick, and thus not able to offer the best of their professional services. There is no doubt that the cost of HIV/AIDS on the education sector is enormous, and a serious threat to sustainable development.

The extent to which young people themselves are affected by HIV/AIDS in the nine countries with which we are concerned is shown in Table 0.4.

Table 0.4 Youth HIV prevalence rates (percentage ages 15–24) 2009

Country	Female	Male
Botswana	11.8	5.2
Namibia	5.8	2.3
South Africa	13.6	4.5
Swaziland	15.6	6.5
Madagascar	0.1	0.1
Lesotho	14.2	5.4
Malawi	6.8	3.1
Zimbabwe	6.9	3.3
Mozambique	8.6	3.1
Average (Excluding Madagascar)	**14.3**	**4.2**

Source: UNDP (2011)

As Table 0.4 shows, the rates of HIV/AIDS infection in eight of the nine countries are high and affect females at a higher rate than males. The exception is Madagascar where rates are low. This has been explained by Madagascar's isolation as an island, which has impeded the flow of infected people from the African mainland (see Chapter 3).

While a number of countries in this book have AIDS education as part of the planned curriculum, the SAQMEQ has devised the HIV/AIDS Knowledge Test (HAKT) which was administered to pupils and teachers in 2,770 schools in late 2007. The results were analysed according to whether respondents had a 'minimal' level of understanding, defined as mastery of half of the official HIV/AIDS curriculum. Almost all teachers (98–100%) in all countries reached the minimal level. However, as Table 0.5 shows, standard six pupils did not have the same levels of minimal understanding.

Table 0.5 Percentage of standard 6 pupils
reaching minimal level in HAKT test

Country	%
Botswana	32
Lesotho	19
Malawi	43
Mozambique	40
Namibia	36
South Africa	35
Swaziland	52
Zimbabwe	30
Average	**36**

Source: SACMEQ (2011)

As SAQMEQ comments, we need to have a better understanding of why there is such gap between well-informed teachers and less well-informed pupils. However, one factor might be the reluctance and/or inability of teachers to discuss controversial issues (of which HIV/AIDS is most certainly one) in the classroom, preferring a content-based, lecture style approach as discussed above. Asimeng Boahene (2007) found that students in Botswana, for example, enjoyed learning about controversial issues, including rival and contradictory opinions, and found it useful in helping them form their own opinions as critical citizens. However, he noted that African teachers may well avoid sensitive topics and that:

> Conducting beneficial discussions on controversial issues is an art that requires skills and practice. However, studies have shown that most African teachers lack this very ingredient, as there is a great shortage of trained and experienced teachers versed in issue-centred approaches to teaching. (236)

A further study in Botswana (Koosmile & Suping, 2011) found that final year pre-service teacher education students were generally reluctant to debate contemporary controversial issues in science education and that their contributions generally lacked critical reflection and thorough analysis. Indeed, the students were challenged by the participatory and interactive thrust of the course and that this has implications for the overall nature of teacher education currently being provided in Botswana. Partly because of a lack of training, many teachers are afraid of teaching controversial issues, even in countries where there is a well-established system of political democracy in place like Britain or a relatively new one like South Africa (Chikoko et al., 2011).

Gender within education

We saw above that in terms of access to schooling the position of females has improved considerably in southern Africa. However, in terms of the experiences of girls *within* schools the picture is not always so promising. A survey carried out by Africa Rights and cited by the World Health Organisation found cases of school teachers attempting to gain sex in return for good grades in both South Africa and Zimbabwe among others (WHO, 2002: 155). Research in Malawi and Zimbabwe carried out for the British Department for International Development and described by Leach (2001, 2002) found evidence of teachers making unsolicited sexual advances and other forms of inappropriate sexual behaviour. In Zimbabwe schools,

> . . . the teachers appeared to pursue their amorous activities both inside and outside the classroom quite openly; in the classroom, boys and girls would whistle or hiss if a teacher called on a particular girl known to be of interest to him to read out loud or come in front of the class . . . Boys were loud in their condemnation of such teachers, not for moral reasons but because they saw it as unfair competition. The teacher was abusing his position of authority; the girls were their peers and therefore 'their property'. (2002)

Moreover, male teachers who behave in this way are indicating to boys that such behaviour is acceptable. One key finding of the research was that sexual abuse of girls by male pupils and teachers is accepted, along with corporal punishment, verbal abuse and bullying, as an inevitable part of much of school life. It exploits unequal power relationships and the authoritarian ethos within schools. Another was that the reluctance of education authorities to address the issue and to prosecute perpetrators allows abuse to flourish unchecked. By their inaction, authorities condone and encourage it. Finally, sexual abuse of girls in school is a reflection of gender violence and inequality in the wider society. Domestic violence against women and children is commonplace, as is rape and forced sex within relationships. Women are considered as 'belonging' to men and hence accorded lower value and status.

A study of child abuse by teachers in secondary schools in Zimbabwe by Shumba (2001) was entitled '*Who Guards the Guards in Schools?*'. This refers to a previous study by the author showing that teachers do carry out sexual abuse and that the great majority of the victims were between 12 and 16 years old. Shumba recognizes that the majority of pupils do not file complaints against teachers for fear of being victimized. He argues that only about 10 per cent of such cases get reported. Shumba nevertheless managed to get access to 212 perpetrators files held by the Ministry of Education, even though these were the 'tip of the iceberg'. Ninety-nine per cent of these were male. Eighty-two per cent of these teachers were trained and 18 per cent were untrained. Not surprisingly, the article calls for an overhaul of the teacher education curriculum to deal properly with issues of sexual abuse and professional responsibility.

USAID (2003: 9–12) also provided a summary of some empirical studies of gender-based violence in schools in Africa. In Botswana, in one study of 800 students 38 per cent of girls reported that they had been touched in a sexual manner without their consent; 17 per cent reported having had intercourse, 50 per cent of which was forced; 34 per cent reported they had sex for money, gifts or favours and 48 per cent reported never having used a condom. In another study in Botswana 67 per cent of girls reported sexual harassment by teachers and 11 per cent of girls were seriously considering dropping out due to ongoing harassment by teachers.

In South Africa in October 1997 the report of the Gender Equity Task Team on gender equity in education was published (Wolpe et al., 1997). This was the first of its kind in South Africa and is a lengthy document that provided an authoritative and comprehensive account of the state of affairs with regard to gender issues in South African education. On the back cover it states that 'South African education is riddled with gender inequities that impact negatively on girls and boys, women and men – but especially on the quality of life and achievements of women. These inequities exist throughout the system and include the extremely worrying elements of sexual harassment and violence'. This document did not really examine the role of teachers in sexual abuse in any detail. However, in 2001 Human Rights Watch produced a detailed report entitled *Scared at School: Sexual Violence Against Girls in South African Schools*. This is based on research in KwaZulu Natal, Gauteng and the Western Cape. The report states,

> Based on our interviews with educators, social workers, children and parents, the problems of teachers engaging in serious sexual misconduct with underage female students is widespread. As the testimony offered below demonstrates, teachers have raped, sexually assaulted and otherwise sexually abused girls. Sometimes reinforcing sexual demands with threats of physical violence or corporal punishment, teachers have sexually propositioned girls and verbally degraded them using highly sexualised language. At times, sexual relations between teachers and students did not involve an overt use of force or threats

of force; rather teachers would abuse their authority by offering better grades or money to pressure girls for sexual favours or 'dating relationships'. (Human Rights Watch, 2001: 37)

Twenty seven complaints of sexual misconduct against teachers were received by the South African Council of Educators between January and October 2008 and in some cases the teacher-pupil relationships took place with the consent of the children's parents based on some kind of financial agreement. The Chief Executive Officer of the Council said,

> It has been very disturbing that there have been cases where students have been minors. Children as young as nine have been found to be involved with teachers. There have also been cases of impregnation. Council finds that completely intolerable. While girl learners are abused by other members of society, we definitely have jurisdiction over teachers. The age of learners, their consent, parental consent or their location in a different school will not mitigate the culpability of a teacher in this regard. (*Mail and Guardian Online*, 8 December 2008)

These problems seem to continue in the countries of southern Africa according to the writers in this book, as noted by Motala in her chapter on South Africa and Mazibuko in his chapter on Swaziland. Felciano Chimbutane also notes in relation to Mozambique in Chapter 5,

> parents' fears to send their daughters to schools where male teachers dominate, which makes them vulnerable to sexual harassment.

Conclusion

As both this chapter and the other chapters in this book demonstrate, there is much to celebrate in southern Africa, especially in terms of improving access to formal education, equalizing access in terms of gender and policy changes in regard to both equity and more relevant curricula but that there is still much to be done. There are still major concerns about the often highly uneven and unequal quality of educational provision and the resulting quality of educational outcomes. Poor school organization and teacher professionalism can also be significant contributory factors in restricting the quality of provision while HIV/AIDS continues to pose a serious problem for education in all the countries bar Madagascar. Classroom interaction and teaching methods tend to still be rather uniformly traditional and teacher-centred, an issue often reinforced, rather than challenged, by the nature of teacher education. Finally, while noting the achievements of greater equity in terms of gender access to formal education this chapter has also highlighted the continuing problem of sexual harassment and violence towards girls within schools.

References

Asimeng-Boahene, L. (2007). 'Creating Strategies to Deal with Problems of Teaching Controversial Issues in Social Studies Education in African Schools', *Intercultural Education* 18, 3, pp. 231–42.

Bartholemew, J. (1976). 'Schooling Teachers: The Myth of the Liberal College', in G. Whitty and M. F. D. Young, *Explorations in the Politics of School Knowledge* (Driffield: Nafferton Books).

Bloch, G. (2009). *The Toxic Mix* (Cape Town: Tafelberg).

Chikoko,V., Gilmour, J., Harber, C. and Serf, J. (2011). 'Teaching Controversial Issues in England and South Africa', *Journal of Education for Teaching* 37, 1, pp. 5–21.

Davies, L. (1993). 'Teachers as Implementers or Subversives', *International Journal of Educational Development* 13, 2, pp. 161–70.

Fuller, B. (1991). *Growing Up Modern* (London: Routledge).

Hammett, D. and Staeheli, L. (2011). 'Respect and Responsibility: Teaching Citizenship in South African High Schools', *International Journal of Educational Development* 31, 3, pp. 269–76.

Harber, C. and Davies, L. (1997). School Management and School Effectiveness in Developing Countries (London: Cassell).

Human Rights Watch (2001). *Scared at School: Sexual Violence Against Girls in South African Schools* (New York: Human Rights Watch).

Humphreys, S. (2006). 'Corporal Punishment As Gendered Practice', in F. Leach and C. Mitchell (eds), *Combating Gender Violence in and Around Schools* (Stoke On Trent: Trentham Books), pp. 61–9.

Johnson, D. (ed.) (2008). *The Changing Landscape of Education in Africa* (Oxford: Symposium).

Kamwendo, G. (2009). 'The SADC Protocol on Education and Training: Linguistic Implications and Complications', *Language Matters* 40, 1, pp. 4–17.

Koosmile, A. and Suping, S. (2011). 'Pre-service Teachers's Attempts at Debating Contemporary Issues in Science Education: A Case Study from Botswana', *International Journal of Educational Development* 31, 5, pp. 458–64.

Kunje, D., Lewin, K. and Stuart, J. (2003). *Primary Teacher Education in Malawi: Insights into Practice and Policy* (London: DfID).

Leach, F. (2001). 'Conspiracy of silence? Stamping out abuse in African schools', *Insights Development Research* August 2001, pp. 1–2.

— (2002). 'Learning to be Violent – The Role of the School in Developing Adolescent Gendered Identity', Paper presented at the conference of the British Association of International and Comparative Education, University of Nottingham.

Lefoka, J. and Sebatane, E. (2003). *Initial Primary Teacher Education in Lesotho* (London: DfID).

Lewin, K. and Stuart, J. (2003). *Researching Teacher Education: New Perspectives on Practice, Performance and Policy* (London: DfID).

Meredith, M. (2006). *The State of Africa* (London: The Free Press).

Motala, S., Dieltiens,V., Carrim, N., Kgobe, P., Moyo, G. and Rembe, S. (2007). 'Educational Access in South Africa: Country Analytic Review', Project Report. Consortium for Research on Educational Access, Transitions and Equity (CREATE), Falmer, UK.

Nagel, T. (1992). *Quality Between Tradition and Modernity: Patterns of Communication and Cognition in Teacher Education in Zimbabwe* (Oslo: University of Oslo Pedagogisk Forskningsintitutt).

Nelson Mandela Foundation (2005) *Emerging Voices* (Cape Town: HSRC Press).

Omolewa, M. (2007). 'Traditional African Modes of Education: Their Relevance in the Modern World', *International Review of Education* 53, 5–6, pp. 593–612.

Oryema, D. (2007). 'Decentralisation Policy and Education Provision in Uganda', PhD Thesis, University of Birmingham.

Palme, M. (1997). 'Teaching Hieroglyphs with Authority', in M. John (ed.), *A Charge Against Society: The Child's Right to Protection* (London: Jessica Kingsley), pp. 62–73.

Prophet, R. and Rowell, P. (1990). 'Curriculum in Action: The "Practical" Dimension in Botswana Classrooms', *International Journal of Educational Development* 10, 1, pp. 17–26.

Riggs, F. (1964). *Administration in Developing Countries: The Theory of Prismatic Society* (Boston: Houghton Mifflin).

Shumba, A. (2001). '"Who Guards the Guards in Schools?" A Study of Reported Cases of Child Abuse by Teachers in Zimbabwean Secondary Schools', *Sex Education* 1, 1, pp. 77–86.

Tabulawa, R. (1995). 'Culture and Classroom Practice: A Socio-Cultural Analysis of Geography Classrooms in Botswana Secondary Schools and Implications for Pedagogical Change', PhD Thesis, University of Birmingham.

Tafa, E. (2002). 'Corporal Punishment: The Brutal Face of Botswana's Authoritarian Schools', *Educational Review* 54, 1, pp. 17–26.

UNDP (2011). *Human Development Report* (Basingstoke: Palgrave Macmillan).

Unterhalter, E. and Oommen, M. (2008). 'Measuring education inequalities in Commonwealth countries in Africa', in D. Holsinger and W. James Jacob (eds), *Inequality in Education* (Hong Kong: Comparative Education Research Centre), pp. 538–57.

USAID (2003). *Unsafe Schools: A Review of School-Related Gender-Based Violence in Developing Countries* (Washington: USAID).

Verspoor, A. (2008). 'The Challenge of Learning: Improving the Quality of Basic Education in Sub-Saharan Africa', in Johnson, D. (ed.), *The Changing Landscape of Education in Africa* (Oxford: Symposium), pp. 13–44.

WHO (World Health Organisation) (2002). *World Report on Violence and Health* (Geneva: WHO).

Wolpe, A.-M., Quinlan, O. and Martinez, L. (1997). *Gender Equity in Education: Report of the Gender Equity Task Team* (Pretoria: Department of Education).

1

Botswana: Aspects of General Education

Richard Tabulawa and Nkobi O. Pansiri
University of Botswana

Introduction

Botswana is a land-locked, semi-arid, middle-income country of 582,000 square kilometres, with a total population of 2,038,228 million people, growing at an annual rate of 1.9 per cent (Republic of Botswana, 2011). It was a British Protectorate for 81 years and gained its independence in 1966 through democratic elections which saw the Botswana Democratic Party (BDP), under the leadership of Seretse Khama, assuming political leadership. Botswana is a multiparty democracy which works side by side with a traditional system of chieftainship. Formal education in Botswana is traceable to traditional chieftainship and missionary initiatives during the 81 years of the colonial period. The former operated community schools while the churches ran mission schools.

The Khama government of 1966 adopted four national principles – namely, unity, democracy, development and self-reliance (Republic of Botswana, 1977a) – as guiding principles in development planning. To date, these principles continue to guide political, economic and social development planning. Under the principle of unity the leadership adopted a language policy which made Setswana a national language and English the official language. Setswana is used in public domains such as local media, community public meetings, community health centres and country-based small-scale businesses. English is used more to link the country to the global community in areas such as education, health, science and technology, commerce (trade and industry), law and justice system, legislature and parliamentary debates and mass media (Bagwasi, 2004). Ethnic minority groups have no linguistic rights.

On the eve of independence in 1965 the government enacted both the Education Act and the Local Government Act. As a result, local authorities or districts were established and mandated to run primary education while the Ministry of Education took responsibility for secondary education. This was the first initiative to extend educational opportunity to every community in the country. At Independence Botswana was one of the poorest countries in the world with an underdeveloped education sector. For example, at independence only 13 per cent of pupils who enrolled at Standard I completed primary education (Republic of Botswana, 1977a) and there were only 40 degree qualification-holding Batswana. The discovery and subsequent mining of diamonds immediately after 1966 saw Botswana develop to the medium-income country that it is today. It boasts an expansive education infrastructure and runs a basic education programme that goes beyond Universal Primary Education (UPE).

It is this phenomenal growth of school education provision that this chapter highlights. The education system of Botswana is broad, changing and growing. Space limitations do not allow for a comprehensive, detailed and critical discussion of this growth. For example, while important, the adult basic, out of school children's programme and skills training programmes, are not detailed in this chapter. It is the formal schooling aspect that is the main focus of the chapter. We have therefore been consciously selective in what we present here, but without sacrificing the depth and breadth of the system's coverage.

Structure of the education system

Botswana operates a 7 + 3 + 2 system of General Education, meaning that Primary Education takes 7 years to complete, Junior Secondary Education 3 years, while Senior Secondary Education takes 2 years (see Figure 1.1). The system is assessed through a national test and national examinations by the Botswana Examinations Council (BEC).

Primary education is free for citizens but not compulsory. It starts at Standard (Grade) 1 and goes up to Standard VII. At Standard IV pupils take a national attainment test to determine the competencies and skills they acquired in the first four years of primary education. Repeating a grade is possible only after consultations between the class teacher, head teacher and parents. At the end of Standard VII (the final year of primary schooling) pupils sit for the Primary School Leaving Examination (PLSE), a formative evaluation exercise meant to

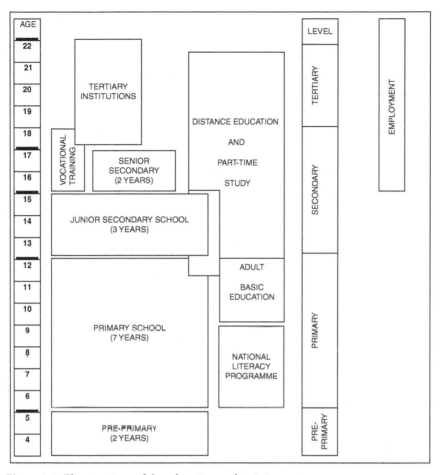

Figure 1.1 The structure of the education and training system
Source: Adapted from Republic of Botswana, 1993

help the system diagnose the basic competencies, skills and knowledge that the seven-year education programme is able to provide.

At the end of the three years of junior secondary education students sit for a Junior Certificate Examination (JCE), a summative and selective examination. Currently, 65 per cent of these students progress to senior secondary while the remaining 35 per cent accesses technical and vocational education or joins the ranks of the unemployed.

Senior secondary education takes two years, at the end of which students sit for the summative Botswana General Certificate of Secondary Education (BGCSE). Successful ones get placed in tertiary institutions for professional training according to their potentialities, abilities, interests and the human resource needs of the country.

Operating side by side with the public school system is a growing sector of private provision of education. The *Education Act* provides for the establishment and running of schools by interested individuals, groups or Non-Government Organizations (NGOs). This has allowed three categories of school systems to emerge. The first category consists of public schools. The second category is that of government-aided schools. These are mostly mission-initiated schools which are financially supported by government. These cover both primary and secondary schools. In both public and government-aided schools human resources, learning/instructional materials, schools supplies, infrastructure including classroom and teacher accommodation and any other learning support needs are provided by government. The third category is that of private schools. These cover preschool, reception classes and primary and secondary education. These are owned, run and managed privately either by individuals or companies. They are, however, registered and are by law subject to Ministry of Education and Skills Development's (MoE&SD) inspection.

The Botswana education system has historically shifted from a decentralized system to a centralized one. Pre-colonial education was tribal/community-based and coordinated by the chiefs. During the colonial period, education trained learners in loyalty, obedience and respect for both the chiefs and colonial power. There was nothing close to an 'education system'. Post-colonial dynamics elevated the nation-building project. The Local Government Act of 1965 established nine local authorities/districts – Central, Kgalagadi, Kweneng, Kgatleng, Gantsi, North East, North West, Southern and South East – and three town districts, namely, Gaborone, Francistown and Lobatse, to which has been added Chobe, Selibe-Phikwe, Jwaneng and Sowa Town Districts. Local authorities wrested control of primary education from the Chiefs and communities, ensuring the State's control of the emerging education system. This control was important for the nation-building project. The central government has since intensified centralization by wresting from local control the entire basic education programme. Paradoxically, this apparent drive towards centralization is taking place in a context of efforts to decentralize education provision. For example, as part of the implementation of the Revised National Policy on Education (RNPE) of 1994, MoE&SD embarked on an Organization and Methods review exercise (O&M) which established education regions slightly aligned and linked functionally to the local authorities but not administratively joined to them. By 2011 ten such regions had been established. But what exactly has been decentralized? Education decision-making and control of the curriculum remain under MoE&SD's control, while teacher recruitment and welfare is the purview of the Department of Public Service Management (DPSM) as the employer of all public servants (including teachers) in Botswana. Education Districts' roles include regularly inspecting schools, settling conflicts between teachers, supervising school heads, recruiting and employing temporary teachers, deploying newly recruited and transferred teachers, making sure teachers have been paid their salaries and presiding over all matters of teacher welfare. Education Districts, therefore, are mere extensions of both the DPSM and MoE&SD, with no control over matters of substance. Thus Botswana's is a centralized as opposed to a decentralized education system.

Basic education programme

General Education is further subdivided into two strata, the Basic Education stratum which comprises the first 10 years of schooling, and the Senior Secondary Education stratum which runs for 2 years.

Botswana introduced the Basic Education Programme (BEP) in the 1980s. It comprised the first 9 (later increased to 10) years of schooling. In Botswana basic education is equated 'with nine [now 10] years of formal schooling' (Youngman, 1993: 192), even though there exists alongside it an out-of-school basic education programme.

BEP required two conditions for it to be 'basic'. First, 'school fees and/or any other prohibitive user-fees had to be abolished, and secondly, there had to be enough places for those who wanted to attend school' (Tabulawa, 2011: 435). Both conditions were fulfilled when in the 1980s the government abolished school fees and provided the required teaching space at both primary and junior secondary levels of education through the Primary Education Improvement Project (PEIP) and the Junior Secondary Education Improvement Project (JSEIP) respectively. In 1987 the nine years BEP was implemented fully. The impact of the programme was astounding: the 394 primary schools with 156,890 pupils in 1979 had increased to 518 primary schools with 209,345 pupils by 1984. The Junior Certificate admissions increased from 38 per cent of its intake in 1984 to 67 per cent in 1991 (Republic of Botswana, 1993). During the implementation of National Development Plan 8 (1997/8–2002/3), Botswana recorded a net enrolment of 85.8 per cent in primary education, and a transition rate of 100 per cent from primary to junior secondary education (Republic of Botswana, 2003).

BEP was enhanced in 1994 when it was increased to ten years. But this was crafted in a policy environment characterized by the integration of neoliberal policies (which included cost-sharing/recovery) into national economic planning. Basic education was not spared the onslaught of these reforms. In 2006 the government re-introduced targeted school fees at the secondary education level, which includes the junior secondary education level, the latter being an integral part of the basic education programme. This violated the first condition for there to be a basic education programme in the country since the concept is not compatible with user-fees. While the government continues behaving as if the original basic education programme is still in place, in theory it is more appropriate to regard Botswana as having reduced basic education to UPE. In practice, however, and to the extent that no child is denied access to the first ten years of schooling on account of failure to pay school fees, the government's insistence that basic education provision in Botswana is still intact makes sense. The government's ambiguous position permits it to sensibly talk of being on track to introducing universal secondary education by 2016 (Republic of Botswana, 1997) without appearing to be contradicting itself.

Pre-primary education

The pre-primary education level is not yet part of the formal structure of General Education. Although the government acknowledged the importance of pre-primary education it insisted that it be left to private individuals, NGOs and Village Development Committees (VDCs) to provide. The government's involvement was limited to creating an enabling environment for private provision by providing regulations, guidelines and policies as well as supervision and management services through the Pre-Primary Education Unit of MoE&SD. There were 514 pre-primary centres in the country in 2010. 56.4 per cent of these were privately owned, 16.5 per cent community owned, 12.5 per cent church owned, district councils owned 2.5 per cent and 0.4 per cent were owned by institutions (Republic of Botswana, 2010: 1). In 2007 the participation rate stood at 17 per cent.

However, the MoE&SD position vis-à-vis pre-primary education shifted in the 2000s when the Human Resource Development Advisory Council (HRDAC), tasked with the responsibility to advice the government on the country's human resource needs, was established. The Council has adopted the position that quality must pervade the entire education system, from pre-primary to tertiary education, implying that the former must be part of the formal public education system. The government has accepted the advice and is working on the modalities of a phased introduction of pre-primary education as a public provision starting in 2013. The Pre-Primary Education Unit of the MoE&SD is currently working on the Pre-School Education Policy for 0–6 year olds which will guide the development of the sub-sector as an integral part of the general education system.

Financing education

Although the policy of cost-sharing is in operation, it is the case that more than 90 per cent of total costs at both primary and secondary levels of education are borne by the State, suggesting that cost-sharing is not as effective as had been envisaged. The unit cost for funding education fluctuates from year to year depending on the inflation rate. At the primary education level, funding covers stationary and feeding programmes at school. While schools are free to levy a development fee on pupils, payment of the fee cannot be a condition for attending school since this would be in violation of the UPE policy to which Botswana has adhered since 1980.

Secondary education funding covers students' feeding (both day and boarding), stationery, laboratory supplies, books, sporting and practical subject equipment. It is at this level that cost-sharing is supposed to augment the State's contribution to education expenditure. But due to the government's ambiguous position of school fees-in-a-free education system cost-sharing has dismally failed.

Goals and priorities of education

The goals and priorities of education in Botswana have shifted over the years. The *National Policy on Education* (1977) aimed to achieve more than just universal basic education. In fact, it is more appropriate to characterize universal basic education as a vehicle meant to deliver the political ideal of nation-building.

Before independence Botswana comprised disparate tribal groupings, with each seeing itself as a 'nation'. Tribal patriotism was (and still is, to some extent) very strong (Marope, 1994). The challenges facing the post-independence government, therefore, were how to achieve political integration as well as promote a national identity. Primary education was identified as the vehicle by which 'the individual child and perhaps even the local community itself derive their sense of belonging to the wider society of Botswana . . ' (Republic of Botswana, 1977b: 53). In addition to the goal of political integration, education in post-independence Botswana had to address the acute human resources deficit that resulted from decades of colonial neglect. Exploitation of natural resources immediately after 1966 created employment opportunities for which few Batswana had the requisite educational credentials. These two factors, together with the need to equitably distribute educational opportunities among the different regions, necessitated a centralized education system. Priorities of education before 1994, therefore, could be summarized as the need to contribute to nation building, the human resource base and regional equality.

Publication of the RNPE in 1994 signalled a shift in the goals and priorities of education. While the earlier goals of nation-building and human resource development were not dropped, priority for education shifted to the need to service a national economy that was increasingly being integrated into the emerging global economy. This is an economy that requires a new kind of worker, one who possesses generic skills such as creativity, critical thinking, problem-solving and communication skills. As knowledge, and not natural resource endowment, becomes the dominant exchange commodity, the role of education in poverty eradication is enhanced. Only by becoming a knowledge-based economy will Botswana achieve economic diversification and, therefore, economic competitiveness in an increasingly competitive global economy. Little wonder, therefore, that National Development Plan 10 (2009/10–2015/16) lists the following as the main goals for the education sector: provision of accessible, equitable and quality education and provision of globally competitive human resources to drive economic growth, the route to poverty eradication.

Equity and access issues

Education in Botswana is considered a human right. Consequently, issues of equity, access and retention are taken very seriously since they are seen to be intertwined with the idea of education as every child's democratic right. To ensure retention in rural areas the government runs a daily feeding programme in schools, and within the basic education stratum automatic promotion is the norm. A major threat to improved retention of girls is pregnancy. Female drop-out rates due to pregnancy increased from 1.5 per cent in 1988 to 3.0 per cent in 1992. To alleviate the situation the MoE&SD reviewed its 1978 policy on student pregnancy by reducing the lay-off period for re-admission of girls who fell pregnant while schooling from 12 to 6 months. This has improved female students' completion rates.

The success of the BEP notwithstanding, access to education reflects a pyramidal shape, meaning that access tapers considerably after the basic education phase. The tapering is confirmed by transition rates from basic education to senior secondary education which show a progressive decline.[1] The following figures illustrate the decline: 1989 (53%), 1990 (35%), 1991 (31%), 1992 (30%) and 1993 (27%) (Bantsi-Chimidza & Mbunge, 1993). The figures show that from 1989 fewer and fewer students (as a proportion of those completing basic education) progressed to the senior secondary phase, meaning that basic education grew faster than the senior secondary level, the result of which was the creation of a bottleneck at the latter level. However, the bottleneck has eased considerably ever since the government's decision to provide universal secondary education during National Development Plan 10 (2009/10–2015/16) (Republic of Botswana, 1997). To demonstrate its resolve the government has so far constructed four additional senior secondary schools and is in the process of upgrading existing ones with a view to increasing their capacity. Little wonder, therefore, that transition rates from junior to senior secondary level increased by 17.7 per cent, from 49 per cent to 66.7 per cent, between 2004 and 2008.

However, this impressive global picture of educational access in the country hides some challenges. For example, it is reported that 10 per cent of school-going children are missing from school (Republic of Botswana, 2010). The majority of these children belong to the marginalized San/BaSarwa people. Of those who enrol many do not complete basic education (Tshireletso, 1997; Koketso, 2001; Polelo, 2005). Table 1.1 shows primary school dropout rates for the period 2004–10.

Table 1.1 Dropout trends in primary education, 2004–10

Year	Enrolment			Dropout Rate			% dropout
	Boys	Girls	Total	Boys	Girls	Total	
2004	166,759	161,933	328,692	2,922	1,775	4,697	1.43
2005	166,963	162,228	329,131	2,844	1,782	4,626	1.40
2006	168,152	162,265	330,417	2,405	1,536	3,941	1.19
2007	168,164	160,961	329,125	2,522	1,518	4,040	1.23
2008	159,313	152,250	311,563	2,364	1,264	3,628	1.16
2009	169,513	161,262	330,775	2,207	1,218	3,425	1.03
2010	169,556	161,640	331,196	2,071	1,124	3,195	0.96
Wastage						27,552	AV = 1.2

The data shows that primary schools still experience holding-power problems. In seven years, 27,552 children (1.2% on average) were lost to the schools system.

Over the years the government has taken a number of steps that have led to a significant decline of drop out rates. For example, between 2001 and 2005 the rate declined from 1.9 per cent to 1.4 per cent.

In 1974 a Remote Areas Dweller Programme (RADP) was introduced which, among other things, sought to address the educational needs of disadvantaged communities, particularly the BaSarwa communities in remote settlements (Koketso, 2001). Through the RADP boarding facilities for primary school children in the North West, Kweneng, Gantsi and Central Districts were built, and the children are provided with food, clothing, toiletry and transport to and from school at the beginning and end of the school term. Primary school entry age for remote areas is between 6 and 10 years, instead of the statutory 6 years. This is, first, in recognition of the fact that many children in remote rural areas live far away from schools – so they need to be old enough to walk long distances daily between home and school. Second, the policy is designed to accommodate children who could not start school on time because there were no schools in their localities. Consequently, it is common in remote areas to find students aged between seven and 20 years enrolled in the basic education programme. Provision of boarding facilities was also extended to junior secondary schools in the remote areas.

Curriculum, assessment and teaching methods

To appreciate the nature of the school curriculum in Botswana first requires an appreciation of the context in which it was crafted. The current curriculum emerged from the RNPE of 1994, the latter being Botswana's response to globalization. Given the policy's genesis, it is little surprising that its thrust 'was the aligning of education to the labour requirements of the economy' (Tabulawa, 2009: 91). Through the pre-vocational preparation strategy, the curriculum was to be re-packaged to ensure that general education developed in learners an awareness and understanding of the world of work. Academic subjects were to be 'taught in such a way that they are related to the world of work' (Republic of Botswana, 2007a: 2). To achieve the vocational orientation of the curriculum, 'skill-based syllabi' were developed across the general education stratum. It is worth noting here that 'skills' for this purpose referred to 'soft' skills such as critical thinking skills, problem-solving skills, interpersonal skills, teamwork spirit and individual initiative. Development of syllabi (from primary to senior secondary education) was to subordinate content to these skills. Suffice it to state here that the structuring of syllabi in terms of specific, assessable and measurable behavioural objectives displayed four features reminiscent of the behavioural objectives movement of the 1970s – knowledge as atomized, skills understood as narrow technical competencies, content as tightly specified and pre-specified/ pre-determined outcomes cast in measurable behavioural terms. These features characterize literally all syllabi from primary to teacher education colleges in Botswana. As shall be shown later, this approach to curriculum development has implications for how teachers teach.

The primary school curriculum is split into two levels: the lower primary (Standard I to IV) and upper primary (Standard V–VII). The first level comprises the following subjects: Setswana, Mathematics, Environmental Science, English, Creative and Performing Arts (CAPA), Cultural Studies and Guidance and Counselling. At the upper level the following subjects are offered: Agriculture, Religious and Moral Education, Setswana, CAPA, Guidance and Counselling, English, Science, Mathematics and Social Studies. This arrangement mirrors the junior secondary curriculum, meaning that the upper level of primary education is a preparatory stage for the former level.

At the junior secondary level, students take between ten and eleven subjects. There are eight core subjects. These are: Setswana, English, Integrated Science, Mathematics, Social Studies, Agriculture, Moral Education and Design and Technology (the latter is offered where facilities allow. Otherwise it is offered as an optional subject). In addition to the core subjects, students take a minimum of two and a maximum of three subjects from the category of Optional Subjects. The latter appear in three groups (see Table 1.2).

Table 1.2 Distribution of subjects for student selection

Core subjects	Optional subjects		
	Vocational subjects	Capa	General studies
• English	• Commerce and Office	• Music	• Religious
• Setswana	Procedures	• Physical	Education
• Mathematics	• Commerce and	Education	• Third Language
• Integrated Science	Bookkeeping/	• Art	
• Social Studies	Accounting		
• Agriculture	• Home Economics		
• Moral Education	• Design and Technology		
• Design and			
Technology			

Source: Republic of Botswana, 2007a: 21

All subjects are expected to infuse and integrate pre-vocational skills. Core subjects carry a weightage of 70 per cent while Optional subjects are weighted at 30 per cent.

The curriculum for the senior secondary level is organized around two broad areas: a Core area for all students and an Optional area which has four subgroups (see Table 1.3).

In addition to the core subjects, students choose a minimum of one subject from each of the Sciences and Humanities and Social Sciences groups and a minimum of two subjects from the Creative, Technical and Vocational group. However, in the latter group students may not make certain combinations. For example, they may not combine Home Management and Food & Nutrition. Students may choose only one subject from the Enrichment list. Pure science (Chemistry, Physics and Biology) students take the three Sciences plus one subject from the Humanities and Social Sciences group and at least one subject from the Creative, Technical and Vocational group. They are exempted from taking an Enrichment subject. The minimum number of subjects students may select is eight.

What is to be made of this curriculum arrangement? In a way it reflects the pre-vocational strategy mentioned above. The curriculum is broad/general and

Table 1.3 Subject groupings at senior secondary level

Core group	Optional groups			
	Humanities & Social Sciences	Sciences	Creative, Technical & Vocational	Enrichment
English	History	Single Science	Design and Technology Agriculture	Third Language
Setswana	Geography	Double Science	Art Food and Nutrition	Physical Education
Mathematics	Social Studies	Chemistry	Computer Studies Fashion & Fabrics	Music
	Development Studies	Physics	Business Studies Home Management	Religious Education
	Literature in English	Biology		Moral Education
		Human and Social Biology (only for private candidates)		

Source: Republic of Botswana, 1998: 9

diversified in that students take a mix of academic, technical and commercial subjects, thus ensuring accommodation of a broader range of abilities and interests. The inclusion of practical subjects in the curriculum is aimed at sensitizing students to the world of work.

Learner-centred pedagogy is the officially mandated pedagogy in schools in Botswana. Also, pre-service and in-service teacher education programmes reflect an emphasis on the promotion of this form of teaching/learning, and substantial resources have been committed to its promotion. The curriculum blueprint for the 10 Year Basic Education programme has as one of its main features the 'learner-centred approach' (Republic of Botswana, 2007a: 3), while that for the senior secondary school programme is committed to utilizing 'innovative learner-centred approaches to teaching' (Republic of Botswana, 1998: 4). In Botswana, leaner-centred approaches are attractive for their democratic pretensions. However, in spite of this commitment little has changed in the way teaching is carried out in the classrooms. Studies on teaching in Botswana schools report a resilience of teacher-centred approaches (Tabulawa, 1997, 2009). Explanations for this resilience range from technical factors such as poorly trained teachers, selective examinations and limited resources, to substantive issues such as culture and the influence of the enveloping social structure. Also militating against institutionalization of learner-centred methods is the behaviourist model of curriculum development discussed above. The highly specified content leaves no room for teacher initiative. Such a situation reduces the teacher's role to that of a 'technician who dispenses pre-packaged chunks of knowledge without any ethical consideration of what they are doing' (Tabulawa, 2009: 101). It is almost impossible for learner-centred pedagogy to thrive under these circumstances.

Assessment

The Botswana Examinations Council, established by an Act of Parliament in 2002, is the body responsible for all assessment, including conducting examinations at primary and secondary levels of education.

The RNPE recommended profound assessment reforms at the primary level. First, it introduced the Criterion Referenced Testing (CRT) to replace Norm Referenced Testing (NRT) which hitherto had characterized testing at this level. Continuous assessment was also introduced. These reforms shifted the focus of assessment from selection to diagnosis and remediation. These reforms should be understood in the context of BEP: the latter made the selection function of the PLSE redundant, thus paving the way for more formative and diagnostic forms of assessment. Primary school pupils take an attainment test at Standard IV in Setswana, English and Mathematics, and the PLSE at Standard VII in seven subjects. In terms of policy, information generated from these performance tests should be used by the teachers to develop student profile records, reflecting their strengths and weaknesses, for use at the next standard/level.

At the junior secondary level the assessment thrust shifts to norm-referenced testing, with the JCE taking precedence over everything else. This is not surprising given that places at the senior secondary level are limited, as shown by the transition rates presented above.

A wide range of assessment techniques is used at the senior secondary level. Continuous assessment in subjects such as the Sciences, Social Studies, Development Studies and Design & Technology contributes towards certification. At the end of Standard V students sit for the BGCSE examinations, which qualifies them for tertiary education studies.

School organization and management

Schools have a duty to ensure that meaningful learning takes place. To achieve this, schools engage in effective collaborative partnership with teachers, learners, parents and community members. Each school is free to determine its long-term goals and objectives, adopt courses of action and deploy and allocate resources necessary to carry out the goals and achieve objectives, but within centrally determined parameters.

Public schools in the same category (i.e. primary, junior secondary and senior secondary) have a standard organizational structure. The larger the school the more management posts it has. The posts are determined and filled by the employer, DPSM. Hierarchically, schools have a head teacher, deputy head teacher, heads of department, senior teachers and teachers. The number of heads of department and senior teacher posts depends on the size of the school. For example, a small primary school with an enrolment of less than 200 learners would not have many posts of responsibility. Private schools are at liberty to decide on their organizational structures. As a result, structures in this category of schools differ from one school to another.

It is policy that 'the Head as the instructional leader, together with the deputy and senior teachers, should take major responsibility for in-service training of teachers within their schools, through regular observations of teachers and organisational workshops, to foster communication between teachers on professional matters and to address weaknesses' (Republic of Botswana, 1994: 47). These cadres constitute the school management team (SMT) and they are their schools' instructional leaders, that is, leaders who are both efficient in school management and effective in their professional practice. The MoE&SD has embarked on a training exercise aimed at improving the instructional leadership qualities of SMTs. *Teaching Service Management Directive No 5 of 2007* exempted from teaching responsibilities all secondary school heads, deputy heads, heads of department and senior teacher Grade I – Guidance and Counseling, while *Teaching Service Management Directive No 6 of 2007* exempted from teaching all primary school heads and deputy heads of Groups 1 and 2 schools.

The exemption from teaching responsibilities is meant to allow incumbents to focus, among others, on:

- Ensuring effective management and supervision of their schools;
- Providing pastoral leadership and expedite remedial/corrective decisions to problems;
- Providing guidance and counselling services to both students and teachers.

Organization and nature of teacher education

There are two types of teacher education programmes in the country: the pre-service and in-service programmes. For primary school teachers, three colleges of education (Serowe College, Francistown College, Tlokweng College) exist and have trained pre-service teachers at the Diploma level since 2000. Before that they trained primary school teachers to the Primary Teachers Certificate (PTC). Francistown College was the last to graduate PTC holders in 1999. The upgrading of the Colleges of Education to diploma offering institutions followed a recommendation in the RNPE. Consequently, the BGCSE became the minimum entry requirement into the colleges' programmes, replacing the Junior Certificate. Also, implementation of the recommendation called for the upgrading of all PTC holders to diploma and degree levels. Francistown College of Education was earmarked exclusively for this task, making it the only College of Education offering in-service programmes. The upgrading of diploma certificate-holding primary school teachers is done in the Department of Primary Education of the Faculty of Education, University of Botswana (UB). Upgrading of teachers is being accelerated as part of the move towards the new vision of an all-graduate teaching profession.

There are two public Colleges of Education (i.e. Molepolole College of Education and Tonota College of Education) that produce teachers for the junior secondary education level. These emerged in the context of JSEIP (1981–91) which led to a phenomenal expansion of the junior secondary education level in preparation for the introduction of BEP. These also admit students with BGCSE. The Botswana College of Agriculture (BCA) offers a diploma in Agriculture Education programme. The upgrading of junior secondary education teachers to degree level is done in the Faculty of Education (University of Botswana) and at the BCA.

In the case of senior secondary education the RNPE stipulated that all senior secondary school teachers must be degree-holders. Two institutions, the University of Botswana and the Botswana College of Agriculture supply most senior secondary schools teachers. The latter offers a Bachelor of Science (Agriculture Education) while UB, through the Faculties of Education (FOE) and Engineering and Technology (FET), offers degree programmes. FET offers the Bachelor of Education (Design and Technology) programme, while the FOE offers a range of Bachelor of Education programmes, both pre-service and in-service, as well as the Post-Graduate Diploma in Education (PGDE) programme.

Two recent developments are likely to change the teacher education landscape profoundly. These are the Bennell and Molwane (2007) study on *Teacher Supply and Demand for Botswana Primary and Secondary Schools: 2006–2016* and the Tertiary Education Council's (TEC) *Tertiary Education Policy: Towards a knowledge-based Society* of 2008 (TEP hereafter) (Republic of Botswana, 2008). The former study predicts a fall in the demand for teachers by 2016 and beyond. It, therefore, calls for a matching of teacher supply and demand to curb the teacher over-production phenomenon that is evident in the country. *TEP*, on its part, wants diploma-granting colleges of education replaced with unified degree-granting university colleges. This move should be understood in the context of the new vision of an all-graduate teaching profession.

The current situation of scattered and marginal colleges of education is said to lack efficiency and economies of scale. Efforts to rationalize these colleges are afoot. The vision is for one or two autonomous teacher education institutions offering degree teacher education programmes.

Teacher recruitment and management

In terms of teacher recruitment and supply, in 1975, the Unified Teaching Service Act was enacted, paving the way for the Department of Unified Teaching Service (UTS), established in 1976 with the mandate to recruit and manage public schools teachers. It was replaced by the Department of Teaching Service Management (TSM) in 1992 which enforced a centralized teacher management system. In 2008, a new Public Service Act was enacted. This Act transferred TSM functions to DPSM, still in their centralized shape and form. Teachers are now recruited by DPSM, but are managed by MoE&SD through TSM.

To ensure that the most suitable candidates are recruited, selection criteria and procedures, such as candidates' screening and short listing, have been developed. Although by and large these procedures are followed, doubts, nonetheless, have been raised about objectivity and fairness in the recruitment and posting of teachers.

Botswana has no salary structure that is specific to teachers. There is a public service salary structure that progresses from A scale (lowest paid) to F scale (highest paid) (see Table 1.4). It applies to all government employees (i.e. administrative, professionals, the armed forces and support service staff). Teachers' salaries range between the C and D scales. Positions of responsibility start from Senior Teacher 1 to Head teacher. The other posts are automatic

Table 1.4 Teachers' salary scales

Salary grade	College teachers	Senior secondary school teachers	Junior secondary school teachers	Primary school teachers
D1	Principal			
D2	Deputy/Head of Department	Headmaster		
D3	Senior Lecturer 1	Deputy/Head of Department	Headmaster	
D4	Senior Lecturer 2	Senior Teacher 1	Deputy/Head of Department	Headteacher
C1	Lecturer 1	Senior Teacher 2	Senior Teacher 1	Deputy/ Head of Department
C2	Lecturer 2	Teacher	Senior Teacher 2	Senior Teacher 1
C3 (Entry scale- degree holder)	Assistant Lecturer	Assistant Teacher	Teacher	Teacher
C4 (Entry scale- diploma holder)			Probationer	Probationer

Source: Adapted from Republic of Botswana, 1996: 26

career progression posts into which any teacher moves upon the school head's recommendation.

Two important observations can be made about teacher remuneration in Botswana. First, lack of salary differentiation overall means that teachers' salary scales do not reflect the nature of their duties, implying some large measure of arbitrariness in assigning the various teacher cadres to the scales. The Job Evaluation and Teacher Appraisal exercises announced in 1989 and 1991 respectively reflected a desire to measure the work of teachers (Pansiri, 2004). The former introduced the concept of job measurement and profiling with a view to determine remuneration. Unfortunately, these exercises did not yield a remuneration package that reflected the uniqueness of the teaching profession. In 1991, a policy on 'parallel progression' was introduced and its objective was 'to attract and retain qualified and experienced officers with scarce skills which are highly needed for economic and technological development' (Republic of Botswana, 1991: 3). There have been delays in implementing the policy in the teaching profession. Its implementation would allow experienced and deserving classroom teachers to progress to the highest possible scale within their level of operation (senior secondary, junior secondary or primary) without being promoted to a position of responsibility, thus ensuring their retention in the classroom.

Second, the concept of 'level of operation' on which teacher remuneration is based (i.e. how a teacher is remunerated depends on whether they operate at the senior or junior secondary or primary school level) is dubious and divisive. The concept is informed by the assumption that teachers' work increases in complexity as they move up the levels. This obviously is controversial. Two teachers holding similar degree qualifications, one teaching in a junior secondary school and the other one in a senior secondary school earn different salaries on account of level of operation. This has generated very negative feelings in the profession.

Before April 2007, a diploma holder entered the service at salary scale C4, irrespective of where it was obtained (i.e. primary or secondary teachers college). Primary schools recruits entered the service as Senior Teacher 2 while the secondary schools ones were recruited as Assistant Teachers (Probationers). The latter, upon successful completion of two years of probation, automatically progressed to the next scale (C3), to a post called Teacher. After another two years, they progressed to salary scale C2, as 'Senior Teacher 2' and remained fixed there until they were promoted to a post of responsibility, meaning that for secondary school teachers salary scales C4, C3 and C2 were progressional scales. Meanwhile, their counterparts at primary school remained stuck at C4 since subsequent salary scales were promotional scales. Clearly, this remuneration policy discriminated against primary school teachers, 79 per cent of whom were women. This policy was revised in April 2007 to make provision for an automatic progressional scale for primary school teachers entering the service. But the secondary school teacher is still advantaged in that they are entitled to two progressional scales, that is, C3 and C2 compared to the one progressional scale for the primary school teacher. Degree-holders posted to a primary school remain the most disadvantaged because they enter service on a fixed salary scale of C3 and they remain there until they are promoted to the next scale, provided there is a vacancy, whereas their counterparts at a secondary school move a scale higher after a successful probationary period of two years and to the next scale (C2) after another two years. A degree-holder recruited to senior secondary enters at C3 and automatically moves to C2 and C1 progressively. While not the only factor, the 'levels of operation' dispensation has contributed significantly to low morale and growing militancy of teachers.

Classifying and then remunerating teachers in terms of 'levels of operation' is, therefore, very contentious. It has contributed to the emergence of fragmented teacher organizations. The Botswana Teachers Union (BTU), once the only voice of all teachers, broke up into four teacher organizations organized according to the levels of operation: the Botswana Primary School Teachers Association (BOPRITA) represents primary school teachers; the Botswana Federation of Secondary School Teachers (BOFESET) represents secondary school teachers; the Association of Botswana Tertiary Lecturers (ABOTEL) represents college lecturers while the old BTU's membership comprises those teachers at the four levels who have remained with the organization (Pansiri, 2004). The fragmentation has weakened teachers' bargaining powers and ability to protect their professional status from governmental assault.

Concluding remarks

Botswana has made big strides in the provision of education since 1966. She is close to achieving both the Education for All goals and the Millennium Development Goals (MDGs) on education. The Net Enrolment Rate (NER) for the 7–13 age group stood at 91.8 per cent in 2009. She is now working towards achieving universal secondary education by 2016. Tertiary education is being transformed with a view to increasing participation. All this is commendable progress. However, a number of challenges remain. As a way of concluding this chapter we would like to flag some of these.

First, quantitative growth has not been matched by improvements in the quality of education. In fact, there is a perception that quality has declined with the quantitative growth of the system. Efforts are underway to develop quality standards for the education system. It is hoped that once these are in place the quality of education will be enhanced.

Second, issues of access and equity remain. The 10 per cent of school-going age children missing from school should be a cause for concern. While a great deal has been achieved to ensure access more needs to be done to increase access and improve school retention particularly in remote areas where dropout rates are high. It is even more worrisome when challenges of access, equity and dropout assume an ethnic dimension. If not attended to promptly this issue has the potential to blemish Botswana's democratic credentials.

Third, teachers' morale and professional concerns need urgent attention. Talk of there being a crisis in Botswana schools should not be taken lightly. Decline (since 2000) in student performance across levels of operation that has been reported can to a large extent be attributed to the teacher factor. A series of teacher industrial actions, the latest being the 2011 public service strike, have adversely affected education quality. Reports of teachers having taken their battle with their employer to the classroom should worry the authorities.

Notes

1   For a detailed explication of this development, see Tabulawa (2011).

References

Bagwasi, M. M. (2004). 'The functional distribution of Setswana and English in Botswana', in M. J. Muthwi and A. N. Kioko (eds), *New Language Bearing in Africa: A Fresh Quest* (Toronto: Multilingual Matters).

Bantsi-Chimidza, L. and Mbunge, J. (1993). *Analysis of Policy Options for Transition Rates from Junior Secondary to Senior Secondary Education* (Gaborone: Botswana Educational Research Association).

Bennell, P. and Molwane, A. (2007). *Teacher Supply and Demand for Botswana Primary and Secondary Schools: 2006–2016* (Gaborone: Ministry of Education and Skills Development).

Koketso, G. (2001). 'The Remote Area Dweller Programme of the Ministry of Local Government', in O. Oussoren (ed.), *Education for Remote Area Dwellers in Botswana: Problems and Perspectives* (Windhoek: Research and Development Unit of the University of Botswana and Workgroup of Indigenous Minorities in Southern Africa).

Marope, P. T. M. (1994). 'Expansion of national systems of education: the case of Botswana', in V. D'Oyley, A. Blunt and R. Barnhardt (eds), *Education and Development: Lessons from the Third World* (Calgary: Detselig Enterprises Ltd).

— (2004). 'Unfair Remuneration of Primary School Teachers', A letter written to the Minister and Assistant Minister of Education – Botswana, 23 November 2004.

Polelo, M. M. (2005). 'School Dropout among the Remote Area Dwellers of Botswana: A Socio-cultural Analysis', *Pula: Botswana Journal of African Studies* 19, 1, pp. 85–102.

Republic of Botswana (1977a). *Education for Kagisano: Report on National Commission of Education* (Gaborone: Government Printers).

— (1977b). *National Policy on Education – Government Paper No 1 of 1977* (Gaborone: Government Printers).

— (1991). *The National Population Census Report* (Gaborone: Government Printer).

— (1993). *The Report of the National Commission on Education* (Gaborone: Government Printer).

— (1994). *The Revised National Policy on Education* (Gaborone: Government Printer).

— (1997). *Long Term Vision for Botswana: Towards Prosperity for All (Vision 2016)* (Gaborone: Government Printers).

— (1998). *Curriculum Blueprint: Senior Secondary School Programme* (Gaborone: Curriculum Development and Evaluation Department).

— (2003). *National Development Plan 8* (Gaborone: Government Printers).

— (2007a). *Curriculum Blueprint: The Ten Year Basic Education Programme* (Gaborone: Curriculum Development and Evaluation Department).

— (2007b). *Teaching Service Management Directive No 5 of 2007* (Gaborone: Ministry of Education and Skills Development).

— (2007c). *Teaching Service Management Directive No. 6 of 2007* (Gaborone: Ministry of Education and Skills Development).

— (2008). *Tertiary Education Policy: Towards a Knowledge Society* (Gaborone: Government Printers).

— (2010). *Education Statistics 2010* (Gaborone: Central Statistics Office).

— (2011). *2011 Population and Housing Census: Preliminary Results Brie* (Gaborone: Central Statistics Office).

Tabulawa, R. (1997). 'Pedagogical Classroom Practice and the Social Context: The Case of Botswana', *International Journal of Educational Development* 17, 2, pp. 189–204.

— (2009). 'Education Reform in Botswana: Reflections on Policy Contradictions and Paradoxes', *Comparative Education* 45, 1, pp. 87–107.

— (2011). 'The Rise and Attenuation of the Basic Education Programme (BEP) in Botswana', *International Journal of Educational Development* 31, 5, pp. 433–42.

Tshireletso, L. (1997). 'They are the Government's Children: School and Community Relations in Remote Area Dweller Settlement in Kweneng District – Botswana', *International Journal of Educational Development* 17, 2, pp. 173–88.

Youngman, F. (1993). 'Issues and trends in Education for All in Botswana', in S. Seisa and F. Youngman (eds), *Education for All in Botswana: Proceedings of the National Conference on Education for All* (Gaborone: Macmillan Botswana), pp. 188–200.

2

Lesotho: Organization, Structures and Challenges

Mapheleba Lekhetho
University of South Africa

Introduction

In Lesotho, formal education was introduced by the Western missionaries in 1838, and from that time it expanded as missionaries spread the gospel throughout the country. In 1871, the British colonial government came on board by providing grants-in-aid to the missionaries to pay teachers' salaries (Matsoha, 2010). This system was phased out, and replaced by the central Teaching Service Unit (TSU) in 1974, later renamed Teaching Service Department (TSD) in 1995, to manage teachers' affairs regarding employment and salaries (Urwick et al., 2005). In 1995 the Teaching Service Commission (TSC), constituted of three representatives from three major churches, and one government representative was established through *Education Act 1995* (Kingdom of Lesotho, 1995). TSC has the executive powers on the employment, promotion, demotion and discipline of teachers. Alongside TSC, there is Teaching Service Department (TSD), which administers teachers' salaries and benefits.

In 2000 the government progressively introduced Free Primary Education (FPE), starting in Standard I until this cohort reached Standard VII in 2006. In the same vein, a bursary scheme for orphaned and vulnerable children (OVCs) in secondary schools was introduced in 2002, and the textbook rental scheme in secondary education in 2004 to reduce the cost of textbooks. Since FPE was implemented, the government has built several government/community primary and secondary schools in underserved areas across the country, and additional classrooms in existing church schools. Finally, from January 2012, the Ministry of Education and Training (MOET) rationalized fees in all public secondary schools to increase access and affordability. It is evident from the above account that, over the years, the government has gradually entrenched its control on the education system. Thus, with the increasing curricular and funding involvement, the governance and control of schools is the shared responsibility of the churches and the state in Lesotho.

A brief overview of Lesotho's political history

With an area of 30,355 sq.km, a population estimated at 2.2 million, and completely surrounded by South Africa, Lesotho is one of the smallest countries in the world. It is largely homogenous, with 99.7 per cent of the population being native Basotho, who speak Sesotho, while the remaining 0.3 per cent is made up of Xhosas, Baphuthi and other ethnic minority groups, Asians and Europeans who speak their languages (Wikipedia, 2012).

A former British protectorate which attained independence in 1966, Lesotho is a constitutional monarchy, where the monarch is the head of state, and the prime minister the head of government. It is a unitary state, with two spheres of government, namely the central and local governments. Local government is fairly new and still in the process of being institutionalized. It was established after the first local government elections in April 2005, which ushered in community councils that are responsible for development and governance issues in a cluster of villages.

Despite being small and culturally homogeneous, Lesotho has had a troubled political history since independence, characterized by power struggles, intermittent political riots, military coups and post-election disturbances triggered by disgruntled opposition members over the election outcome. All these symptoms indicate that Lesotho is a divided society along political lines. According to Makoa (1996), political instability which had become so entrenched in society and organs of state during the repressive regimes of one-party state and military dictatorships, from 1970 to 1993, continue to polarize the country even after the restoration of democracy in 1993.

From 1965 to 1998, a major factor that caused political instability in Lesotho was the first-past-the-post (FPTP) electoral model, which turned Lesotho politics into a zero-sum game because of one dominant party, Basutoland Congress Party (BCP), led by the late Prime Minister, Ntsu Mokhehle, which overwhelmingly won all the constituencies in 1993. Due to political infighting, Mokhehle left BCP in 1997 to form Lesotho Congress for Democracy (LCD), and won the 1998 elections convincingly. This 'winner take all' outcome was a source of political disputes instigated by some disgruntled members of the opposition parties that lost the elections. The most devastating political crisis that crippled Lesotho's economy was the 1998 post-election violence, which led to the intervention of Southern African Development Community (SADC) force, made up of South Africa and Botswana, to restore order. This sparked massive looting and torching of businesses by disgruntled gangs and some disaffected members of the Lesotho Defence Force. After major hostilities, the SADC force retrained the Lesotho army, and now there is some order in the army, and relative stability in the country.

Following the 1998 political crisis, the FPTP model was modified to Mixed Member Proportional (MMP) in the 2002 elections to ensure that smaller parties which do not get seats in the 80 constituency-based FPTP seats are allocated compensatory seats from the 40 proportional representation (PR) seats available. Since MMP was adopted, there has been relative political stability, though there are still some tensions over different political issues. After the 2012 general elections, which resulted in a hung parliament, the three smaller parties, All Basotho Convention (ABC) led by the current Prime Minister, Mr Motsoahae Thabane, Lesotho Congress for Democracy (LCD) and Basotho National Party (BNP) formed a coalition government ousting the newly formed Democritic Congress (DC), which had won most seats but without an outright majority. This new form of government in Lesotho history was occasioned by the defection of the former Prime Minister, Mr Pakalitha Mosisili from the ruling LCD to form DC due to political infighting. Though there is some relative stability under the current coalition government, there are still some intra-party and inter-party conflicts charactersised by public spats and tensions between the once-ruling DC and other parties, which often coalesce against it. All these are the hallmarks of political instability and dysfunctionality, which inhibit the country from forging a common national purpose (Maundeni, 2010).

An overview of the socio-economic situation

Lesotho is classified as a poor, least-developed country ranked 158 of 186, and in the group of *low human development* countries in the Human Development Index (HDI) in 2013 (UNDP, 2013). This is partly because it has limited resources, with only small deposits of diamonds and a weak industrial base that contributes very little to the national fiscus. The only significant natural resource that Lesotho has is water, with a hydropower component, which it sells to South Africa, and supplies to Gauteng province, its economic hub. Lesotho Highlands Water Project (LHWP) manages this project, which started with construction works after Lesotho and South Africa signed a treaty in 1986.

A major threat to Lesotho's development efforts is a high prevalence rate of Human Immunodeficiency Virus (HIV)/Acquired Immunodeficiency Syndrome (AIDS), estimated at 23.2 per cent of adults and the third highest in the world, with more than 120,000 children orphaned by AIDS (WFP, 2007; UNICEF, 2008). Over half of the 260,000 adults living with HIV in Lesotho are women (Avert, 2012). Crippling poverty coupled with the HIV pandemic has reduced the life expectancy to 48.2 years (Avert, 2012). HIV/AIDS affects many children academically in that some of them are sick and fear stigmatization, while some care for terminally ill parents and devote little time for their studies. According to Avert (2012: n.p.), 'out of all countries with an HIV prevalence greater than 1 per cent, Lesotho has the largest percentage of children who have lost one or both parents'.

Approximately, 43.4 per cent of Lesotho's population lives below the international poverty line of US $1.25 a day (UNDP, 2011). Three-quarters of Lesotho's population of approximately 2.2 million people live in the mountainous districts, and about 68 per cent are considered poor (WFP, 2007; Wikipedia, 2012). Lesotho's economy is integrated with, and heavily dependent on, that of its larger and more affluent neighbour, South Africa, to a point where it is often said that when South Africa sneezes Lesotho catches cold. Despite Lesotho's weak economy, its expenditure on education of around 12 per cent is considered high by international and regional standards, compared to the world average of 4 per cent. As a result, compared to other sub-Saharan countries with similar economies, Lesotho has a high adult literacy rate of 82 per cent.

With a high unemployment rate estimated at 26 per cent in 2008, the majority of Lesotho's inhabitants subsist on farming and migrant labour earnings, mainly from the male population working in the South African mines, and receipts from Southern Africa Customs Union (SACU) (Bureau of Statistics, 2012; Wikipedia, 2012). However, in recent years, thousands of Basotho mineworkers have been retrenched due to heavy job losses in the mining sector (Linking Lives, 2009). Nonetheless, the traditional migrant labour system is still intact since many professional and unskilled Basotho workers continue to work in various sectors of the South African economy.

The manufacturing sector, particularly textile manufacturing, with around 43,000 workers is Lesotho's biggest employer, partly due to the African Growth and Opportunities Act (AGOA), implemented in 2001. Through AGOA, the US government gave 34 eligible sub-Saharan African countries duty-free access to the US markets. However, in recent years many factories have been closed down due to the global economic meltdown which affected many Western economies. This added to the economic woes of the country and deepened poverty as many workers were laid off.

In the previous budget speeches, the Minister of Finance and Development Planning, Dr Timothy Thahane (2008; 2012) cautioned that one of the risks facing Lesotho is its 'overdependence (over 60%) on SACU revenues'. The current Finance Minister, Dr Leketekete Ketso (2013) also expressed similar concerns in the budger speech that the dependency on SACU revenues makes Lesotho vulnerable to external shocks, and harms its development effors. SACU consists of South Africa, Botswana, Namibia, Lesotho and Swaziland and its primary goal is to promote economic development within member states through harmonization of trade. Among others, SACU raises revenue by charging common external tariffs on all goods imported into the Union from the rest of the world, and uses a revenue-sharing formula for the distribution of customs and exercise revenues collected by the Union.

Brief history of education in Lesotho

The first missionaries from the Paris Evangelical Missionary Society (PEMS), later renamed Lesotho Evangelical Church (LEC), arrived in Lesotho in 1833, followed by the Roman Catholic Mission (RCM) in 1862 and the Anglican Church of Lesotho (ACL) in 1875. The advent of the first group of missionaries ushered in the opening of the first school for infants and a reading centre for adults in 1838 (Ministry of Education, Sports and Culture, 1982). The main focus of the first schools was the acquisition of functional literacy at an elementary level and reading of the Bible. The curriculum of the time was tailored to expand the evangelical work of the missionaries.

As they spread the gospel throughout the country, the early missionaries also established schools, operated in poorly constructed buildings or in the open air. The establishment of schools, which is a public good, was, to a large extent, driven by competition for religious expansionism and dominance among the three major churches, and other religious groups that followed later. Due to denominational rivalry, throughout the history of formal education in Lesotho, church membership determined the school an individual attended and the type of education he or she received (Odendaal, 2000). This is particularly the case at secondary level when schools select students into Form A from different primary schools. In many cases, church affiliation is a major consideration for parents and children when selecting schools, and for some secondary schools when selecting applicants.

Up to now, the three main churches: RCM, LEC and ACL still operate the largest number of schools in Lesotho. Other churches in conjunction with the government own a relatively smaller number of schools. In 2012, the churches owned 81 per cent primary schools, while the government and community owned 11 per cent and 4 per cent respectively (MOET, 2012). Although the RCM arrived long after the LEC, the former overtook it in terms of religious and educational dominance, partly because it has superior physical structures in most of its missions and schools, and good schools that generally produce better results in the national examinations. This could be attributed to the fact that their missions have maintained strong links with the sister missions in wealthy Western countries such as Canada, which provide strong financial backing, while the protestant churches are financially independent, with limited income streams.

Vision, goals, objectives and values of Lesotho education

The Constitution of Lesotho stipulates that Lesotho shall endeavour to make education available to all, and shall adopt policies that ensure that:

1. education is directed to the full development of the human personality and sense of dignity and strengthening the respect for human rights and fundamental freedom;
2. primary education is compulsory and available to all;
3. secondary education, including technical and vocational education, is made generally available and accessible to all by every appropriate means, and in particular, by the progressive introduction of free education; and
4. higher education is made equally accessible to all, on the basis of capacity, by every appropriate means, and in particular, by the progressive introduction of free education. . . . (Kingdom of Lesotho, 1993)

The above goals underscore the importance of education in moral development, and cultivating a culture of human rights, democratic values and respect. Though the constitution stipulates that secondary education should be made accessible to all, Lesotho has not fully achieved this goal since fees in many secondary schools are still prohibitive for many parents. To expand access, MOET rationalized fees in all public secondary schools in 2012. However, there are reports that some schools have resisted this policy on the grounds that it is financially unfeasible to run schools on the capped fees. Though fee rationalization has increased affordability and access, many children still fail to proceed to secondary schools on account of abject poverty.

With regard to higher education, it is only a tiny minority that gains access because of high wastage and inefficiency at lower levels. The stark differences between schools in terms of resources, staff profile, socio-economic status and selectivity widen the gaps in achievement between students in the national examinations, particularly in COSC, and thus access to higher education. To increase access to higher education, the government provides scholarships to all qualifying students to study at different tertiary institutions, including specialized fields outside the country. However, due to economic crisis that Lesotho has been through, the government has capped the budget allocated to the National Manpower Development Secretariat, an agency that administers the scholarship fund, despite the increasing student demand. As a result, some students are not granted scholarships.

The vision of the MOET regarding the country's education is that:

> Basotho shall be a functionally literate society with well-grounded moral and ethical values; adequate social, scientific and technical knowledge and skills by the year 2020. (MOET, 2005)

To operationalize this vision, the Ministry formulated the following objectives, among others:

1. To improve access, efficiency and equity of education and training at all levels;
2. To improve the quality of education and training;
3. To ensure that curricula and materials are relevant to the needs of Lesotho ... and gender responsive;
4. To promote gender equality and ensure empowerment [of the] disadvantaged groups.

Some government interventions to achieve these objectives

Access

As mentioned earlier, to achieve universal access to primary education, the government introduced FPE in 2000 and built additional classrooms in existing schools and new government schools where there was need. To reduce costs and expand access to secondary education, fees in all new government secondary schools have been capped at M650 per annum. Finally, starting in 2012, fees in all day public secondary schools have been rationalized, capped at M1,300 per annum, while fees for boarding schools have been set at the maximum of M2,400 per annum.

Despite access being open, many children, especially boys in the remote rural areas, do not attend school due to poverty and child labour, particularly looking after livestock to supplement their families' income. To tackle this, the government enacted *Education Act 2010*, which makes primary education free and compulsory (Kingdom of Lesotho, 2010). However, the challenge is that, in general, there is weak law enforcement in Lesotho. Hence, it is questionable whether the government has the capacity and political will to prosecute parents or guardians who do not send their children to school.

Quality

To improve education quality, the government provides textbooks and stationery to primary schools through School Supply Unit (SSU). Similarly, textbook rental scheme for secondary education was introduced in 2004 to reduce the costs to parents. To improve the quality of teachers, Lesotho College of Education (LCE), the country's only teacher training college, increased the admission requirements for its full-time programmes, upgraded all its qualifications from certificate to diploma level in 1998 and introduced Distance Teacher Education Programme (DTEP) for unqualified and under-qualified primary school teachers in 2002. Similarly, the National University of Lesotho (NUL) reintroduced a part-time Bachelor of Education (Primary) degree as a fully-fledged programme in 2007. The MOET also offers several in-service training workshops for teachers in primary and secondary schools on a range of topics. Finally, in recent years, the government improved the salaries of teachers in order to motivate and retain them in the teaching service.

Equity

Equity is achieved by promoting education of both boys and girls, children of ethnic minorities, those with special educational needs and access and retention. The Special Education Unit within the Ministry of Education was established in 1991 to run the special education programme. The emphasis here is on the integration of children with special needs into regular schools, and developing appropriate life skills. It also runs sensitization workshops for teachers in selected primary schools and for primary inspectors depending on the availability of funds.

Although the children of minority groups like Xhosas and Baphuthi in the districts of Quthing and Qacha's Nek have access to education, they are not taught in their home languages in the first years of primary, but in the dominant Sesotho language. This creates a language hurdle for many of them and deprives them of their cultural identity. Finally, there are no targeted interventions for improving the achievement of learners in failing schools, particularly those in inaccessible rural areas.

Relevance

Primary and secondary curricula are reviewed from time to time to ensure that they respond to the changing needs of the country, and are sensitive to the local context and sociocultural circumstances of learners. There are also ongoing efforts to entirely localize COSC curriculum and assessment. The localization process started in 1989 with marking, but not the setting of the examinations, which is still done in Cambridge. Already in 1995, the former Registrar of the Examinations Council of Lesotho, Mr Pule noted that the United Kingdom itself was changing to a new system of curriculum and examinations to meet their own needs, hence Lesotho had to follow suit (Mavugara-Shava, 2005).

An historical overview of school and teacher management

Unlike other British colonies, the pre-independence colonial government left the ownership and control of education in the hands of the missionaries in Lesotho. Until the enactment of *Education Act 1995*, teacher management was the domain of the church-appointed school manager, who was responsible for the immediate appointment, transfer and discipline of teachers at parish level, but had to work in collaboration with the relevant denominational educational secretary, who had executive powers (Ministry of Education, 1996; World Bank, 1999). This joint responsibility in school and teacher management favoured the church, and prompted the government to agitate for equitable power sharing with denominational authorities, so that it could be more actively involved in school governance. What the government actually wanted was a well spelled out partnership with the church, with a clear-cut delineation of functions. To this end, the Education Department was established in 1927 and 'undertook the formulation of a uniform syllabus and a system of school inspection' and standard examinations for primary and secondary schools (Ministry of Education, Sports and Culture, 1982: 2).

Matooane (1980) states that in 1945, Britain established the Commission on Education led by Sir Fred Clarke, otherwise, known as the Clarke Commission on Education, to examine:

- the organization and control of schools;
- the place of missionary effort; and
- the financial provision made and the method of administering it.

Some of the key developments that resulted from the commission included the promulgation of a comprehensive Education Act which defined the roles and responsibilities of the government and churches in the management of policy and schools, the establishment of the central and district advisory committees to guide education policy, education management, uniform syllabuses and a system of school inspection (Clarke Commission, in Muzvidziwa and Seotsanyana, 2002). By implication, the Commission delineated the roles and responsibilities, and the ambit of control of the church proprietors and the government as stakeholders (Ministry of Education, Sports and Culture, 1982). In 1982 the Ministry of Education, Sports and Culture (1982: 3) reported that education in Lesotho 'is organized under two distinct institutions: the government and churches'. Though not mentioned here, the local communities (parents) are considered to be an integral part of the tripartite. This enduring partnership is further accentuated by *Education Act 2010*, which provides for the involvement of each of the three partners in the management of schools.

Educational secretaries

In terms of *Education Act 2010*, the educational secretaries are appointed by their respective churches to coordinate and supervise the educational work of schools and to liaise with the MOET on matters of management of schools (Kingdom of Lesotho, 2010). The government is responsible for the remuneration of educational secretaries of churches with more than 20 schools. In the past, the educational secretaries had greater powers and clearly-defined roles, which included handling teachers' employment matters. However, in recent years, their powers have been gradually curtailed by the creation of central structures such as TSC, and the human resources officers based in all the ten district education offices of the country. These offices work in conjunction with TSD and have taken over most of the employment-related responsibilities from the church authorities.

Though it is often stated that parents form the third leg in the metaphorical three-legged pot in the management of schools in Lesotho, their involvement is minimal and mainly in the form of support to the other two stronger legs (government and churches). The role that they play in schools is mainly to respond to the requests of these two main role-players, particularly school authorities by paying fees, attending parents' meetings, contributing labour in school projects, discipline of their children and supporting their learning. Otherwise, their formal participation in school governance is by means of representation on the school board.

Figure 2.1 depicts the typology of a three-legged pot often used to describe the arrangement of education management in Lesotho. This metaphor reflects

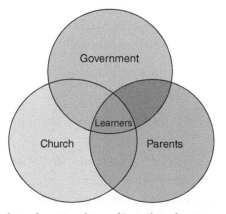

Figure 2.1 The three-legged pot typology of Lesotho education system

that all the three major partners – the government, the church and parents (communities) – are interconnected and interdependent. As such, they should work harmoniously and support one another's efforts. Learners are at the centre or intersection to show their centrality and that they are the pivot around which the education machinery revolves. Thus, all the educational efforts of the different partners should be geared towards serving their best interests, and optimizing student learning and academic success.

There are different views on the impact of this shared responsibility or dual control system. Many educators, parents and members of the community argue that the dual management arrangement of schools causes confusion as there are two distinct authorities in control of schools. They argue that this causes a dysfunctional education system and a weak school management as no single authority is responsible for education in the country. This means that before the government can implement any new education policy or legislation, it has to engage in extensive discussions with the church authorities in order to get their assent. The section below discusses the organizational structure of MOET (as illustrated in Figure 2.2).

The MOET is responsible for the provision, management and regulation of education. It is headed by the Minister assisted by the Deputy Minister both of whom are members of parliament, appointed by the Prime Minister to lead the Ministry. The Principal Secretary is an administrative head responsible for running the Ministry. This is a strategic, fixed-term contract position. The principal secretary is a link between the Minister and the operational staff of the Ministry and other stakeholders. He is assisted by the deputy principal secretary, and a team of senior managers responsible for different programmes. The Ministry has seven programmes, namely, primary, secondary, teaching services, tertiary, curriculum services, planning and technical and vocational training, each headed by a chief education officer (CEO) or a director. Each programme has different departments or sections headed by departmental heads or line managers.

National Curriculum Development Centre

The National Curriculum Development Centre (NCDC) was established in 1980 to oversee the development of curriculum that responds to the socio-economic needs of learners and the country. The primary task of NCDC is to develop the curriculum, develop appropriate materials and methods, devise and carry out

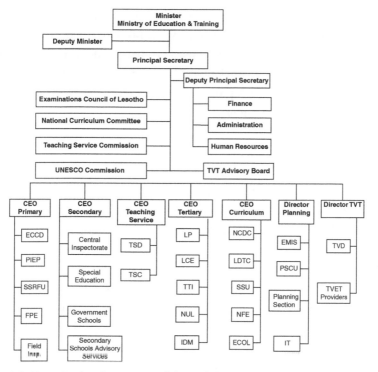

Figure 2.2 Organizational structure of the MOET

Source: MOET (2006)

Key

ECCD	**Early Childhood Care and Development;**	**LP**	**Lerotholi Polytechnic**
PIEP	Primary In-service Education Programme	LCE	Lesotho College of Education
SSRFU	School Self-Reliance Food Unit	TTI	Thaba-Tseka Technical Institute
FPE	Free Primary Education	NUL	National University of Lesotho
Field Insp.	Field Inspectorate	IDM	Institute of Development Management
TSD	Teaching Service Department	NCDC	National Curriculum Development Centre
TSC	Teaching Service Commission	LDTC	Lesotho Distance Teaching Centre
SSU	School Supply Unit	NFE	Non-Formal Education
ECOL	Examinations Council of Lesotho	PSCU	Public Section Coordinating Unit
EMIS	Education Management Information System	IT	Information Technology
TVT	Technical and Vocational Training	TVET	Technical and Vocational Education and Training
CEO	Chief Education Officer		

plans for disseminating the curriculum materials and methods to schools and teachers and organize in-service training workshops for teachers. NCDC works through subject panels that consist of teachers, teacher training institutions, the inspectorate and teachers' associations. All curriculum materials intended for use in the schools must be approved by the government on the advice of the National Curriculum Committee.

Central inspectorate

The Central inspectorate, responsible for the inspection of secondary schools, was established in 1988, and encompasses ten subject specialists (Ministry of Education, 2000). Their major task is to inspect, support, supervise, monitor, evaluate the work of schools and to ensure that the curriculum is offered effectively and in accordance with the norms and standards prescribed by the Ministry (Ministry of Education, 1992). The main function of the inspectorate is to ensure that there is good practice in schools, both in pedagogy and administration. The subject inspectors do this by organizing in-service workshops for teachers, visiting schools to demonstrate aspects of curriculum policies and providing support services to the school administration.

Field inspectorate

The Field inspectorate, also called primary inspectorate is responsible for the professional support, supervision and inspection of primary schools. Primary inspectors are based in all the ten districts of the country, and they oversee all the educational work in the district including post-primary schools. However, since FPE was introduced in 2000, the bulk of the inspectors' work has shifted from the core function of supervision and inspection of schools, to administrative duties such as processing payment of caterers and cooks in schools, settling disputes in schools and attending to assignments from headquarters in Maseru.

Assessment

Most of the assessments are school-based, prepared and conducted by grade teachers in primary schools, and subject teachers in secondary schools, using a variety of assessment techniques such as tests, quizzes, assignments, mid-term and end-of-year examinations. The Examinations Council of Lesotho

(ECOL) is a semi-autonomous body constituted to conduct three major national examinations, namely the Primary School Leaving Examinations (PSLE) at Grade VII, Junior Certificate (JC) examinations at Grade X, and Cambridge Overseas School Certificate (COSC) examinations at Grade XII, as well as assessment tests for other institutions in a manner that will promote the culture of learning and teaching, and maintain the quality and standards of education in Lesotho. The results of the examinations are used to select students for admission into the next phases of education. One of the objectives of ECOL is 'to provide feedback on the effectiveness of the curriculum development and other educational endeavors which are intended to improve the quality of teaching and learning in schools' (Ministry of Education and Training, 2012: n.p.).

Structure of the education system

Formal education in Lesotho follows a 7–3–2–4 structure, representing seven years of primary, three years of junior secondary (Form A-C), two years of senior secondary (Form D-E) and four years of tertiary for a Bachelor's degree. However, there are differences in course duration between different tertiary institutions depending on the qualification pursued. Figure 2.3 graphically presents Lesotho's education system, showing the different grades in which learners are expected to be at particular ages. However, the reality is that because of low efficiency and high repetition rates, many learners complete older than the expected official ages. Unlike the school calendar which runs from January to December, the academic years of many tertiary institutions start in August and end in May of the following year. So, this delays students from completing at the illustrated ages.

Pre-primary education

Historically early childhood education was not part of formal education in Lesotho. Many children started school at the age of six or older. However, since the 1990s, the number of pre-primary schools, also known as early childhood care and development (ECCD) centres has grown dramatically throughout the country, fuelled by the sensitization campaigns run by MOET. These centres are largely owned by individuals, communities and churches, and they serve as a source of income for the unemployed women who operate them.

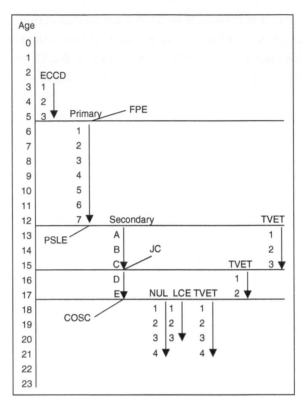

Figure 2.3 Lesotho's education system
Source: World Bank (2005)

Key

FPE	**Free Primary Education**	NUL	**National University of Lesotho**
PSLE	Primary School Leaving Examinations	LCE	Lesotho College of Education
JC	Junior Certificate	COSC	Cambridge Overseas School Certificate
TVET	Technical and Vocational Education and Training		

Pre-primary education is for children aged 3 to 5 and is non-compulsory. It uses a practical approach, providing children with 'hands on' learning experiences. The main focus is to develop children's cognitive, motor and communicative skills needed for successful primary education and to prepare them emotionally and behaviourally in order to achieve their potential. Unlike the higher phases of schooling, the ECCD centres are not publicly-funded, and do not follow any prescribed curriculum. However, there is an ECCD unit within

MOET that coordinates and oversees the early childhood activities. This was started as a project in 1985, and later integrated into the Ministry's structure in 1995.

In 1999, the Ministry appointed ten national teacher trainers (NTTs) based in the ten districts of the country to provide professional support to preschool teachers. In 2006, the Ministry launched a pilot project for reception classes attached to 11 government primary schools for children aged five, and paid caregivers wages. In 2012, the Ministry provided capitation grants to 227 reception classes attached to primary schools for school feeding and payment of caregivers' wages, and fees for 2,786 orphaned and vulnerable children in ECCD, exceeding the target of 2,690 (Khaketla, 2012).

Primary education

The major goals of primary education are to achieve basic literacy and numeracy for all pupils, and to lay a foundation for secondary education. In primary school, ten subjects are taught, namely English, Sesotho, mathematics, science, social studies, art, religious education, health, home economics and agriculture. The first five are examinable in PSLE, while the rest are ancillary. A teacher is expected to teach all the subjects. However in many schools, there is an increasing trend of 'subject-teaching' where a grade teacher arranges with her colleagues to teach certain subjects, usually one or two that they are more competent in. Moreover, since the introduction of FPE in 2000, the government shoulders most of the costs of primary education, which include the supply of textbooks, stationery and instructional materials to primary schools including those in inaccessible mountain areas using helicopters.

Feeding scheme

In order to mitigate the effects of poverty, promote school attendance and enhance learning, there is school feeding programme assisted by World Food Programme (WFP) for primary schools in the highlands, which started in 1965. Under this programme, the government engages cooks to prepare and serve food at a cost of M1.50 per child, per day on fixed-term rotational contracts. Between 1990 and 1994, WFP gradually began to phase out schools in the lowlands and foothills. To replace WFP assistance, the government introduced School Self-Reliance Project (SSRP) in 1989, which provided farm inputs for schools in the foothills and lowlands, assisting them to establish school gardens and rear livestock in order to grow their supplies for school meals (Ellis et al., 2009). However, the efforts of SSRP, which was later renamed School Self-Reliance and Feeding Unit (SSRFU), were unsuccessful since most schools lacked adequate resources and capacity to sustain their self-reliance projects. Due to failure of self-reliance projects in schools, SSRFU has focused on training cooks and caterers on food handling, basic hygiene, preparation and nutrition.

For schools in the lowlands, caterers are engaged on fixed-term rotational contracts to acquire, cook, deliver and serve a prescribed menu at the cost of M3.50 per child per day to all children under FPE programme. This cost is reviewed from time to time to keep up with inflation. This scheme has helped some unemployed women to generate income for their families, and created a market for local agricultural food products.

The state of physical facilities

Since 1994 the government has intensified the construction of additional classrooms and provision of furniture in most primary and secondary schools with a substantial number of learners. This was given a further boost after the introduction of FPE, with funding from various development partners such as the Government of Japan, Irish AID, African Development Bank (ADB) and the World Bank. As a result, schools in high population density areas in the lowlands, and some in the highlands, have decent standard classrooms, physical facilities and furniture.

In contrast, many schools with small enrolments in sparsely populated, hard-to-reach mountain areas are terribly under-resourced and educationally unviable. In most cases, teaching is conducted in decrepit, poorly constructed buildings, usually church halls or in the open air. Most teachers in these one- or two-teacher schools are unqualified and yet they do multigrade teaching. These wide disparities in the quality of facilities between schools based on geographic area predetermine the quality of teachers who teach in them, and the quality of education pupils receive, in the sense that it is usually the unqualified teachers who teach in schools in the hardship areas.

Coverage and gender equity in primary education

Despite primary education being free, in 2012, the net enrolment rate (NER) was 81.1 per cent; 79.6 per cent for males and 82.6 per cent for females (MOET, 2012). This shows that a substantial proportion of primary school-age learners, 18.9 per cent, is not in school, and that males have lower participation. During the same period, the average pupil-teacher ratio was favourable at 34:1, way below the official of 40:1. This is mainly because pupils and teachers are not evenly distributed, with some schools having larger enrolments and proportionally fewer teachers, and vice versa.

Unlike many African countries where the participation of boys in school is higher than that of girls, in Lesotho the situation is different in the sense that more females than males attend school. The 2012 education statistics reflect that from Standard I to IV there are usually more males than females enrolled in primary schools. This could be a reflection of the overall population distribution of boys and girls at this age. However from Standard V through Standard VII, the enrolments of females surpass those of males. For instance, in 2012 there were 36,438 males and 31,033 females enrolled in Standard I, but in Standard VII there were 21,860 males and 24,962 females (MOET, 2012).

The lower participation of male students in school has a cultural explanation in that in the Sesotho culture women and girls are supposed to be treated tenderly and with sensitivity because they are considered to be delicate, while men and boys are supposed to be treated in a harsher way to prepare them for the vagaries of life. The second reason is the traditional migrant labour system where young Basotho men used to work in the South African mines to earn a living and support their families. Moreover, due to widespread poverty in the remote rural areas, young boys are forced to look after livestock in order to supplement their families' income.

The initiation school (*lebollo* in Sesotho), a secret rite of passage for boys marking transition from boyhood into manhood, also accounts for their lower participation because it usually runs from July to February in a secluded area, and clashes with the school calendar, which runs from January to December. Many boys often abandon school in the middle of the year to undergo this ritual. Since most schools are run by the churches, the initiation school is considered to be a pagan practice, and at variance with the Christian teachings. Hence, when they come back from the 'mountain' (*thabeng*) for reincorporation into society, many schools refuse the initiates and require that they should take one year cooling off period to readjust to normal life.

Secondary education

Secondary education is the intermediate level between elementary and tertiary education. The curriculum followed is largely general, with some technical and vocational subjects that prepare students for college or university education. Secondary education consists of junior and senior levels. Junior secondary runs from Form A-C (Grade VIII–X), at the end of which, students sit for the JC examinations, while senior secondary or high school level or O-level, runs from Form D to Form E (Grade XI–XII). At the end of this level, students write the school-leaving COSC examinations.

In the past, COSC examinations were notorious for being difficult, with only a tiny minority who qualified for admission at the NUL, the country's only public university. However, in recent years, performance has improved steadily, and more students qualify for university admission. But in comparison with other countries, COSC performance is still very poor, given that in 2012, for instance, the pass rate was 55.4 per cent. This is low since it includes 33 per cent of candidates who passed in third class, and can hardly be admitted to any tertiary institutions. Only 4.8 per cent and 17.6 per cent candidates obtained first and second class passes respectively. Many of the candidates who obtain second class without a credit in English language or credit passes in mathematics and science subjects are not admitted at NUL and other tertiary institutions that offer science-based courses. The problem has been exacerbated by lack of adequate facilities in these institutions.

Coverage, participation and gender parity in secondary education

In 2012, the total enrolment in registered secondary schools was 127,852 (MOET, 2012). Girls constituted 57 per cent and boys 43 per cent of this total. During the same period, the national average student-teacher ratio was 25:1, way below the official ratio of 35:1 (MOET, 2012). However, because of an uneven distribution of teachers and learners, some teachers in some schools or critical subjects such as mathematics and science are often overloaded, while others are underutilized.

Gender parity revealed that the number of female students was higher than that of males at appropriate ages in all the grades at this level. However, as age increased, the number of male students surpassed that of females. This could be linked to the fact that the Sesotho culture favours females because they are considered to be vulnerable. There is a common belief that educating a girl is a worthwhile investment since girls usually stand by their parents at all times. Education is also viewed as a safety net for girls if they encounter challenges later in life.

In 2012 the gross enrolment ratio (GER) was 55.4 per cent exactly the same as that of the previous year (MOET, 2012). This shows that a large percentage of secondary school age youth (44.6%) are not in school. Compared to primary, secondary school GER is quite low, possibly due to high dropout rates in primary schools and prohibitively high fees in secondary schools. However, as opposed to primary schools where GER has been decreasing, in secondary schools, the rates have been going up, arguably because of a government bursary scheme for orphaned and vulnerable children where regulated fees in government schools is capped at M500.00 to ensure affordability. In 2012, GER for males and females were 46.9 per cent and 64.0 per cent respectively, which signifies that a relatively larger percentage of females than males is enrolled in secondary schools (MOET, 2012).

Performance in primary, junior secondary and senior secondary school

Compared to the neighbouring countries, Lesotho's performance is dismal at all levels of the education system. For instance, in 2012, the PSLE pass rate was 87.2 per cent, 68.4 per cent at JC and only 55.4 per cent at COSC (Examinations Council of Lesotho 2013a, 2013b, 2013c). Though PSLE and JC performance looks better than COSC, it is argued that COSC examination actually evaluates teachers, and indirectly monitors the standards in the lower levels of primary and junior secondary education (Maqutu, 2003). Thus, to a large extent, students' poor performance in COSC examinations could be traced back to the poor quality of primary education. This gap in performance, often blamed on curricular disjuncture between these three levels has exposed that the standard of teaching and learning is weaker at the lower levels, especially at primary level. Therefore, to fix the perennial problem of poor performance at COSC, the government and other stakeholders should focus efforts on improving the quality of teachers, particularly for primary level through high selectivity, intensive training, effective school management and strong support from MOET.

In the 2010 Southern and Eastern Africa Consortium for Monitoring Educational Quality (SACMEQ III) project where 15 countries participated in the reading and mathematics tests for Standard 6 pupils, Lesotho came way below the averages of 512 and 509.7 respectively, with mean scores of 467.9 in reading and 476.9 in mathematics (SACMEQ, 2010). In contrast, Botswana and Swaziland, which have similar colonial and education histories fared better, with reading mean scores of 534.6 and 549.4, and mathematics mean scores of 520.5 and 540.8 respectively. The SACMEQ III mean scores of Botswana and Swaziland correlate positively with their superior school-leaving examination results, which have been consistently better than those of Lesotho.

Some of the factors that contribute to the dismal performance in mathematics and science in COSC include a critical shortage of teachers of these subjects, inexperienced, unqualified and under-qualified teachers and a high staff turnover due to their high demand in the job market, and the resurgent brain drain to the neighbouring South Africa because of better salaries. Maqutu (2003) identifies high mobility of mathematics and science teachers as a major cause of poor performance in COSC. A shortage of mathematics and science teachers is directly linked to their low production by educational institutions within the country, especially the leading NUL (Moru et al., 2009).

Teachers in primary and secondary schools as quality indicators

The phenomenon of attrition and teacher wastage is higher among secondary school teachers, particularly graduates, than primary school teachers (Halliday, 1989; Ministry of Education, 1992). This is arguably because graduate teachers possess saleable skills that are in demand in the job market.

Primary school teachers

In 2012, the total number of teachers in registered primary schools was 11,200, signifying a drop in the numbers of teahers in recent years (MOET, 2012).

A disaggregation of this total by gender reflects that primary school teaching is dominated by female teachers with a total of 8,579 (77%), compared to 2,621 (23%) males. A similar pattern is discernible in the number of qualified teachers, with 6,095 (81%) females and only 1,470 (19%) males. This imbalance is a result of the stereotypes that teaching or nurturing younger children is suitable for women. The distribution of teachers by district in general, and qualified teachers in particular, reflects that they are concentrated in the lowland districts, while the districts in the mountains, namely Thaba-Tseka, Mokhotlong and Qacha's Nek have the smallest proportion of qualified teachers (MOET, 2012). Secondary school teachers

Whereas primary school teaching is female-dominated, the gap closes considerably at secondary level where, out of a total of 5,094 teachers in 2012, there were 2,208 (43%) males and 2,886 (57%) females (MOET, 2012). Of the total 3,969 qualified teachers, 1,615 (41%) were males, and 2,354 (59%) females. However, in terms of subject specialization, male teachers usually outnumber females in mathematics and science. Qualified teachers are concentrated in the lowland districts and urban areas, while the districts in the mountain areas have comparatively fewer qualified teachers in both primary and secondary schools.

Conclusion

A dominant feature of Lesotho's education system is a dual control between the church and state. This partnership sometimes poses challenges as there are conflicting expectations between these two partners on the management of education. Some examples of policies that were challenged by some church authorities include the introduction of Free Primary Education 2000 and the rationalization of fees in secondary schools in 2012, partly because of failure by the government to absorb some of the costs that were covered through school fees. These initiatives have been introduced with a goal of expanding access to primary and secondary education. With regard to quality, a cohort analysis and analysis of examination results reveals that Lesotho's education is inefficient, as seen by high dropout, repetition and failure rates, especially at COSC level. Lesotho's poor performance in the regional SACMEQ test confirms this. Some of the factors that lead to this poor education quality include the stark inequalities in resource and teacher distribution between urban and rural schools, inefficient teachers, weak macro- and micro-level management of schools and a shortage of mathematics and science teachers at secondary school level, especially in the rural schools and the country's unstable political situation and poverty.

References

Avert (2012). *HIV and AIDS in Lesotho* [Online] Available at: www.avert.org/aids-lesotho.htm. Accessed on 12 May 2012.

Bureau of Statistics (2012). *Key Indicators* [Online] Available at: www.bos.gov.ls. Accessed on 15 May 2012.

Ellis, F., Devereux, S. and White, P. (2009). *Social protection in Africa* (Cheltenham: Edward Elgar Publishing Limited). [Online] Available at: books.google.co.za/books?isbn=1848442580.... Accessed on 15 May 2012.

Examinations Council of Lesotho (2013a). *2012 PSLE Passslist* (Maseru: ECOL).

— (2013b). *2012 JC Passlist* (Maseru: ECOL).

— (2013c). *2012 COSC Passlist* (Maseru: ECOL).

Halliday, I. (1989). *Teacher Management and Records in National Educational System: Resource Book for Educational Administrators* (London: Commonwealth Secretariat).

Ketso, L. V. (2013). 'Promoting Growth for Economic and Social Development: Budget Speech to Parliament for the 2013/2014 Fiscal Year', Maseru, 22 February 2013.

Khaketla, M. (2012). Minister of Education and Training Seeks Budget Allocation in Parliament. [Online] Available at: www.education.gov.ls/index2.php?=com_content&do ... Accessed on 25 May 2012.

Kingdom of Lesotho (1993). *The Constitution of Lesotho* (Maseru: Government Printer).

— (1995). *Education Act 1995* (Maseru: Government Printer).

— (2010). *Education Act, 2010* (Maseru: Government Printer).

Linking lives (2009). *About Lesotho* [Online] Available at: www.linkinglives.org.uk/about-lesotho.html. Accessed on 20 January 2012.

Makoa, F. K. (1996). 'Political Instability in Post-military Lesotho: The Crises of the Basotho Nation-state', *African Security Review* 5, 3, pp. 13–20.

Maqutu, T. Z. (2003). 'Explaining success in O-level Physical Science in Lesotho: A Survey of Physical Science Teachers', *African Journal of Research in SMT Education* 7, pp. 97–107.

Matooane, J. L. (1980). 'A Historical Interpretation of Lesotho's Educational System', DEd Dissertation. Rutgers: Graduate School of Education, State University of New Jersey.

Matsoha, F. M. (2010). 'Transforming Society to Meet the Community Needs and Enhance the Quality of Life: A Case Study of Bishop Allard Vocational School', MPhil assignment. Philosophy Stellenbosch: University of Stellenbosch.

Maundeni, Z. (2010). 'Political Culture as a Source of Political Instability: The Case of Lesotho', *African Journal of Political Science and International Relations* 4, 4, pp. 128–39.

Mavugara-Shava, F. M. (2005). 'Teaching for Mathematical Literacy in Secondary and High Schools in Lesotho: A Didactic Perspective', PhD thesis. Bloemfontein: University of the Free State.

Ministry of Education (1992). *Education Sector Development Plan: 1991/92 – 1995/96* (Maseru: Government Printer).

— (1996). *The Development of Education 1996 – 1998* (Maseru: Government Printer).

— (2000). 'Impact Assessment for the Education Sector: 1997 and 1998', Unpublished Report, Maseru: Ministry of Education.

Ministry of Education and Training (2005). *Education Sector Strategic Plan: 2005–2012* (Maseru: Government Printer).

— (2012a). *Education Statistics Bulletin* (Maseru: Planning Unit).

— (2012b). MOET localises COSC qualification. [Online] Available at: www.education. gov.ls/index2.php?option=com_content&do . . . Accessed on 24 May 2012.

Ministry of Education, Sports and Culture (1982) *The Education Sector Survey: Report of the Task Force* (Maseru: Government Printer).

Moru, E. K. Persens, J. and Breiteig, T. (2009). 'Investigating a Possible Gap between Students' Expectations and Perceptions: The Case of a Pre-Entry Science Program', *International Journal of Science and Mathematics Education* 8, pp. 323–46.

Muzvidziwa, V. N. and Seotsanyana, M. (2002). 'Continuity, Change and Growth: Lesotho's Education System', *Radical Pedagogy.* [Online] Available at: radicalpedagogy.icaap.org/content/issue4_2/01_muzvidziwa.html. Accessed on 12 February 2012.

Odendaal, A. (2000). *Peacebuilding in Lesotho: An Analysis of Political and Social Conflict in Lesotho and the Role of Centre for Conflict Resolution.* [Online] Available at: ccrweb.ccr.uct.ac.za/archive/staff_papers/odendaal_lesotho.html. Accessed on 14 March 2012.

SACMEQ (2010). SACMEQ III Project – *Trends in Achievement Levels of Grade 6 Pupils in the SACMEQ Countries.* [Online] Available at: www.sacmeq.org/sacmeq3.htm. Accessed on 12 March 2012.

Thahane, T. T. (2008). 'The Race for Jobs, Better Life, High and Sustainable Growth Must Be Won: Budget Speech to Parliament for the 2008/2009 Fiscal Year', Maseru, 13 February 2008.

— (2012). 'Strengthening Fiscal Resilience and National Competitiveness for Accelerating Economic Growth and Development: Budget Speech to Parliament for the 2012/2013 Fiscal Year'. Maseru, 18 January 2012.

UNDP (2013). *Human Development Report 2013 – The Rise of the South: Human Progress in a Diverse World* (New York: Palgrave Macmillan).

UNICEF (2008). *Lesotho.* [Online] Available at: www.unicef.org/har08_Lesotho_countrychapter.pdf. Accessed on 31 May 2012.

Urwick, J., Mapuru, P. and Nkhoboti, M. (2005). *Teacher Motivation and Iincentives in Lesotho* (Maseru: Lesotho College of Education).

WFP (2007). *Development Project – Lesotho 10582.0 – Strategic Focus of WFP Development Project: Support Access to Primary Education.* [Online] Available at: one.wfp.org/operations/current_operations/project . . . /105820.pdf. Accessed on 12 November 2011.

Wikipedia (2012). *Lesotho* [Online] Available at: en.wikipedia.org/wiki/Lesotho. Accessed on 27 April 2012.

World Bank (1999). *Education Sector Development Project* (Draft) (Maseru: Ministry of Education).

— (2005). *Primary and Secondary Education in Lesotho: A Country Status Report for Education* (Africa Region Human Development Working Paper Series No. 101. Washington, DC).

World Food Programme (2007). *Development Project – Lesotho 10582.0: Strategic Focus of the WFP Development Project: Support Access to Primary Education* [Online] Available at: one.wfp.org/operations/current_operations/project . . . /105820.pdf. Accessed on 13 April 2012.

3

Madagascar: From Political Divisionism to Unified Development

Carrie Antal
USAID

and

Romain Kléber Ndrianjafy
Chargé d'étude au Secrétariat général du MEN, Madagascar

Introduction

Madagascar is in many respects a world apart from its geopolitical neighbours in southern Africa. Indeed, the isolation afforded to this fourth-largest island in the world by the Mozambique Channel to the west and the expanses of the Indian Ocean to the east once allowed its internationally renowned but highly threatened wildlife to evolve undisturbed over the course of millions of years. When the first settlers arrived around 350 BCE from South Borneo in their outrigger canoes, having stopped periodically en route at points along the Asian and African coasts to trade (and, according to some theories, to establish short-lived settlements and intermarry), they discovered a virgin land rich with bizarre flora and fauna in a variety of novel forms: giant lemurs of all types, the one-ton elephant bird, the pygmy hippopotamus and many thousands of other distinctive species, over 80 per cent of which are currently identified as endemic to the island. Soon after the arrival of humans, the largest indigenous animal species were set upon the path to extinction through the combined forces of hunting and habitat destruction for cultivation and grazing (Crowley, 2010). Today, after the loss of an estimated 90 per cent of the island's original forest cover, conservationists' efforts to save this biodiversity hotspot's remaining plant and animal species continue to attract international attention and calls to action.

Relative to their island's exotic wildlife, the people of Madagascar have benefitted somewhat less from the international concern about their nation. Typically condemned in the foreign press for their role in burning forest cover for cultivation through the traditional practice of *tavy*, as well as for occasional forays into the consumption and trade of bush meat or harvesting of protected rainforest hardwoods, the Malagasy living in rural areas (who comprise around 70 per cent of the total population of 22 million) struggle, like their urban compatriots, against severe poverty to meet their basic needs. Madagascar has achieved significant advances in national development over the past two decades and particularly in the period 2003–7 when the annual economic growth rate averaged 5.3 per cent. Nonetheless, the average Malagasy continues to earn around $470 per year, with approximately 81 per cent of the population living on less than $1.25 per day and 25 per cent of the adult population unable to read. Life expectancy hovers around 63 years for men and 67 for women.[1] Cyclical political instability regularly slows or reverses development gains made during periods of growth (Marcus & Razafindrakoto, 2003).

The challenges that successive Malagasy administrations and development partners work to overcome are often characterized as problems typical to the development of Africa. While Madagascar shares a number of development challenges with its geopolitical neighbours, in several respects this perception both ignores and masks key distinctions between Madagascar and other southern African states in numerous areas. Although research and debate into the prehistory of the island are ongoing, most historians believe that for centuries, Austronesians were the only human settlers on the island, joined later by small numbers of Arab and Indian traders, and only around 1000 CE by a large influx of Bantu-speaking migrants from eastern Africa. As a result of assimilation and intermarriage, the ethnicity and culture of the average Malagasy reflect a relatively homogenous blend of Asiatic and African influences that shape the values explicitly and implicitly promoted within schools (Ade Ajayi, 1998). Furthermore, the natural oceanic barriers that long protected the island's wildlife have likewise helped to preserve the Malagasy people from the type of border conflicts, refugee migrations and pan-African epidemics of diseases such as Human Immunodeficiency Virus (HIV)/Acquired Immunodeficiency Syndrome (AIDS) that have complicated the development process in many African countries. The topography of the island, with its steep, rainforest-clad escarpments to the east, and scorching plains bordered by malarial swamps along the western coasts, were especially instrumental in minimizing the presence and influence of Europeans and other potential invaders until the nineteenth century.

These protective features, coupled with the mild climate of the central highlands and the interior's suitability for rice cultivation techniques imported by the earliest settlers, supported high population density, particularly among the Merina people, who form the largest ethnic group on the island. The Merina were united in the sixteenth century by Andriamanelo, who founded the Kingdom of Imerina with its capital at the highlands city of Antananarivo. Soon surpassing the predominance of the rival kingdoms of the Sakalava to the west and Betsimisaraka to the East, as well as numerous smaller kingdoms, principalities and fiefdoms established by the island's 18 main ethnic groups, the Kingdom of Imerina extended its sovereignty over much of the island by the mid-nineteenth century, when its successive monarchs were recognized by its principal trading partners, England and France, as the rulers of a unified Madagascar. This unique political history, in combination with the island's shared language and indigenous religion, have helped to foster a common Malagasy identity that has spared Madagascar from the degree of internal conflict that has hindered development efforts in many other African states post-independence (Hauge, 2011). It also facilitated the establishment of the most advanced pre-colonial formal school system in sub-Saharan Africa, laying the foundation for all future developments in the education sector.[2]

This chapter will explore the ways in which the uniquely insular condition of Madagascar, by its dual nature as an island and a state, has shaped the development of education on the island. The discussion will illustrate the benefits and challenges that this isolation has provided to successive administrations and development partners, framing contemporary issues within their historical and political contexts. Special attention will be given to the ramifications of this country's distinctive sociocultural and geopolitical conditions for schools, which have been continually refashioned as vehicles to serve the prevailing political mood, and for the teachers obliged by their civil servant status to enact the policies handed down by central government. The discussion will conclude with observations regarding the future of schooling in Madagascar and key challenges to be met if education is meant to serve as a successful catalyst for enduring progress and sustainable development for the Malagasy people and their nation.

History of schooling in Madagascar

The emergence of formal schooling in nineteenth-century Imerina can be traced back to the initial encounter in 1818 between King Radama I (1810–28) and the first envoys of the Protestant London Missionary Society (LMS), who had arrived and established the first Western-style school in the coastal town of Toamasina earlier that year.[3] Radama was a forward-thinking ruler eager to develop economic and political ties with foreign powers to consolidate his authority over newly subjugated neighbouring ethnic groups. Recognizing the power of the learning the LMS missionaries offered, he invited them to use the Latin alphabet to transcribe the Merina dialect of the Malagasy language (which he declared the sole official form in 1822) and teach this new form of writing to the children of nobles living at his Rova palace in Antananarivo. The value Radama placed on this new form of education was symbolized by the convening of the Palace School within Besakana, an ancient building constructed in the traditional style and first erected (according to oral history) by the renowned Andriamanelo himself. For at least five centuries prior, the Malagasy language had heretofore been transcribed using Arabic letters in a script known as *sorabe* – a privileged form of knowledge formerly accessible only to certain astrologers (*ombiasy*) and sovereigns. Traditional education beyond these elite groups typically consisted of informal transmission by elders to youth of the skills, lore and role-based values relevant to an individual's class and gender, as dictated by local community standards (Raharijaona, 1968). Radama took an unprecedented step by adopting a formal Westernized setting for the expansion of access to elite knowledge areas such as literacy, Western science, mathematics and technology to a wider population within Imerina. He declared school attendance compulsory among the Merina upper classes in 1825, although resistance among certain families led them to send slaves to be educated instead, spreading the reach of this new education throughout all levels of the social strata. As a result of Radama's policy and the subsequent construction of schools in larger towns throughout his kingdom, over 4,900 students were enrolled in the palace school, town schools and LMS technical school one decade after the missionaries' first contact with the king (Rafaralahy-Bemananjara, 1983).

A backlash against the growing influence of foreigners in Imerina led to the closure of Radama's schools from 1835 to 1861 under his traditionalist successor, Queen Ranavalona I (1828–61), only to see many of these schools reopened again during the brief reign of her pro-European son, Radama II.

However, the abrupt and drastic reversal of many of his mother's protectionist policies fomented dissatisfaction among Radama's courtiers who had grown tired of being subject to the caprices of absolute monarchs, leading a faction of the king's advisors to mount a coup d'état in 1863 and immediately establish a government in which power was to be shared between the sovereign and the prime minister. The following year, Queen Rasoherina assigned the role of prime minister to her commander-in-chief, Rainilaiarivony, who would wield the bulk of administrative power throughout the remainder of her reign and those of her successors Ranavalona II and Ranavalona III, until the mounting conflict with the French concluded in the capture of the royal palace in September 1895 and dissolution of the monarchy two years later.

Under Rainilaiarivony, primary schooling was once again made compulsory for children of the Merina aristocracy in 1872, then all Malagasy children across the island in 1881, with 133,695 students enrolled by 1883 (Rafaralahy-Bemananjara, 1983). A system of secondary schools and teacher training institutes was also established, staffed by missionaries and Malagasy – many of whom had completed a full course of training in Europe. The state education system in imperial Madagascar delivered basic literacy and numeracy to the masses while creating cadres of formally trained Malagasy teachers, doctors and civil servants who staffed the modernizing nation's hospitals, government administrative bureaus, schools and more.

Throughout the formative period of formal education under the Merina monarchy, its institutions of learning were deliberately employed as political tools to transform the values of the school-going public according to the objectives of the powerful. Radama I (and later Prime Minister Rainilaiarivony) adapted the curriculum to transmit messages in the classroom that sought to reinforce obedience to state laws and Merina domination of the island. For their part, the LMS envoys and other European missionaries who taught in these schools used the translated Bible for literacy and ethics instruction in an attempt to inculcate their own normative values in their students. Throughout Madagascar, a worldview grounded in reverence for leaders, elders and ancestors (*ray aman-dreny*) and conformity to their dictates – whether through the decrees of the living or the pervasive taboos (*fady*) established by those now dead – moulded Malagasy society and facilitated popular adoption of the many innovations introduced by sovereigns and foreigners in the nineteenth century, including those delivered via the medium of public education. Teachers were perceived as ray aman-dreny to be respected and obeyed, facilitating the receptiveness of learners to the messages taught at the royal schools.

The school system established under the rule of the Merina monarchs was retained and gradually expanded following French conquest of Madagascar to reach approximately 10 per cent of the school-age population a decade after colonization. Under the administration of General Joseph Gallieni, schools for Malagasy children were initially designed to create obedient subjects capable of contributing to the French exploitation of the island's resources, with over half the curriculum dedicated uniquely to the study of the French language. Malagasy teachers' difficulties in managing large class sizes (in 1930, the average student to teacher ratio was 86:1), and obstacles to comprehension posed by the use of French as the instructional language, led to a pedagogical overreliance on lecture and chorused responses to teachers' questions. Certain European contemporaries began to express concern that the education system was creating a passive and intellectually dull populace. By contrast, beginning in 1906 French children living in Madagascar enjoyed modern educational facilities and a curriculum on par with European standards. That same year the secularist *Loi Cadre* in France prompted new restrictions on mission schools in Madagascar, forcing the closure of several thousand without the construction of an adequate number of new state schools to offset the loss. As teachers in Malagasy primary schools were also forbidden to educate children over the age of 13, the access of Malagasy students to educational opportunities was severely restricted in the early colonial period (Razafimbelo, 2004).

Under Gallieni, Rainilaiarivony's secondary schools and teacher training institutes were gradually closed, leaving one lone secondary school – the government-run l'Ecole le Myre des Vilers – to train Malagasy upper primary teachers and civil servants. In a symbolic gesture of authority, the French established this school within the palace of Ranavalona I on the grounds of the Rova, the former seat of Merina power. The curriculum of teachers in training here included *morale*: civics lessons that trumpeted French contributions to the island's development and taught submission to the colonial regime with the intent of transmitting these messages to primary school students by way of their teachers. But while the French colonial education system restricted Malagasy access to power and knowledge, the administration was unknowingly planting the seeds of its own destruction. The Malagasy elite trained at le Myre des Vilers inhabited a dormitory on the grounds where nationalism and the politics of independence were privately debated, producing the future leaders of an independent Madagascar – including the country's first president, Philibert Tsiranana, and later president Albert Zafy.

Evidencing the French roots of Madagascar's political system, this island state has undergone four consecutive Republics since gaining independence in 1960 and its people, schools and teachers have likewise been subject to the State's successive political philosophies. Throughout the First Republic (1960–75), ties with France remained strong. The education system remained heavily reliant on French residents of Madagascar as Ministry officials and secondary-school instructors, and the use of French as the language of instruction, textbooks imported from France and the French-language exam system were carried over from the colonial period to the newly independent state. High-performing students were offered scholarships to institutions of higher learning in France, enabling the former colonial power to continue exerting its influence through the Malagasy education system. Attempting to redress the challenges to educational access which were especially acute in coastal areas, President Tsiranana – himself a former teacher – enacted reforms of the education system in 1962 that mandated the establishment of at least one primary school per *fokontany* (an Imerina kingdom administrative division typically composed of several neighbouring villages). The resulting annual enrolment growth rate of 4.5 per cent marked a rare success among post-colonial African states striving to make progress in the education sector. Improvements in quality and particularly in moving away from didactic, teacher-centred methods of instruction nonetheless remained a challenge in spite of efforts to transform pedagogy at Madagascar's new teacher training institutes (Goguel, 2006).

Frustration with pervasive French influence on the island contributed to the ousting of Tsiranana and the establishment of the fiercely nationalist and socialist Second Republic under Admiral Didier Ratsiraka (1975–91). A cornerstone of his new vision for Madagascar was the notion of *malgachization* – restoring the pre-eminence of Malagasy language and traditions at the expense of cultural and economic ties to France and other Western powers. French nationals were abruptly expelled from their teaching posts and the language of instruction was changed to Malagasy, rendering all existing textbooks obsolete without adequate means to replace them with local-language texts. New schools were constructed with the aim of providing one primary school in each fokontany, one middle school in each commune and one high school in each district.

These two policies necessitated rapid, wide-scale recruitment of new teachers. At the lower secondary level, the State recruited a large portion of its new teaching force from among Malagasy high school graduates who were assigned to fulfil the new two-year national service requirement as instructors in rural schools and literacy centres. Adults holding a *brevet* (middle school leaving certificate) were recruited to teach at the primary level and provided an intensive three-month teacher training programme before being assigned to a school. Teacher training was delivered regionally at communal centres and consisted of education in curricular content, socialist ideology and student-centred pedagogy rooted in discussion and independent research (Ranaivoson, 1980). Despite efforts to reform instructional practices, the accelerated training and influx of inexperienced teachers coupled with inadequate classroom materials led to deterioration of education quality across the island and a sharp increase in repetition and attrition rates at the primary level. Far from achieving the socialist-nationalist ideal of equality for Malagasy across all classes, inequity was exacerbated by the growing trend for well-off families to send their children to French-language private schools in Madagascar or abroad.

As was the case in many other African states, the socialist-nationalist experiment in Madagascar failed to respond adequately to global and national pressures, resulting in rapid economic collapse by the end of the 1970s. Growing popular dissatisfaction with Ratsiraka's policies led the administration to overturn malgachization in the mid-1980s in favour of once again teaching in French. However, by this time many new recruits to the profession had only minimally studied the former colonial tongue and struggled to master its use as the language of instruction. Due to the deepening decline of education quality following these policy shifts, many Malagasy refer to those schooled during the period as the lost generation (Sharp, 2002).

When the instatement of multiparty democratic rule by popular demand ushered in the Third Republic (1992–2010), the successive administrations of Presidents Albert Zafy (1993–6), Didier Ratsiraka (1997–2002) and Marc Ravalomanana (2002–9) were confronted with the legacy of previous educational policies. Dilapidated infrastructure, inadequate materials, teachers possessing disparate levels of competence and training, continued prevalence of teacher-centred pedagogy and almost universally low teacher mastery and student comprehension of French as the language of instruction collectively raised intransigent barriers to progress. Despite significant donor support to the education sector in Madagascar in the 1990s, both access and quality continued to lag behind: primary enrolment rates stagnated over the course of the 1990s, and students' repetition and attrition rates remained among the highest in Africa (World Bank, 2002).

Stifled progress

Over the course of the Ravalomanana administration, renewed government commitment to the beleaguered education sector was complemented by an upsurge in donor support to achieve the objectives of Education For All in Madagascar. The transformation of the national education landscape began in 2003 when the challenge of inadequate access was addressed through the elimination of primary school fees and the introduction of a programme to annually distribute basic school supplies to students. These policies produced a leap in primary enrolment from 67 per cent in 2001 to 97 per cent in 2005 (World Bank, 2005), accompanied by the rehabilitation or construction of 2,000 classrooms each year to improve school proximity in rural areas and prevent an unmanageable inflation in class sizes (MENRS, 2003).

The staffing of primary schools was accomplished in the short term by parent-teacher associations (FRAM) who recruited and paid thousands of new teachers selected from among the most qualified members of the local community. The number of FRAM teachers increased from around 8,000 in 2003 to over 35,000 in 2007. As an investment in improving the quality of education, the Ravalomanana administration committed to providing formal training and salary subsidies to these FRAM teachers, in addition to recruiting and formally training 2,000 state primary teachers and 1,000 state *collège* teachers each year (MENRS, 2003). Education quality was further supported by the setting in 2007 of a minimum educational requirement for state-recruited sixth- and seventh-grade teachers at the level of the baccalaureate (high school leaving certificate). In addition, the primary teacher training curriculum itself was revised in 2004, placing a strong emphasis on *approche par les competences* (APC), a participatory competency-based approach made practicable by the distribution to schools of oversized slates to be used in group work activities (MENRS, 2005).

In 2007, Madagascar's Education For All strategy was revised to effect sweeping changes for improved quality and access throughout the system. For the first time since national independence in 1960, the primary curriculum was to undergo a complete overhaul that would have clustered lessons around the themes of Malagasy and social sciences, foreign languages (English and French) and the trio of science, maths and technology. In addition to developing children's knowledge in these subject areas, the new curriculum was designed to engage children as active participants in the learning process, strengthen their critical thinking skills and love of learning, and enable them to become well-rounded, open-minded citizens. This reform was intended to bring the Malagasy curriculum into line with international standards, reduce the achievement gap between rural and urban students, improve local relevance by devolving selection of non-core subjects taught (namely drawing or song and dance) to the school level and reduce the number of subjects taught while enriching the curriculum through technologies and the earlier introduction of English in Grade 4. In an effort to improve student achievement and support the development of critical thinking skills and habits of classroom participation, the use of Malagasy as a language of instruction was extended from the first three years of primary to the first five, accompanied by the teaching of French (from Grade 1) and English (from Grade 4) as foreign languages following a 2007 constitutional amendment making English an official language alongside Malagasy and French. The 2014–15 school year was set as the anticipated completion date for the roll-out of the new curriculum to all primary grades and all schools nationwide.

These extensive reforms in basic education were designed to be complemented by a number of related programmes and reforms in the education sector. A programme to develop the capacity of primary school libraries was slated for the 2011–12 school year. A series of objectives were likewise defined for the eventual reform of the middle-school curriculum, including the development of knowledge and skills enabling students to compete on the job market, ingraining in students the habits of research and life-long learning, and strengthening students' decision-making and problem-solving abilities for use throughout their personal and professional lives. A strategy was to be developed to further strengthen the professionalization of FRAM teachers. In addition, a national programme for early childhood education was launched in 2008 that provided access to non-formal education for parents of children aged 0–3 and preschool education for children aged 4–5 (of whom only 7.4% were enrolled in the 2007–8 school year).

However, beginning in January 2009, Andry Rajoelina, then mayor of Antananarivo, led a series of popular protests against Ravalomanana's perceived abuses of power and increasingly autocratic practices. This resulted in Ravalomanana's pressured transfer of power to military leaders in March 2009, who immediately conferred upon Rajoelina the authority of head of state – a political transition that was declared constitutional by the High Constitutional Court, but widely condemned by the international community as a coup d'état. Madagascar has since been suspended from a variety of regional and international organizations, its top leaders placed on a no-fly list and its relationships with many key development partners reduced to humanitarian-only assistance.

The island suffered negative economic growth in 2009, experienced by many families as a deepening of poverty through an increase in basic commodity costs coupled with a drop in monthly income. A new constitution preserving the multiparty democratic nature of the state was approved by voter referendum in 2010, ushering in the Fourth Republic administered by Rajoelina and his *Haute Autorité de Transition* interim government (HAT). At the time of writing, the island remains politically and economically marginalized by key partners who demand the election of a legitimate government.

The political upheaval and subsequent suspension of some donors' support to the education sector had an immediate and dramatic impact on the Ministry of National Education's (Ministère de l'Education Nationale, MEN) capacity to deliver services and implement the revised vision of Education For All in Madagascar. The Ministry's budget declined by 20 per cent in 2009 (UNICEF, 2010), then dropped further still the following year, from $82 million in 2008 to 14.5 million in 2010 (United Nations, 2011). Institutional memory and technical capacity throughout the system was diminished over the same period following the replacement of the school district (CISCO, circonscriptions scolaires) chiefs and many of the ministry's technical directors and regional managers, leading to confusion among local level staff about which education programmes the MEN intended them to continue implementing (UNICEF, 2010). The sharp drop in donor support to the education budget has posed significant challenges to the transitional government's capacity to offset the costs of school kits for students, or pay its share of subventions to FRAM teacher salaries, leading to teacher strikes that have disrupted service delivery and infringed upon education quality and access, particularly among students from underprivileged families who attend the public schools where FRAM teachers are employed.

Ripple effects have been observed throughout the education system. Student enrolment has declined from 85 per cent in 2005 to 73 per cent in 2010, and school dropout rates have tripled since 2009. A 2010 poll revealed 75 per cent of parents were experiencing difficulty in allocating resources to pay costs associated with schooling, such as books, supplies, uniforms and the FRAM teacher salary contributions (UNICEF, 2010). According to the Malagasy government's National Institute for Statistics, a growing trend towards public schools requesting higher fees from economically vulnerable parents to supplement the salaries of FRAM teachers has pushed an estimated 700,000 children out of the public education system since the crisis began (UNICEF, 2012). Education quality has been affected as well as access, with a marked deterioration in pedagogical quality observed during the political crisis. This decline coincides with delayed disbursement of school capitation grants, late payment (or non-payment) of state teacher salaries, and increased vulnerability of teachers and students (and indeed, the majority of the population) to nutritional deficiencies and illness as a consequence of the decline in living standards since 2009.

Budget constraints and ideological differences led the HAT to initially suspend a number of the previous administration's education policies (UNICEF, 2010). Pressure from key development partners in the education sector has since led MEN to continue partial policy implementation in such areas as curriculum reform, school canteens in southern Madagascar, school construction and partial subventions to FRAM teacher salaries. The World Bank's catalytic fund has been administered since 2009 according to an agreement by which the resources are managed directly by UNICEF and pass to local-level structures rather than to MEN itself (World Bank, 2011). At the time of writing, selected development partners and MEN are coordinating to develop am interim three-year strategy to meet the nation's most pressing education needs. However, Madagascar's political future remains uncertain, and wider-ranging improvements to the condition of education are likely dependent on the organizing of internationally-sanctioned presidential elections, which have been repeatedly scheduled and postponed since 2009. The administration that follows will be tasked with ensuring access and quality of education, building upon the structure and capacity of the educational system discussed in the remainder of the chapter.

Structure of the Malagasy education system

The objectives and guiding principles that form the foundation of the contemporary Malagasy education system were defined early in the Third Republic.[4] The 1995 education policy (*Loi No.94–033*) sought to modernize and democratize schooling in line with prevailing international norms, describing education as a human right that enables the physical, intellectual, moral and artistic development of each individual. Consistent with Madagascar's effort to cast off its socialist past and rejoin the broader democratic and humanist international community of nations, the objective of state education is to enable individuals to contribute to the social, economic and cultural development of the country. This objective was reiterated in the 2006 *Madagascar Action Plan*, the Ravalomanana administration's medium-term development strategy (2007–12), which underscored government responsibility to support a world-class national education system capable of developing the economic competitiveness of each

Malagasy citizen and enabling all to participate actively in the development of their country (IMF, 2008). The administration committed to achieving the objectives of Education for All in 2003 and received $60 million in World Bank catalytic funds to support education upon being named a Fast Track Initiative beneficiary country in 2005, followed by an additional 85 million allocated in 2007 but largely frozen as a result of the political crisis.

Under Ravalomanana, a series of education reforms further defined and clarified the structure and management of education in Madagascar, which is compulsory for all Malagasy children from ages six to 14. Reforms from 2003 to 2004 subdivided education into the categories of primary education, secondary education, tertiary education in academic or professional fields and technical and vocational education. Under the 5–4-3 system defined by *Loi n° 2004–004* of 26 July 2004, Madagascar's 2.9 million primary-age students could begin their nine years of basic education through five years of study at one of approximately 24,400 *écoles primaires*, with around 20 per cent of students enrolled in private primary schools. Around 35 per cent of the 2.1 million children of lower secondary school age complete Grade V, and only around 55 per cent of those will continue their studies at one of approximately 2,500 collèges, with 34 per cent enrolled in private institutions. Around 15 per cent of children of upper secondary age are enrolled at that level, of which 9 per cent are at an academic *lycée* and 6 per cent in technical schools; approximately 6 per cent of students complete schooling at the upper secondary level. Boys and girls enrol and complete their schooling at near equal rates across primary and secondary levels (UNESCO Institute of Statistics website, 2012).[5]

In July 2008, a policy was adopted to transition from the 5–4-3 model to a 7–3-2 model. A revised curriculum was to be rolled out to all seven primary grades by the 2012–13 school year, in which the two additional years of primary schooling (Grades VI and VII) were to be taught by teachers 'semi-specialized' in one of three areas: Malagasy and social sciences, foreign languages (namely French and English) and science, mathematics and technology. The first cohort of semi-specialized teachers was trained during the 2008–9 academic year in anticipation of a limited rollout in October 2009. In addition, the Ravalomanana administration anticipated constructing or rehabilitating 2,400 classrooms and recruiting 2,800 teachers per year beginning in 2008 to achieve its vision of providing ten years of free basic education to all Malagasy students by 2012. This restructuring, however, has been indefinitely suspended since Ravalomanana's resignation in March 2009, and the 5–4-3 model remains in place.

Advancement through the system is determined by results on exams administered at the end of the school year, which typically runs from September to June. Schools deliver the national curriculum to students in a single five and a half hour shift, totalling 27.5 hours of schooling per week. In public primary schools, one teacher delivers lessons across all subjects, while subject-specialist teachers migrate between classrooms at the lower and upper secondary school levels. Completion of primary schooling (*éducation fondamentale niveau 1* or EF1) earns the graduate a *Certificat d'études primaries et élémentaires* (CEPE diploma), and students who complete their lower secondary schooling (*éducation fondamentale niveau 2* or EF2) are awarded a *Brevet d'études du premier cycle de l'enseignement secondaire* (BEPC diploma). Alternatively, those holding a CEPE diploma can pursue a course of technical training to receive a *Certificat d'aptitude professionnel* (CAP) diploma after two years of study or a *Brevet d'étude professionnel* (BEP) diploma after three years of study.

Graduation from high school is accomplished by successfully passing one of several French-language baccalaureate exams similar in content and form to the high school leaving exam administered in France, which confers the eponymous diploma. Three years of upper-secondary study are required to pass the exam for languages, humanities, science, mathematics or technical education (the latter offered at technical high schools), or four years of study for the professional baccalaureate. Vocational and technical training is also available at the secondary level in the form of two-year courses at *Centres de formation professionelle* (CFP) training centres that award technical certificates, and at the tertiary level through various technical schools.

Madagascar's first higher education institution, the Institute for Advanced Studies, was established at Antananarivo in 1955 and renamed the University of Madagascar in 1961, having since expanded to include branch campuses in each of the island's six largest urban centres (Antananarivo, Antsiranana, Fianarantsoa, Mahajanga, Toamasina and Toliara). Other public tertiary institutions include branches of the *Institut Supérieur de Technologie* in Antananarivo and Antsiranana, a national institute for nuclear science, and the *Centre National de Télé-enseignement de Madagascar* (national distance learning centre) with its 24 regional branches. In total, 21 public and private institutions of higher education are operating on the island in 2012. A baccalaureate is prerequisite to admission at all tertiary institutions in Madagascar.

Until recently, the duration and structure of university-level programmes of study varied according to the particular subject area. Technical programmes offered at universities and Normal Schools typically last two to three years.

Within academic programmes, a diploma in the humanities (DUEL) or sciences (DUES) could be earned within two years. Similar to the French system, a *license* could be earned in three years, a *maîtrise* in four and a *diplôme d'études approfondies* (DEA) – the highest degree conferred – within five years of study, although university students commonly spend much longer to complete their degrees. A reform was adopted in 2008 to transition to a standardized, credits-based system that would confer bachelors, masters and doctoral degrees in line with European higher education standards. Universities are currently in the process of transitioning between systems in anticipation of complying with European norms by 2015. The state offers limited need-based financial assistance and subsidized housing near campus for some university students, although demand routinely outstrips supply.

From 2003 to 2008, the management of the education system was overseen by the MEN and Ministry of Scientific Research (*Ministère de l'éducation nationale et de la récherche scientifique*, MENRS), composed of three offices: Basic Education and Literacy, Professional and Technical Training and Higher Education and Research. Following ministry restructuring in 2008, education is overseen by the MEN under the direction of the Minister of National Education and a Vice-Minister of Higher Education and Technical and Professional Training. MEN implements all national education policy relevant to its three general bureaus (*directions générales*): basic education and literacy; secondary, technical and professional training and tertiary education and scientific research. These guide the activities of offices (*directions*) responsible for a variety of specialized areas, including pre-primary and basic education, initial professional and technical training, curriculum development, training for professional qualification, literacy, secondary education, higher education, administrative and financial affairs, research, human resources, reform of higher education and research, information technology, planning and oversight (including education statistics), regional management and school registration.

Educational administration remains highly centralized, despite the prominence of the theme of government institutional decentralization in Malagasy political discourse since the 1990s. Higher education is managed both centrally and through administrative and scientific councils located within each university, with nationwide conferences periodically called by the Minister of National Education to facilitate communication between MEN and the universities.

The administration of basic and secondary education is managed by the nation's 22 administrative sub-offices (*direction régional de l'éducation nationale*, DREN). Under the authority of the DREN, the island's 114 school districts

(CISCO) ensure that primary and secondary education policy is adopted at the local level, manage student registration, organize local data collection, conduct studies and evaluations and deploy pedagogical advisers (*conseillers pédagogiques*) to perform teacher assessments and provide in-service support to the professional development of school staff. Each district is subdivided into zones (*zones d'appui pédagogique*, ZAP), headed by ZAP chiefs who provide further support to CISCOs at the school level. This complex system of decentralization stands in contrast to the management of technical schools, which are principally administered through an office located within each of the island's six largest cities.

Systems of professional development for teachers exist at both the pre-service and in-service levels. The status of in-service training stands in sharp contrast to pre-service training, managed under MEN by the National Pedagogical Training Institute (*Institut national de formation pédagogique*, INFP) and delivered throughout the country at 25 regional centres (CRINFP) that offer a a one-year course for primary and collège teachers and a 32-month course for pedagogical counsellors. Reformed in 2004, the year-long primary teacher training course is designed to alternate between months spent in theoretical study at the CRINFP (720 hours total) and in an equal amount of hands-on experiential learning and practice within a local primary school with guidance and supervision offered by a more experienced teacher. The majority of instructional time within the CRINFP (486 hours, or 67.5%) reviews primary course content and related methods of instruction, while the remainder of the CRINFP-based training (234 hours, or 32.5%) develops teacher competencies in such areas as educational theory, pedagogy, classroom management, school administration and child psychology. Learner-centred, participatory forms of pedagogy are taught theoretically and student-teachers are encouraged to attempt them while in the primary classroom (MENRS, 2005). These reforms built upon an already promising foundation: a UNESCO study conducted prior to Ravalomanana's teacher education reform found that while the majority of CRINFP instruction time (70%) was lecture-based, 20 per cent was dedicated to group work activities, with another 10 per cent dedicated to research and individual learning activities (Mungala, 2003). By contrast, the training of high school teachers, CRINFP teacher trainers and secondary-level pedagogical counsellors occurs at Normal Schools affilliated with the national university system, through courses that rarely deviate from a traditional lecture format.

In-service professional development for school personnel is dominated by specialized trainings designed to raise teacher awareness of expected changes in practice associated with the adoption of new education policies such as APC or APS. These trainings are provided to basic education teachers by CISCOs with support from ZAP chiefs, but capacity limitations among these training providers restrict the frequency of teacher support at the school level, necessitating regional off-site trainings that many teachers lack the means or motivation to attend. Trainers are further hindered by the lack of a comprehensive national in-service training plan or systematic delivery strategy to build specific teacher competencies beyond the immediate needs dictated by policy changes.

The education reforms initiated in 2007 will be critical to achieving quality education for all in Madagascar as the gains made in education access and quality during Ravalomanana's first term have improved but not maximized results on a number of key measures. According to the UNESCO Institute for Statistics Website, repetition rates decreased between 1990 and 2004 but have since stabilized at around 20 per cent. Primary completion rates increased under Ravalomanana from 51 per cent in 2004 to 66 per cent in 2009, but levels have not yet reached the MEN goal of 82 per cent primary completion by 2012. Student performance on exams remains low, although passing rates on primary leaving exams and the baccalaureate showed modest improvements between 2004 and 2008, increasing from 60 per cent to 66 per cent and from 44 per cent to 45 per cent respectively. Passing rates for the lower secondary leaving exams decreased over this same period, from 50 per cent in 2004 to 46 per cent in 2008, underscoring inconsistencies in quality improvements across levels within the education system.

Conclusion: Education at the intersection between *fihavanana* and global development

The experience of education reform in Madagascar is one characterized by the tension between sweeping top-down reforms and gradual but enduring changes at the community level. The establishment of formal schooling and its many transformations has been driven less by local demand than by state objectives in line with the authority in power at any given point in time. Peaceful transfers of power have been the exception rather than the rule in Madagascar, and successive regimes have utilized the school as a vehicle to achieve state objectives, occasionally to the detriment of the public. The political and social messages either implicitly or explicitly communicated through schools have trickled through layers of state bureaucracy to reach the public with varying degrees of clarity and resonance. But regardless of how effectively state schools have communicated prevailing ideologies, the ramifications of political change are evident in Madagascar's education sector. The cyclical process of building, tearing down and rebuilding the island's political system (and, by extension, the state education system) has created profound discontinuities in the quality and content of state-delivered education, with consequences felt throughout Malagasy society.

The immediate source of destabilization in these systems originates uniquely from within the island itself, and particularly the ability of a particular state administration to respond to the challenges confronting it or the public it governs. This reality stands in contrast to that of Madagascar's southern African neighbours, whose efforts to improve their education systems are challenged not only by governance and state capacity issues but by the complexities arising from heterogeneities within their borders and exogenous factors passing through their frontiers. Madagascar's geographic isolation has protected it from the destabilizing effects of the AIDS epidemic, refugee influxes, small arms surpluses, border disputes and other challenges to state service delivery in many African states. The strong cultural, linguistic and spiritual unity of the Malagasy people and their promotion of the traditional value of *fihavanana* (solidarity) have minimized violent conflict and averted civil war even throughout the most highly charged periods in the island's political history. Effective, stable and responsive governance, including the strengthening of education access and quality to responsibly educate Madagascar's citizens, holds significant potential to contribute to a rise in living standards across the island, relatively unimpeded by external shocks.

In recent years, top-down reforms in the Malagasy education sector have become increasingly aligned with international standards as expressed in such declarations as Education For All and the Global Partnership for Education. To a growing degree, MEN priorities have reflected those trending globally, as manifested in the focus on expanding access while improving quality through such strategies as reduced class sizes, greater use of learner-centred pedagogy, better availability and quality of teaching materials and setting standards that shape curriculum and facilitate learning assessments. Although the most recent 2008 reforms were interrupted too early to assess their full impact on educational outcomes, quantifiable change has already been achieved under Education For All reforms since 2003 in terms of increased access, reduced repetition, smaller class sizes and improved attainment at the primary level. The decision to expand schooling at the primary level from five to seven years was intended to ensure that an even higher average level of educational attainment would be readily accessible to children throughout the country. These reforms, coupled with improvements to education quality beginning with the simplification of the primary curriculum, use of Malagasy as a language of instruction in Grades I to V and teachers' increasing adoption of participatory methods of instruction, represented an ambitious education strategy grounded in good practices. The impact of this latest phase of the Education for All strategy in Madagascar, however, can only become evident with the resolution of the political impasse of 2009. This resolution must result in more than the emergence of a legitimate and stable government capable of effectively implementing education policies: it must forever abandon its historic tendency to view schooling as a means to advance a political agenda, and instead continue the recent dedication to improve the life quality of the Malagasy people and sustainable development prospects of the nation.

Notes

1 For the most recent demographic and education indicators for Madagascar, please consult the primary source for this chapter, the Data Centre within the UNESCO Institute for Statistics Website.

2 A detailed discussion of the features of the pre-colonial school system at its height in the late nineteenth century can be found in Chapus and Mondain (1953).

3 A thorough analysis of the history of formal schooling in Madagascar from Radama I to Zafy can be found in Koerner (1999).

4 Further information regarding the structure of Madagascar's education system, including organizational charts, can be found in UNESCO-IBE (2010).

5 http://stats.uis.unesco.org/unesco/TableViewer/document.aspx?ReportId=198

References

Ade Ajayi, J. F. (1998). *General History of Africa: Africa in the Nineteenth Century until the 1880s* (Paris: UNESCO).

Chapus, G. S. and Mondain, G. (1953). *Un Homme d'Etat Malgache: Rainilaiarivony* (Paris: Editions Diloutremer).

Crowley, B. E. (2010). 'A Refined Chronology of Prehistoric Madagascar and the Demise of the Megafauna', *Quaternary Science Reviews* 29, 19–20, pp. 2591–603.

Goguel, A. M. (2006). *Aux Origines du Mai Malgache: Désir d'Ecole et Competition Sociale, 1951–1972* (Antananarivo: Editions Karthala).

Hauge, W. (2011). 'Madagascar between Peace and Conflict – Domestic Capabilities for Peaceful Conflict Management', *Conflict, Security & Development* 11, 5, pp. 509–31.

IMF (2008). 'République de Madagascar: Document de stratégie pour la reduction de la pauvreté. Rapport d'avancement annuel pour 2007 et le premier semestre 2008: Rapport de progrès de la mise en oeuvre du MAP, Année 2007'. Direction du Suivi et Evaluation des Programmes, March 2008.

Koerner, F. (1999). *Histoire de l'Enseignement Privé et Officiel à Madagascar (1820–1995): les Implications Réligieuses et Politiques dans la Formation d'un Peuple* (Paris: Harmattan).

Marcus, R. R. and Razafindrakoto, P. (2003). 'Madagascar: A New Democracy?', *Current History* 102, 664, pp. 215–21.

MENRS (2003). 'Draft Plan d'actions pour le système éducative malgache. Madagascar – Plan d'actions du gouvernement, amelioration du secteur de l' éducation et de la formation. Période de 2003 à 2006', Malagasy Government Printing Office.

— (2005). *Curriculum de Formation des Elèves-Maîtres* (Antananarivo: Malagasy Government Printing Office).

Mungala, A. S. (2003). *Rapport de la mission d'évaluation des ENS – Madagascar. UNESCO Technical Report No. 402966* (Paris: UNESCO).

Rafaralahy-Bemananjara, M. (1983). *Enseignement des Langues Maternelles dans les Ecoles Primaires à Madagascar: Division des Structures, Contenus, Méthodes et Techniques de l'Education* (Paris: UNESCO).

Raharijaona, H. (1968). *Le Droit de la Famille à Madagasikara, le Droit de la Famille en Afrique Noir et à Madagascar* (Paris: UNESCO).

Ranaivoson, S. (1980). *La Formation du Personnel Enseignant de l'Education de Base à Madagascar: Une Etude de Cas. Quelques Reflections Interessant la Programmation de l'Assistance de l'UNICEF* (Paris: UNICEF).

Razafimbelo, C. (2004). 'La Formation des Enseignants au Temps des Colonies', *Didaktika: Revue de Didactique* 1, 1, pp. 5–11.

Sharp, L. A. (2002). *The Sacrificed Generation: Youth, History and the Colonized Mind in Madagascar* (Berkeley: University of California Press).

UNESCO-IBE (2010). *Madagascar: World Data on Education, VII Ed. 2010/11. Données mondiales de l'éducation.* 7è edition, 2010/11. (IBE/2010/CP/WDE/MG).

UNICEF (2010). *Newsletter on the Situation of Children and Families in Madagascar* (UNICEF Madagascar).

— (2012). *Communiqué de Presse: L'UNICEF Présente une Etude pour Favoriser l'Inclusion de Tous les Enfants dans les Ecoles Primaires de Madagascar* (UNICEF Madagascar).

United Nations (2011). 'La Lettre d'information du système des Nations Unies à Madagascar', Edition 00, Juin 2011; www.unicef.org/madagascar/Final_ONU_ Newsletter_2011.pdf.

World Bank (2002). *Education and Training in Madagascar: Toward a Policy Agenda for Economic Growth and Poverty Reduction* (Washington, DC: World Bank).

— (2005). *Madagascar Development Policy Review: Sustaining Growth for Enhanced Poverty Reduction* (Washington, DC: World Bank).

— (2011). *Madagascar: FTI Progress Report – April 2011* (Washington, DC: World Bank).

Malawi: Contemporary and Critical Issues

Gregory Kamwendo
University of KwaZulu-Natal

Introduction

It was the pioneer Christian missionaries who introduced formal education to Malawi. Initially, the missionaries' aim was to provide education that could facilitate the process of evangelization. As time went by, the missionaries ended up establishing some of the best schools/colleges in Malawi. One of the most famous is the education facility which the Protestant Scottish missionaries had established at Livingstonia Mission in Northern Malawi (McCracken, 1977). Despite the fact that over the years the government has turned into the biggest provider of education to Malawians, the contribution of religious denominations to the education sector remains significant. Currently some of the most reputable schools are those that are owned by Catholic and Protestant churches. The current chapter is a critical discussion of some key aspects of education in post-colonial Malawi. The focus is on the following three sectors of education: pre-school, primary school and secondary school. The chapter takes the following sequence. First, we provide a brief historical and political background to Malawi's education system. In the next section, we highlight the goals and values of education in Malawi as per the country's key policy documents. This is followed by an outline of the current basic structures of education in Malawi. The next section of the chapter is on equity in, and access to, education, and we make specific references to: (i) social status (ii) gender (iii) ethnicity and religion and (iv) disability. This is followed by sections that discuss curriculum, teaching methods and assessment through public examinations. Next we consider the language factor in education. In the next section, we discuss the way(s) in which schools are managed, that is, school governance and management. The following section is on teacher education.

After this section, the focus turns to teacher recruitment and teacher supply. The last but one section discusses teacher remuneration, motivation, satisfaction and professionalism. The final section is a summary of the chapter.

Malawi: Historical, political and socio-economic background

Malawi, previously known as Nyasaland during British colonial rule, is a landlocked country situated in Southern Africa. Covering a geographical area of 118,484 square kilometres, and with a population of 13 million people (Malawi Governmment, 2008a), Malawi shares borders with Mozambique, Zambia and Tanzania. In 1891, Nyasaland became a British protectorate. On 6 July 1964, the country gained independence and from 1964 to 1994 Malawi was ruled with the iron fist of President Dr Hastings Kamuzu Banda and his Malawi Congress Party (MCP). A reign of terror, abuse of human rights and intolerance towards political dissent characterized President Banda's rule. Political opposition was non-existent, and any trace of opposition to President Hastings Banda would be brutally suppressed. In 1993, internal and external pressure on the Hastings Banda regime led to a national referendum. The goal of the referendum was to decide whether Malawi was to remain a one-party state or become a multiparty state. The referendum went in favour of a multiparty system. In response, multiparty general elections were held in 1994, and President Hastings Banda and his MCP lost power. Following Hastings Banda's fall from power, Bakili Muluzi and his United Democratic Front (UDF) formed the next government (United Democratic Front, 1993a, b). One of the major initiatives of the Muluzi government was the launch of free primary education (FPE). During the electoral campaign, the UDF made a pledge that if voted into office, it would implement FPE in order to increase access to education. The target was the poor and disadvantaged pupils who were unable to access school due to economic barriers. While the FPE was a noble cause, its implementation was not smooth and was characterized by a multitude of challenges and hurdles (see, for example, the literature on the subject by Kadzamira & Rose, 2003; Chimombo, 2005; Kendall, 2005; World Bank, 2010 and others).

During the Muluzi era, donor support for the FPE was made available but there were numerous reports of corruption and mismanagement of donor funds. The Muluzi regime was so corrupt that the donor community froze the flow of aid to Malawi. Things improved in 2004 when Bingu wa Mutharika rose to the presidency. He broke away from the UDF, accusing it of ruining the economy of Malawi through corrupt practices. The first term of Mutharika's presidency (2004–9) was generally a success. Donor support had been restored. Food security was strengthened and the government sent a clear message of zero tolerance for corruption. However, the second term of Mutharika's presidency (2009–12), was much less successful. For example, the human rights record deteriorated significantly. One result was that intolerance towards dissenting views went so high that Malawi soured relations with Britain, the former colonizer. The two countries expelled each other's ambassadors. The country was plunged into economic crisis, resulting in critical foreign exchange and fuel shortages and an inability on the part of the government to adequately support education and other sectors. Mutharika's second term of the presidency ended abruptly following his death as a result of a cardiac arrest on 5 April 2012. The then Vice President, Joyce Banda, took over the presidency in line with the constitutional provisions. Joyce Banda's administration has the uphill task of restoring donor confidence as well as promoting prudent use of financial and other resources, and the respect of the rule of law. It remains to be seen how the Joyce Banda administration is going to impact on Malawi's education sector.

Malawi, in general, has not been spared from the negative impact of the Human Immunodeficiency Virus (HIV)/Acquired Immunodeficiency Syndrome (AIDS) pandemic. The education sector, in particular, has suffered and continues to suffer from the impact of HIV/AIDS. For instance, HIV/AIDS is responsible for the deaths of some teachers. An education system that is already suffering from an acute shortage of trained and experienced teachers gets a serious blow when the little it has (in terms of number of teachers) is taken away through HIV/AIDS deaths. Deaths of parents is another challenge, given that some learners are left without any parents to look after them. Some of these children drop out of school and engage in wage-giving activities for economic survival while others go into socially unfavourable activities such as crime and prostitution. Some of the children, due to the deaths of their parents, are forced to step into positions of responsibility and take care of their siblings. Some girls may have to play a motherly role to their siblings, and this may lead to lack of concentration in school. It is not uncommon for such girls to be absent from schools so that they are able to attend to siblings' illnesses. HIV/AIDS has also led to more funerals than was previously the case before the rise of the pandemic. Such numerous funerals disrupt school activities as parents, teachers and learners have to attend them. Furthermore, those teachers who are living with HIV/AIDS are often sick, and thus not able to offer the best of their professional services. There is no doubt that the cost of HIV/AIDS on the education sector is enormous, and a serious threat to sustainable development (Malawi Government, 2008b; World Bank 2010).

Goals and values of education

In this section, we discuss the goals and values of education in Malawi. We should not treat these goals and values as isolated items. These goals and values are extracted from policy and official documents such as the national education sector plan of 2008–17 (Malawi Government, 2008b), and the appraisal/reviews of Malawi's education sector plans (e.g. Malawi Local Education Donor Group, 2009; World Bank, 2010). It is important to see how the national goals and values connect with, or fail to connect with, regional initiatives or expectations (e.g. the SADC protocol on education and training), continental obligations (e.g. the African Union's second decade of education for Africa – see African Union, 2006) and international obligations such as Education for All (EFA) goals and the Millennium Development Goals.

The vision for Malawi's education is 'to be a catalyst for socio-economic development, industrial growth and instrument for empowering the poor, the weak and voiceless. Education enhances group solidarity, national consciousness and tolerance of diversity' (Malawi Government, 2008b: 1). This vision clearly underscores the critical role that education can and/or should play in national development. The mission of education in Malawi is 'to provide quality and relevant education to the Malawi nation' (Malawi Government, 2008b: 1).

Malawi's first education plan came nearly a decade after independence. The plan, covering the period from 1973 to 1980, prioritized secondary and tertiary education. The objective was to create human resources that would fill in the gaps created by the departure of the former colonial (white) personnel. The second education plan did not come immediately after the end of the first plan. The decade 1985 to 1995 marked the time span of the second education plan for Malawi. Its focus was on universal primary education. However, this objective was never achieved. The FPE was expected to reduce household direct costs of education. In addition, FPE was to increase access, equity and relevance of primary education.

Current basic structure of education

Malawi follows what is known as the 8–4-4 system of education. This translates into a primary school system that is 8 years long, a secondary school system that runs for 4 years, and another 4 years of university undergraduate education. Below we discuss the key trends that prevail in three sectors of education, namely: pre-school, primary school and secondary school.

Pre-school sector

The pre-school sector in Malawi falls under the responsibility of the Ministry of Women and Child Development. According to the Malawi Government (2008b), there are 6,277 Early Childhood Development (ECD) centres serving as pre-schools, and only 30 per cent of the targeted children attend ECD centres. It should also be mentioned that the majority of these pre-schools are located in urban areas. This means pre-school is largely non-existent for the majority of Malawian children, and that pre-school is largely an urban phenomenon.

The Malawi National Education Sector Plan, covering the period 2008 to 2017 (Malawi Government, 2008b), has identified the following eight major challenges for the ECD sector:

- Lack of systematic monitoring and evaluation;
- Poor conditions of ECD centres due to lack of support from government and communities at large and poor coordination of stakeholders;
- Lack of integration of special needs in ECD provision;
- Poor advocacy for and information on the importance of ECD;
- Lack of community and parental involvement in the provision of ECD;
- Acute shortage of trained teachers of ECD;
- Lack of standard instructional materials such as syllabuses and operational guidelines; and
- Insufficient public funding for ECD activities.

ECD services in Malawi can be placed into two categories. The first category consists of baby-care centres for children aged 0 to 2 years. These baby-care centres are usually offered by the private sector. The second sector of ECD services consists of preschools or nurseries for children aged between 2 and 5 years. Both the government and the private sector are involved. Government contribution comes in the form of providing training to caregivers and, sometimes, through the provision of learning and teaching materials. Enrolment into the ECD sector picked up between 2002 and 2007, reaching a 27 per cent increase. This increase is, in part, attributed to the support and intervention of non-state institutions such as the United Nations International Children's Educational Fund (UNICEF) and Non-Governmental Organizations (NGOs). The ECD sector is in need of serious government intervention as it is an underdeveloped sector of education. The majority of Malawian children still enter primary school without having been exposed to ECD services (World Bank, 2010).

Primary school sector

As mentioned earlier, primary school education lasts for 8 years. At the age of 6, children are expected to enrol into primary schools, but in reality older children enrolling into primary school is not unusual (Williams, 2006; Malawi Government, 2008a). The primary school sector is divided into three sections, namely: the infant section (i.e. Standards I and II), the junior section (i.e. Standards III–V) and the senior section (i.e. Standards VI–VIII). At Standard VIII, learners take a national examination known as the Primary School Leaving Certificate of Education (PSLCE). This is a qualifying examination into the secondary school sector.

The primary school sector 'harbours most the challenges in the entire education system in Malawi due to increasing enrolment without adequate funding and management' (Malawi Government, 2008b: 11). Challenges in the primary school sector include:

- Shortage of qualified primary school teachers;
- Poor strategic management of teachers;
- Inadequate teaching and learning materials;
- Poor monitoring and supervisory systems;
- Poor access for children with special needs;
- Negative impact of HIV/AIDS; and
- Poor participation of school committees and their communities in school management.

Due to inadequate space in public secondary schools, not every eligible pupil finds their way into secondary schools. Few students are selected into public secondary school. The primary education sector faces a number of challenges (see Kadzamira & Rose, 2003; Kunje et al., 2003; Kendall 2005). To begin with, there is no legal framework that obliges parents and/or guardians to send children to school. This means that while primary school education is free, it is not compulsory. Second, there are delays in starting schooling. Officially, Malawian pupils are expected to start school at the age of six but in reality some pupils start school at a more advanced age. Some pupils in their twenties can be found in primary schools (Williams, 2006). Chimombo (2007: 69) has also noted that in Malawian primary schools, there are 'wide variations in age'. Third, there are high non-enrolment and dropout rates due to poverty and the need for children to join the labour force. Some of the dropouts are caused by early marriages or pregnancies. The fourth challenge is that there is an acute shortage of qualified teachers, aggravated by insufficient teacher training facilities and high attrition rates due to unattractive terms of employment (Kunje et al., 2003). Fifth, the teaching profession is not viewed as an option for high achievers (Kunje et al., 2003). Primary school teaching is 'regarded by many as dead-end, a dumping ground for those who have not done well in national examinations and cannot therefore be absorbed anywhere else' (Abura, 1998: 47). Another challenge is that generally Malawian schools are poorly supplied with teaching and learning resources. For example, it is not uncommon to find some pupils learning under trees while others learn in thatched huts. Some classrooms have no desks and pupils have to sit on the floor. Books and other teaching and learning materials are also in inadequate supply. When books are available, they may have to be shared among the pupils. Overcrowded classrooms pose another serious challenge in Malawi (see Kadzamira & Rose, 2003; Williams, 2006).

Secondary school sector

The four year secondary school system is divided into two sections. The first section comprises the junior secondary school, made up of Forms I and II. At the end of Form II, learners take what is known as the Junior Certificate of Education. The senior secondary school comprises Forms III and IV. The Malawi School Cerificate of Education (MSCE) examination is an ordinary level public examination that leads into tertiary education. Some challenges have been identified in the secondary school sector as follows:

- Inadequate access to secondary education with emphasis on special-needs students, orphans and needy young people;
- Inadequate supply of qualified teachers, especially in community day secondary schools;
- Inadequate basic infrastructure and teaching learning materials;

- Poor retention, especially for girls, due to long distances to schools and an unfavourable gender environment among other reasons;
- Partial implementation of the curriculum, which in turn affects public examinations and results negatively;
- Poor learning achievement with only 50 per cent of students passing end-of-cycle examinations;
- Inefficient use of existing resources such as infrastructure, time and staff;
- Negative impact of HIV/AIDS on teachers and students; and
- Lack of financial prudence, management and information systems, thereby compromising standards (Malawi Government, 2008b).

The secondary school sector feeds into the tertiary education sector. The quality of the former obviously impacts on the quality of the latter. As such, the current situation and challenges being faced in the secondary school sector do not augur well with the desire to produce students who are well prepared to face the tertiary education sector or the world of work.

Access and equity issues in education

EFA goals speak about equity: they speak about inclusiveness so that no one is left out of education due to their social status, gender, race, ethnicity or disability. This is not just about access to education by all as it is also critically important that once a learner can access education they should experience good quality education. EFA goal 2 is very inclusive, ensuring that by 2015 all children, particularly girls, children in difficult circumstances and those belonging to ethnic minorities, have access to, and complete, free and compulsory primary education of good quality. Malawi, through its current national education sector plan, has three intervention areas, one of which reads: 'expand equitable access to education to enable all to benefit' (Malawi Government, 2008b: 1).

Social status and access to education

EFA goal 1 is most relevant here given that it aims at expanding and improving comprehensive early childhood care and education, especially for the most vulnerable and disadvantaged child. It is in this spirit that FPE, within the UDF government's poverty alleviation programme, was conceived. Abolishing school fees and the removal of the compulsory school uniform requirement were some of the measures aimed at making education accessible to children from economically weak families.

Gender and access to education

The point of departure is MDG 3 which aims at promoting gender equality and empowerment of women. One of the targets of this MDG is to eliminate gender disparity in primary and secondary education, preferably by 2005, and at all levels by 2015. This MDG echoes EFA goal number 5. The Second Decade of Education for Africa also has the goal of eliminating gender disparities and ensure gender equality, girls' and women's empowerment throughout the education system, while enriching the system with positive aspects of African cultural values (African Union, 2006). According to Malawi's national education sector plan, gender equity features as one cross-cutting intervention at all levels of education (Malawi Government, 2008b). Malawi has, for example, been taking a number of measures to ensure that its entire education system is gender-friendly and gender-sensitive. This can be noticed in areas such as curriculum development and learning and development of teaching materials. For example, school curricula at various levels have been revised to make them gender-sensitive. One also cannot fail to acknowledge the establishment of the Gender Appropriate Curriculum Unit at the Malawi Institute of Education. This Unit offers training on gender sensitivity and ensures that curriculum textbooks have been engendered. Teacher education is also another avenue through which gender issues are emphasized (see Kamwendo, 2011 on gender issues in primary teacher education). There is expansion of girls' only schools (and hostels). In Addition, some donors are assisting in the development and establishment of gender-balanced schools. The goal is also to bring schools closer to communities for the purpose of reducing girls' walking distances to school. There is also a policy that allows pregnant girls to leave school, and then later resume school after giving birth. Overall, FPE has improved access for both boys and girls (Maluwa-Banda, 2003).

Ethnicity, religion and access to education

Historically, ethnicity and religion have had considerable impact on access to education and success in education. As it was mentioned earlier on in this chapter, it was the pioneer Christian missionaries who introduced education to Malawi. Generally, ethnic groups in Northern Malawi (e.g. the Tumbuka and the Tonga) were prominent in warmly embracing Western education (see McCracken, 1977) while on the other hand, the Yao (who were predominantly of Islamic faith) were reluctant to embrace education. Since education was initially provided by Christian missionaries, the Yaos feared that they would end up losing their religious faith and then convert to Christianity. As a result, the Yaos were slow to allow their children to go to school. Though today Yaos no longer harbour that fear, one still finds that their level of attainment of education is lower than other ethnic groups. The Northern Region, on the other hand, made big headway in the attainment of education during the missionary/colonial days, and today education remains well embraced in the Northern Region.

Disability and access to education

Christian missionaries were the first providers of special needs education (SNE) in Malawi. Later, the government took over responsibility. SNE covers the following areas:

- Learners with sensory impairment (vision, hearing, deaf-blind);
- Learners with cognitive difficulties (e.g. intellectual difficulties);
- Learners with socio-emotional and behavioural difficulties; and
- Learners with physical and health impairments (e.g. asthma, bifida and epilepsy) (Malawi Government, 2007; Itimu & Kopetz, 2008).

There are three modes through which learners access SNE in Malawi, namely: residential special schools, resource rooms within ordinary schools and itinerant programmes within which SNE teachers travel to schools within their zone or district and provide SNE to learners with disabilities. The SNE education faces the following challenges: acute shortage of teachers, long distances that SNE teachers have to travel to attend to learners, inadequate resource centres and lack of support from parents and regular teachers (Itimu & Kopetz, 2008). Ideally, disability of any kind should not bar a learner from accessing education and succeeding in education. Unfortunately, this is not the situation in the poorly resourced education system of Malawi. In line with EFA goals, education must be made available to all, irrespective of their disabilities. This goal can be enhanced in a number of ways. First is to provide SNE facilities. One way is to provide specialist schools to handle specific disabilities. In addition to the SNE facilities, one also needs to stress the importance of having well-trained and skilled teaching and support personnel. To this end, there is an urgent need for teacher education institutions to include or expand their SNE programmes.

Third, it is important to work on campaigns whose goal is to erase stigmas that are associated with disabilities.

Curriculum

Curricula review is a normal process in any education system. With regard to Malawi, our focus will be on the primary and secondary sectors of education. In 2007, the Ministry of Education introduced a new primary school curriculum at Standard I level. The rollout of the new curriculum has taken a phased approach with Standard I being coved in 2007, Standards II, IV and VI coming in 2008, and Standards III and VII in 2010. The rollout will be supported by appropriate in-service training of teachers. The new curriculum, which is outcome-based, places a lot of emphasis on literacy, numeracy, expressive arts and continuous assessment. The curriculum seeks to address contemporary social, economic and political issues.

A secondary school curriculum review is also on the drawing board. The curriculum was last reviewed in 1995. The new curriculum will have to be aligned to the revised primary school curriculum. The new curriculum is expected to include health and social, political and economic trends that have emerged since the last review. It is against this background that it is expected that the new curriculum will address issues such as democracy, governance, human rights, environmental degradation and climate change. Two critical processes have to accompany the new curriculum, that is, improving teachers' capacity to implement the new curriculum and provision of relevant learning and teaching materials.

Teaching methods

Despite these changes in the curriculum teacher-centredness remains predominant in both primary and secondary schools in Malawi (Mizrachi et al., 2010). There is still a need for teachers to embrace active-learning or student-centred pedagogies. This paradigm shift is of critical importance if Malawi is to improve quality in education. This paradigm shift will not be easy as a number of challenges stand in the way. For example, large classes (a common feature in Malawi) restrict some teachers from adopting learner-centred pedagogies. Another reason for the non-adoption of the learner-centred pedagogies is that there is an acute shortage of learning and teaching resources. Third, some of the teachers lack the skills and expertise needed for the implementation of learner-centred pedagogies. Another challenge is that while some teachers (especially the recently trained teachers) may possess the relevant skills, they find that their counterparts in the schools are opposed to learner-centred pedagogies. The advocates for learner-centred pedagogy therefore become outnumbered and isolated, and they naturally succumb to tradition, that is, teacher-centred pedagogies. Another challenge is the fact that Malawi has an examination-oriented culture. How well or badly a school performs in national examinations is of critical importance. Progression to the next level of education is decided on the basis of the results coming out of national examinations. Very few learners pass the examinations and, as such, parents, teachers and learners are all anxious to find ways of passing and succeeding. One of the strategies is to teach in ways that specifically prepare learners for examinations. In this way, what matters is that students pass an examination – whether they learnt anything is not important. In line with this thinking, students are drilled for examinations (Mizrachi et al., 2010).

Assessment through public examinations

As mentioned earlier, at Standards VIII, Froms II and IV, learners take national examinations. The Malawi National Examination Board (MANEB) is responsible for running all these examinations. These public examinations are used for determining which students can proceed from one level to the next one. Very few make it the next level, thereby creating a pyramid shape for students who proceed with education in Malawi. The bottom of this pyramid is at primary school while the top (and narrow end) of the educational pyramid is made up of tertiary education students.

Public examinations have had some challenges. One of them has been low pass rates, a situation that can be attributed a number of factors (such as poor learning and teaching conditions and low student interest in education). The public examination system has to an extent lost the support and trust of the very public it is supposed to serve. Leakage of public examination questions has been one such situation. MANEB has on a number of occasions been faced with the embarrassment of finding examination papers being sold by vendors on the streets. Some school heads, teachers, examination invigilators, security personnel/law enforcers, students, parents and other stakeholders have been involved in public examination-related irregularities and/or scams. Some of the culprits have been prosecuted and sentenced in courts of law. MANEB then has the tough task of restoring confidence in public examinations. This has involved tightening examination security measures and conducting civic education against examination-related malpractices.

Language in education

Language is by no means an uncontroversial issue in any education system, including Malawi. Like other African countries, Malawi is multilingual. According to the 1998 population census, the major languages of household communication in Malawi were identified as follows: Chichewa (70%), Yao (10.1%), Tumbuka (9.5%), Sena (2.7%), Lomwe (2.4%), Tsonga (1.7%) and other languages (3.6%) (see Malawi Government, 1998). Chichewa (also known as Chinyanja) is the national language. The official language is English – a legacy of British colonialism. This then places Malawi within the category of the so-called English-speaking African countries. The tendency to describe Malawi as an English-speaking nation is somewhat misleading because the language is confined to a small minority. The vast majority of Malawians communicate in the national language and other local languages.

Following Chichewa's elevation to national language status in 1968, the language became the only indigenous language used in the education domain. In all public schools, Chichewa is the medium of learning and teaching from Standards I to IV. Thereafter, English takes over as the medium of learning and teaching. English, as a subject, is offered straightaway in Standard I up to Standard VIII.

Both English and Chichewa are offered as subjects throughout the eight years of primary education (Kamwendo, 2001). A proposal to introduce more indigenous languages (dominant languages of a school's catchment area) as media of teaching and learning was made in 1996 but the policy still remains unimplemented due to a lack of resources (see Kamwendo, 2008). This policy directive stemmed from the electoral campaign manifesto of the then ruling political party, the UDF (see United Democratic Front, 1993a, b). The mother tongue policy declaration came barely two years after the installation of FPE, and the latter has been poorly resourced (Chimombo, 2005; Kendall, 2005). It is therefore not surprising that aid-dependent Malawi (see Kendall, 2005) could not assemble the necessary resources needed for the implementation of the mother tongue education policy.

The medium of teaching and learning in primary schools brings mixed fortunes. On a positive note, both pupils and teachers acknowledge that learning through Chichewa is easier than learning through English. Pupils are actively involved – in contrast to English-medium classes in which the learners remain silent due to their lack of proficiency in English. But there is the other side of the story – the negative side of the use of Chichewa as a medium of instruction. According to action research conducted by some primary schools teachers (see Kamwendo et al., 2003), the switch from Chichewa to English (Standards V–VIII) hinders effective teacher-pupil communication since some of the Malawian pupils find it hard to understand the new medium of instruction. In Malawi, like most of Africa's so-called English-speaking countries, the majority of the pupils have little out-of-the classroom exposure to English. Given this linguistic situation, the current transitional bilingual education system in Malawi impacts negatively on the quality of teaching and learning. Some pupils perform poorly because they are unable to express themselves competently in English. This trend also appears during national examinations.

Kamwendo et al. (2003) noted that teachers have a number of strategies that help them to cope with English as a medium of teaching/learning problem. The first strategy involves the teachers' use of simple English words. To this end, the teacher tries as much as possible to avoid using complex vocabulary. However, it is not easy to stick faithfully to this practice all the time. There are times when the use of complex vocabulary becomes inevitable. As a second strategy, teachers code switch between English and Chichewa/or any other appropriate indigenous language. The third strategy amounts to the use of some school-based language policies and/or practices that are perceived to promote pupils' competence in English. One of such school practices is to hold debates – the aim being to improve pupils' oral proficiency in English. In addition, as part of what can be called school-based language policy, some teachers reported that in their schools/classrooms, they impose a 'speak English only rule'. That is, pupils are required to speak solely in English. A pupil who breaks the rule by speaking Chichewa or any other indigenous language attracts punishment.

As regards the medium of teaching/learning problem, some recommendations were made by the teachers (Kamwendo et al., 2003). One recommendation was that Chichewa should cease to be the medium of learning and teaching in Standards I to IV. According to the teachers who advanced this view, mother tongue instruction does not allow pupils to have maximum exposure to English.

Pupils only get exposed to English during English lessons. Given that after Standard V, all subjects (except Chichewa) are taught and examined in English, the teachers argued that it does not make sense to delay the introduction of English as a medium of instruction. According to such teachers, the earlier English is introduced as the medium of teaching/learning, the better the ability of the learners to use this linguistic medium.

School governance and management

One of the three areas of intervention coming under Malawi's National Education Sector plan for 2008–17 is to 'improve governance and management of the sytem to enable more effective and efficient delivery of services' (Malawi Government, 2008b: 1). Of special interest here is community participation in school governance. All schools do have Parents/Teachers Associations (PTA) or school committees. School committees are supposed to consider issues such as: teachers' professionalism, pedagogy, financing and others. Low education of parents, especially in the rural areas, makes it difficult for many parents to serve effectively on the school committees. They are not well conversant with the issues at hand, hence they are unable to make meaningful contributions to school governance.

Teacher education

The demand for teachers at primary and secondary school levels has put immense pressure on teacher education. For example, the FPE has created a huge demand for primary school teachers. Unfortunately, teacher education programmes and institutions are not able to satisfy demand for teachers. Teacher education, at both primary and secondary levels in Malawi, is confronted by the following critical challenges:

- Lack of coherent policies and clear strategies to address overwhelming demand which in turn has put a strain on and/or compromised both the quantity and quality of primary and secondary school education;
- Total output has remained at less than 3,000 for primary school teachers and 400 for secondary school teachers annually. This translates into a continuing huge demand for qualified teachers;

- Inadequate funding for teaching and learning of teachers;
- Qualified teachers rarely attend professional development activities;
- A significant number of secondary school teachers are under-qualified;
- Lack of teacher education coordinating bodies mandated to link the Ministry of Education and teacher education institutions in order to produce a qualified, dedicated and flexible teaching force;
- Problem of coordination in teacher management;
- The impact of HIV/AIDS on teachers (and other education staff) is worrisome;
- Recruitment and deployment of teachers is inefficient;
- Poor inspection of schools and teachers has led to weak supervision of the quality of teaching and learning;
- Need for qualified special needs teachers and necessary inputs for primary and secondary schools (Malawi Government, 2008b).

One thing that is clear is that both primary and secondary school sectors have created teacher demand levels which teacher education institutions cannot satisfy at the moment. Public institutions providing teacher education are Teacher Training Colleges (for primary school teachers) while Domasi College of Education, University of Malawi and Mzuzu University cater for the training of secondary school teachers. In view of the high demand for teachers and the low supply, there is need for expansion in enrolments in teacher education programmes. There is also need to introduce additional programmes in teacher education, one of which is a special education teacher education programme. Gender is another key aspect that has to be infused into all teacher education programmes (see Kamwendo, 2011 on gender issues in primary teacher education). It is also important to appreciate that as new programmes are introduced, and enrolment goes up, facilities at the teacher education institutions should be both increased and improved. One common mistake is to increase enrolment without increasing and improving a training institution's capacity. There is also need to explore ways of providing teachers with professional development through short courses, seminars and other avenues.

Teacher recruitment and supply

Malawi faces an acute shortage of teachers, especially at the primary school level (World Bank, 2010). It is important to mention that the quality of people who enter the primary school teaching profession has an impact on the quality of the teaching/learning outcomes. Generally, the teaching profession, especially at primary school level in Malawi, is not viewed as an option for the high achievers (Kunje et al., 2003). What Schmied (1991) says about the low prestige of the teaching profession is applicable to Malawi:

> The best students want to attend universities and colleges (they often have higher admission terms as to quality and quantity of A-level passes) and the lower ranks go to teacher training colleges, whose best students leave for careers in administration, business and politics. (Schmied, 1991: 113)

Equally relevant and applicable to the Malawian situation is Abura's observation that in Kenya, primary school teaching is 'regarded by many as a dead-end, a dumping ground for those who have not done well in national examinations and cannot therefore be absorbed anywhere else' (Abura, 1998: 47).

Teacher remuneration, motivation, satisfaction and professionalism

Levels of remuneration affect teachers' satisfaction and motivation (Kadzamira, 2006). Private schools generally offer remuneration packages that are better than those offered to teachers in public schools. Generally, teacher motivation and satisfaction in Malawi are not favourable (Kadzamira, 2006). This is true of pre-school, primary and secondary sectors. Workload, promotion prospects, career growth possibilities, prospects for further training, availability or non-availability of housing and learning/teaching resources are some of the factors that can motivate or demotivate teachers or increase and/or decrease teachers' job satisfaction. For example, high workloads, accompanied by low pay leads to low motivation and low teacher satisfaction. The location of a school is another critical factor. Schools that are located in rural areas are generally not the first choices for teachers. This is because the working and living conditions in rural areas are far from being pleasant. Poor or no housing, lack of electricity, lack of running water and poorly resourced schools are some of the reasons why teachers generally do not like being posted to teach in rural areas.

Student behaviour is another factor worth considering when discussing teacher motivation and satisfaction. Disruptive student behaviour and unruly students make teaching an unfavourable profession. Student behaviour in Malawi has deteriorated since the advent of the democratic dispensation in 1994. Some students misunderstand democracy and human rights, and therefore, think that they have the freedom to be anything in school. In the Hastings Banda era (an era of dictatorship), student discipline was at its highest point. Unfortunately, the culture of democracy has been misinterpreted and abused. Student respect of teachers has gone down considerably and, in some cases, students have threatened teachers' personal security.

While within the private school category there are some schools that are of low quality, it has generally been observed in Malawi that teacher morale is higher among those working in private schools than public schools. On average private schools have better learning and teaching resources than public schools. Furthermore, most private schools have more favourable teacher/learner ratios.

There have been complaints about what can be called lack of professionalism among teachers. The media in Malawi has been inundated with reports or allegations of teachers who display unprofessional conduct. For instance, the media contains stories or allegations of teachers who sexually harass their, usually female, learners (see, for example, Maluwa-Banda, 2003). Some teachers engage in excessive and irresponsible drinking habits. Some teachers are frequently absent from duties on no good grounds. For instance, some teachers run away from duties and engage in private jobs that would earn them income to supplement their low salaries. As noted above, some teachers even indulge in examination-related malpractices such as leaking public examination papers to students. Usually such teachers do so on account of being promised some financial rewards. These situations impact negatively on their performance as teachers. They also fail to serve as good models for their young learners. They lose the confidence and trust of society. There is a feeling that while in the past teachers were a highly respected and self-respecting group of professionals and were the custodians of socially acceptable behaviour, this is no longer the case. Teachers are fast becoming perceived as less and less professional in their conduct and performance. This state of affairs cannot be attributed to one factor alone. One has to consider a range of factors such as: lack of proper training, the increasingly young age of teachers, poor remuneration and a weak supervisory system.

Summary and conclusions

The question of resources is particularly critical to Malawi's quest for quality education. Malawian public schools are poorly resourced. The situation is worst in rural schools. When it comes to secondary schools, it is the conventional secondary schools that are better resourced than the community day secondary schools. In 1994, FPE was introduced. It led to a huge leap in the enrolment figures. While an increased enrolment has been registered, no effective learning and teaching takes place in some of the schools due to deteriorating teacher/ pupil ratios, insufficient learning and teaching materials, substandard and ageing school infrastructure and inadequately trained and poorly motivated teachers. As a result, the FPE has meant a serious compromise on the quality of primary education (Chimombo, 2005; Kendall, 2005; World Bank, 2010). In fact, according to the Civil Society Coalition for Quality Basic Education in Malawi, the country is 'very far from achieving the 2015 targets in education because of poor implementation of policies' (Ndaferankhande, 2006). The poor implementation of policies is due to the fact that the education sector is inadequately funded by the Government of Malawi. The entire education sector is heavily dependent on donor funding. The danger of this dependence is that donors sometimes take over the policy agenda, and leave the government powerless in deciding on national policy issues. One can summarize Malawi's challenges in education as: access, equity, quality, relevance, management and finance. These challenges exist in the three sectors of education considered in this chapter (i.e. pre-school, primary school and secondary school).

References

Abura, J. (1998). 'Towards more Communicative Approaches to the Teaching of English as a Second Language: Primary Teachers' Colleges in Kenya', *Southern African Review of Education* 4, pp. 41–8.

African Union (2006). *Second Decade of Education for Africa: 2006–2015* (Addis Ababa: African Union).

Chimombo, J. P. G. (2005). 'Quality versus Quantity in Education: Case Studies in Malawi', *International Review of Education* 15, pp. 155–72.

Itimu, A. N. and Kopetz, P. B. (2008). 'Malawi Special Needs Education (SNE): Perspectives and Comparisons of Practice and Progress', *Journal of Research in Special Education Needs* 8, 3, pp. 153–60.

Kadzamira, E. (2006). 'Teacher Motivation and Incentives in Malawi', Unpublished document.

Kadzamira, E. and Rose, P. (2003). 'Can Free Primary Education meet the Needs of the Poor? Evidence from Malawi', *International Journal of Educational Development* 23, pp. 501–16.

Kamwendo, G. (2001). 'Malawi's Approach to Language in Education: A Review of Key Issues', in R. Trewby and S. Fitchat (eds), *Language and Development in Southern Africa: Making the Right Choices* (Windhoek: Gamsberg Macmillan), pp. 86–93.

— (2008). 'The Bumpy Road to Mother Tongue Instruction in Malawi', *Journal of Multilingual and Multicultural Development* 29, 5, pp. 353–63.

Kamwendo, J. (2011). 'Gender Mainstreaming in Initial Primary Teacher Education Curriculum: The Case of Blantyre Teachers College-Malawi', Unpublished M.Ed thesis, University of Botswana.

Kamwendo, J, Dolozi, A. and Mteleka, L. (2003). 'Problems in the Teaching of Primary Science: Views from Zomba Urban Teachers', Poster Presentation at the 11th Southern African Association for Research in Mathematics, Science and Technology Education Conference, 11–15 January 2003, Swaziland.

Kendall, N. (2005). 'Free Primary Education in Malawi: The Practice of Global Policy in Aid-dependent States', in D. Baker and A. Wiseman (eds), *Global Trends in Educational Policy* (Amsterdam: Elsevier), pp. 125–43.

Kunje, D., Lewin, K. and Stuart, J. (2003). 'Primary Teacher Education in Malawi: Insights into Practice and Policy', Multi-Site Teacher Education Research Project (MUSTER) Country Report. DFID Educational Paper No. 49D.

Malawi Government (1998). *Malawi 1998 Population Census Report* (Zomba: Government Printer).

— (2007). *Special Needs Education Policy (Revised)* (Lilongwe: Ministry of Education).

— (2008a). *Population Census Report* (Zomba: National Statistics Office).

— (2008b). *National Education Sector Plan: 2008–2017* (Lilongwe: Ministry of Education, Science and Technology).

Malawi Local Education Donor Group (2009). *Appraisal of Government of Malawi's Education Sector Plans NESP 2008–2017, ESIP 2009–2013.*

Maluwa-Banda, D. (2003). 'Gender Sensitive Educational Policy and Practice: The Case of Malawi', Background paper presented for the Education for All Global Monitoring Report 2003/4, UNESCO.

McCracken, J. (1977). *Politics and Christianity in Malawi 1875–1940* (Cambridge: Cambridge University Press).

Mizrachi, A, Padilla, O. and Susuwele-Banda, W. (2010). *Active-learning Pedagogies as a Reform Initiative: The Case of Malawi.* USAID.

Ndaferankhande, C. (2006). 'Malawi far from MDGs, Civil Society says *The Nation*', www.nationmalawi.com. Accessed 19 September, 2006.

SADC Protocol on Education and Training. Accessed from: www.sadc.int

Schmied, J. (1991). *English in Africa* (London: Longman).

United Democratic Front (1993a). *Towards a better Malawi: Manifesto.* N.P.

— (1993b). *Draft Policy on Education and Culture.* N.P.

Williams, E. (2006). *Bridges and Barriers: Language in African Education and Development* (Manchester: St Jerome Publishing).

World Bank (2010). *The Education System in Malawi.* World Bank working paper 182 (Washington, DC: World Bank).

5

Mozambique: Binding Quantitative and Qualitative Goals

Feliciano Chimbutane
Universidade Eduardo Mondlane

Introduction

The government of Mozambique has defined education as a key element in its development strategy. The assumption is that education is central for improving living conditions and alleviating poverty. Among other things, this has led the government to focus its attention on the expansion of basic education. Ensuring basic primary education for all has been one of the key government goals since independence in 1975, but it was after the civil war (1976–92) that the conditions for meeting this goal started to be in place. The government abolished enrolment fees in primary education, provided free textbooks to pupils, constructed more schools with donors' and communities' involvement and built teacher training institutes nationwide. As a consequence of these measures, there are now more people attending school in Mozambique, there are more trained primary school teachers, primary completion rates have improved, from 14 per cent in 1999 to 58 per cent in 2010 (MEC, 1999; MINED, 2011b), and illiteracy has dramatically dropped from 93 per cent at independence (Comissão Nacional do Plano, 1985) to nearly 48 per cent in 2007 (INE, 2010).

Improvements in access to basic education have led to new challenges. On the one hand, the increase in numbers of primary school graduates has put pressure on secondary schools, hence the current need to expand access to this level of education and beyond. On the other hand, the expansion of access seems to have compromised quality of teaching and learning, hence the current focus on improving quality of education at all levels, but particularly at primary level. The changing needs of the emerging economy, increasingly based on knowledge and technology, also challenge the education system to produce skilled graduates who can compete in regional and international markets.

These new challenges have pushed the government to articulate planning for access with planning for quality and diversification of education opportunities. Indeed, as will become apparent throughout the chapter, education plans developed in the past 10 years have sought to improve education quality and relevance while ensuring increasing access to post-primary levels, including technical and vocational components. Within this framework, policy and planning now focus more on improving the quality of teaching and learning, assuming that can be achieved, among other things, through improvements in teacher training, monitoring of teaching activities and pupils performance, increasing of instructional hours and curriculum reforms aiming at better results in the areas of skills. Despite the relevance of quality-oriented policies, these seem not to have substantial impact on education processes and outcomes, at least for the time being – education quality is on the decline without a clear indication of improvement. The absence of a nationwide system to monitor and enforce quality-oriented policies (Crouch, 2011) may explain, at least in part, why these policies have not been translated into improvements in teaching quality and learning outcomes.

This chapter is a result of a desk study, mainly based on a review of research reports and policy documents on education in Mozambique. I also draw on my experience as researcher and consultant, in particular in the area of language-in-education policy and practice. The analysis offered in this chapter focuses on basic education, though post-primary education is also considered. This is because basic education is the most researched and well documented level of education in Mozambique as well as the best barometer to gauge the quality of education in the country. This is a consequence of the fact that, until recently, education planning and policy gave priority to basic education, making it the main target of government and donor efforts and resources.

Historical and political background

Mozambique became independent from Portugal in 1975, after 10 years of bloody war. The struggle for independence was led by the *Frente de Libertação de Moçambique* (Mozambican Liberation Front, hereinafter Frelimo). Frelimo formed the first government of the Republic of Mozambique (then The People's Republic of Mozambique) and established a one-party socialist state.

Following a Marxist-Leninist orientation, Frelimo set revolutionary policies which included nationalization of land, industry, education and health care. The policies adopted by Frelimo prompted internal and external opposition to the regime. It was within this climate of discontent that the *Resistência Nacional Moçambicana* (Mozambican National Resistance, hereinafter Renamo) was formed and, with the support of the Rhodesian and Apartheid regimes, waged a war against the Frelimo government.

The guerrilla raids by Renamo were first documented in 1976, but it was in the 1980s that the country witnessed the escalation of the conflict into a devastating civil war. By the mid-1980s, the country experienced complete stagnation: health and education systems collapsed, communications were cut off, agricultural production ceased as citizens abandoned the unstable rural areas and sought refuge in urban areas and in neighbouring countries. By 1990, the war had claimed nearly a million lives and about 4 million were refugees in neighbouring countries or displaced within the country (Newitt, 1995). Education was one of the sectors severely hit by the civil war. Indeed, the country witnessed massive killings of pupils and teachers and destruction of educational infrastructure. Schools and teachers were some of the main guerrilla targets, chiefly because Renamo viewed these as part and parcel of the ideological force of the Frelimo regime. Schools and teachers were respectively seen as the arenas and agents for dissemination of socialist ideologies and for forging new socialists.

The 16 years of conflict between Frelimo and Renamo ceased in October 1992, after the Rome Peace Agreement. Since then a multiparty political system has been introduced in the country, paving the way for competitive political activity. As a consequence, the country has already held four general elections, out of which Frelimo won presidential and parliamentary majorities.

Since the advent of peace in 1992, Mozambique started its long process of social and economic recovery with relative success. For example, poverty decreased from 69 per cent in 1996/97 to an estimated 54.7 per cent in 2008/09 (RM, 2010), with growth of around 8 per cent per annum achieved over the last decade. Based on its capacity for keeping peace, democratization and economic progress, the country has been regarded as one of the post-war success stories in the world (IMF, 2007; World Bank, 2007). However, despite the relative economic success, Mozambique remains one of the poorest countries on earth, ranking 184 out of 187 countries in 2011 (HDR, 2011). More than half of its population (estimated at 20.2 million people) lives below the poverty line, without access to basic services such as education and health. This is one of the African countries hardest hit by the Human Immunodeficiency Virus

(HIV)/ Acquired Immunodeficiency Syndrome (AIDS) pandemic, with 2010 data showing a prevalence of 11.5 per cent among adults (INS et al., 2010). More than 40 per cent of the state budget still depends on external assistance (RM, 2010).

Portuguese is *the* official language of the country, in spite of the fact that this is only spoken by about 50 per cent of the population, of which only 10.7 per cent claim to speak it as a first language (INE, 2010). In contrast, 85.3 per cent of the population speak a Bantu language as a first language.

Mozambican education system

The current National Education System, which has been in force since 1992, represents an adjustment of the 1983 system due to new sociopolitical circumstances. Indeed, in addition to pedagogical factors, the review of the system was also influenced by political and socio-economic changes that took place in the 1990s, including the introduction of a multiparty political system and a market-oriented economy.

The structure of the National Education System of Mozambique has three main components: Pre-school Education (or early childhood education), Formal Education and Non-formal Education (RM, 1992). Pre-school education, which is not compulsory, is provided for 1- to 5-year-old children in *creches* and *jardins infantis* (kindergartens). Education at this level is mainly provided through private operators and a few public institutions. Unlike the other subsystems, which are under the supervision of the Ministry of Education (MoE),[1] pre-school education is under the Ministry for Women and Social Welfare.

Formal education is provided from primary through to tertiary level. There are two modalities of formal education: regular (or normal) and special modalities. The regular modality encompasses general education (primary and secondary education), technical and vocational education and higher education. Primary Education comprises two levels: lower primary education (Grade I to V) and upper primary education (Grade VI and VII). The same organization also applies to secondary education, which comprises lower secondary education (Grade VIII to X) and upper secondary education (Grade XI and XII). The special modality encompasses special education (for children with disabilities), adult education, distance education and teacher education.

Non-formal education includes literacy and professional development programmes provided outside the formal education system, mainly by Non-Governmental Organizations (NGOs) and community-based institutions.

Since 2003 there have been two programmes in place at primary level in Mozambique: a monolingual Portuguese programme which, given its representativeness across the country, can be regarded as the mainstream programme, and a bilingual programme, in which, in addition to Portuguese, a local language is also used as a medium of instruction. So far, the bilingual programme has only been gradually introduced into selected rural schools. Despite its popularity among rural communities, this programme is facing severe limitations, such as lack of trained human resources and learning/teaching materials (for details, see Chimbutane, 2011).

Much of the Mozambican population has only access to the lower levels of primary education: in 2011, the primary level absorbed about 84.9 per cent of the school population, being 71.9 per cent at the lower levels (Grades I–V) and only 14.0 per cent at higher levels (Grades VI and VII) (MINED, 2011a). The demand for education is so high that the majority of primary schools accommodate two shifts a day (in fact, in urban areas many schools accommodate up to three shifts), which, among other things shortens school day for pupils and hinders the quality of education offered to them.

Goals and priorities for education

The Constitution of the Republic of Mozambique states that education is a right, as well as a duty, for every citizen (RM, 1990, 2004). Since 1995, this statement has been translated into a National Education Policy, which sets out the goal of providing basic education for all children.

Goals and priorities for education in Mozambique are set out in a number of key planning documents, including the National Poverty Reduction Plans (PARPA), Five-year Government Plans and Sector Plans. There are always attempts to articulate the different plans in terms of key goals and priorities for each government sector. For example, education goals and priorities are also translated into the Poverty Reduction Plans and also into the Five-year Government Plans. These are also articulated with international educational goals and priorities, such as those set for the Education for All (EFA) initiative. However, there are often questions about coordination at the implementation level.

The strategic plans for the education sector, which have been developed since 1999, mirror the overall goal of providing basic education to all citizens. The first Education Sector Strategic Plan covered the period 1999–2005, the second covered the period 2006–10/11 and the third covers the period 2012–16. The first strategic plan reaffirmed education as a basic human right and translated the view that basic education was key in guiding the priorities and commitments of the government. In order to effect this, three strategic objectives were defined: (i) the expansion of access to basic education, (ii) the improvement of the quality of education services and (iii) the strengthening of the institutions and the administrative setup for effective and sustainable delivery of education (MEC, 1999).

The improvement in the access to basic education is regarded as the major achievement of the implementation of the first strategic plan. However, this improvement seems to have been achieved at the expense of quality. In addition to that, massive access to basic education and the consequent high completion rates have led to an increased demand for post-primary education. These and other issues were addressed in the second strategic plan.

Unlike the first strategic plan, the second plan (2006–10/11) covered the entire education sector, although priority was devoted to primary education for all. In line with this new orientation, the plan defined the following strategic objectives: (i) extending access to all school age children, (ii) providing educational opportunities for out of school youth and adults and (iii) improving quality and relevance of education to ensure that increasing numbers of children have access to post-primary levels (MEC, 2006).

Above all, this second plan emphasized the government's commitment to working towards meeting the objectives of the Millennium Development Goals (MDGs), by focusing on ensuring the completion of seven years of primary education for all Mozambican children by 2015. According to the plan, these seven years of basic education should give all the children life skills and enable them to participate in a responsible manner in society as well as provide them the opportunity to continue their studies beyond primary level.

The focus on providing children with access to post-primary levels was a response to the demand resulting from improvements in access and completion at primary level and also reflected the recognition that a basic education for all is not enough to keep pace with economic development. This prompted the government to expand access to secondary education and reform technical and vocation education so as to respond to labour market demands and lead to (self) employment opportunities.

The third strategic plan (2012–16) reaffirms the government's aim to ensure good quality primary education for all. One of the main innovations of the plan is the attention devoted to pre-school education, regarded as a crucial stage for children's physical and cognitive development. The plan defines the following main strategic objectives: (i) inclusiveness in access to education and improvement of retention rates, (ii) improvement of education quality, particularly in terms of student learning, (iii) expansion of post-primary education and diversification of programmes and curricula offered at this level and (iv) improvement of education management (MINED, 2012).

As can be understood, this is a follow up of the previous strategic plans. Despite the introduction of new priorities, the fundamental ones remain the same: expansion of access to education, improvement of education quality and diversification of education opportunities, mainly in response to new economic development demands.

Improvements in access to basic education and in primary school completion rates can be regarded as the major results of the education policies pursued since independence, but particularly during the last decade. The increase in primary school completion rates can be taken, at least in part, as a consequence of the implementation of two policy decisions: abolition of school fees and introduction of semi-automatic promotion, a policy through which pupils can only be made to repeat if they fail in examinations at Grades II, V or VII.[2] Indeed, the abolition of school fees has led to an increased access to primary education (there are more children in schools than before) and the semi-automatic promotion dramatically reduced the rates of repeaters.

Equity issues

Equity is an ongoing issue in education in Mozambique. Equity concerns in this sector are chiefly related to disparities in terms of regions, provinces, the rural/ urban divide, gender and social status. The disparities observed have a bearing on access to education as well as on educational processes and outcomes. This section focuses on geographic and gender discrepancies, although other forms of disparity are also considered.

Geographic disparities

Despite government efforts, disparities among regions and provinces remain high, mainly affecting children in rural areas. Indeed, enrolment rates in basic education tend to be higher in the southern region, compared to the centre and north of the country. For example, in 2011, enrolment rates for school age children (6-year-olds) in the southern provinces of Maputo City, Maputo Province, Gaza and Inhambane were 87 per cent, 96.8 per cent, 84.1 per cent and 79.2 per cent, respectively, while in the central provinces of Manica, Sofala, Tete and Zambézia they were 61.1 per cent, 68.8 per cent, 65.6 per cent and 78.2 per cent, respectively. The northern province of Nampula had the lowest school enrolment rate at national level, with 48.4 per cent (MINED, 2011a: 24).

Substantial geographical disparities can also be attested in terms of completion rates. In 2010, the provinces of the southern region had higher completion rates at lower primary level, with the highest being for Maputo City (93.7%). Tete (53.9%), in the central region, and Niassa (52.8%) and Nampula (57.7%), in the north, had the lowest completion rates (MINED, 2011b).

Statistical data compiled by the MoE are consistent with results from the few national learning assessments conducted in the country. For example, SACMEQ III[3] found disparities between provinces in average learning achievement. In a reading test, in which the national mean score was 476, Maputo City's score was 540 while the central province of Tete scored 427 and the northern provinces of Niassa and Cabo Delgado scored 440 and 448, respectively. In mathematics, where the national mean was 483, Maputo City scored 506 while Tete scored 457 and Niassa and Cabo Delgado scored 445 and 460, respectively (Passos et al., in preparation).

Gender disparities

Gender disparities in Mozambican education, especially in rural settings, are commonly linked to a set of social, cultural and economic factors, including: (i) the prevalence of cultural habits leading to the non-enrolment or dropout of girls from schools, such as premature marriages and the absence of recognition on the part of the parents of the importance of schooling for girls; (ii) parents' fears to send their daughters to schools where male teachers dominate, which makes them vulnerable to sexual harassment (see RM, 2010).

Despite still being a matter of concern, in general gender disparities in primary education are gradually narrowing, especially at lower primary level.

The gender parity index in net enrolment ratios at primary level (Grade I–VII) has improved from 0.90 in 2004 to 0.93 in 2008 and 0.95 in 2011. However, gender discrepancies become evident when the different regions and provinces are taken into account. The discrepancies are more pronounced in the northern and central provinces than in the southern provinces, where the numbers of girls and boys enrolled in lower primary education tend to be equal. More recent assessments indicate that in spite of progress made towards gender equity in primary education enrolment, disparities remain significant at the higher levels of schooling (see Bartholomey et al., 2010 and references therein).

Gender discrepancies can also be found when completion rates are considered. Completion rates in primary school tend to be slightly lower for girls. For example, in 2010, the completion rates for girls in lower primary school was 61.7 per cent, while for boys was 71.3 per cent. Although boys are still outperforming girls, the gender parity index for primary school completion shows a significant rising trend. As a matter of fact, from 61 in 2003, the index rose to 72 in 2007 and to 87 in 2010. These improvements may be a result of government and societal initiatives aiming at gender parity in the country.

As would be expected, primary school enrolment and completion rates tend to be related to the level of wealth of the students' households. Boys and girls from higher wealth quintiles tend to have higher enrolment rates as well as higher completion rates than girls and boys from lower wealth quintiles (RM, 2010 and references therein; Passos et al., in preparation). This has led some analysts to conclude that the fact that primary schooling is free in itself does not guarantee that children from poorer households' stay at school until completion (RM, 2010: 37).

The disadvantage of girls in terms of school outcomes have also been captured through learning achievement tests. For example, SACMEQ III found that gender-related differences in learning achievement at Grade VI were not significant in the reading test, where the mean score for boys was 478 and 473 for girls. However, the differences were slightly higher in the mathematics test, where boys scored 488 points and girls 479 (see Passos et al., in preparation). These results are consistent with the ones obtained in SACMEQ II.

As pointed out in Bartholomey et al. (2010), improvements in gender indicators (e.g. enrolment and completion rates) seem to suggest that policies related to gender equity in education have been somewhat successful. Indeed, gender equity has been at the centre of different levels of policy and planning in Mozambique. Gender is conceived as a cross-cutting issue, one that is dealt within all areas of activity. The government goal has been to guarantee gender equality both in terms of socio-economic benefit and women's participatory role in decision-making processes. The government recognizes the link between gender and poverty, thus assuming the education of women as central for the reduction of poverty. One of the underlying rationales has been that provision of universal basic education for women will, among other things, lead to their autonomy and contribute to the reduction of child mortality and to the improvement of mother health (see RM, 2010).

Curriculum, teaching methods and assessment

Curriculum

Concerns about the quality of education coupled with both national and international sociopolitical and economic transformations have led to curriculum reform initiatives mainly targeting basic education, secondary education, technical and vocational education. The general perception has been that the structure and content of the curricula are not following the rhythm of economic and social transformations taking place in the country and internationally. It was within this climate that a new curriculum for basic education was introduced in 2004 and another one for secondary education in 2008. Since 2006, the government has also been engaged in a long-term reform programme for technical and vocational education, known as *Programa Integrado de Reforma da Educação Profissional* (PIREP).

The curriculum reform for basic education brought about some important changes into the system. Some of the crucial innovations of the new curriculum included the introduction of seven years of complete and integrated primary schooling, bilingual education and semi-automatic promotion. As discussed later in this chapter, the latter innovation has been a source of tensions among educational stakeholders. The reform also introduced what is called *currículo local* (*local curriculum*), which consists of teaching local knowledge (local history, geography, agriculture, fishery, crafts, etc.) for 20 per cent of instructional time. This portion of the curriculum is expected to be developed locally, a move which is part of a process of decentralizing curriculum development and monitoring. As part of the introduction of the new curriculum, textbooks are provided to pupils free of charge, which adds to the free primary education provision.

The new curriculum for secondary education aims to equip students with some notions of professional competences so that graduates can choose between entering the labour market and proceeding to tertiary education. The aim of PIREP is to transform technical and vocational education into a more demand-driven system with curricula, assessments and certifications designed to address the needs of employers in a variety of sectors. The new curricula are being designed so as to ensure that training leads to the production of graduates with skill sets that meet the specific needs of particular industries and services. The programme has defined the sectors of administration, accountancy, agriculture, tourism, hotel management and mechanics as the major targets of the curriculum reform. In order to ensure that the curricula and training systems in fact produce graduates with skill sets that respond to the specific needs of particular industries and services, the programme counts on active involvement of important labour force stakeholders, such as labour unions and employers. These are regularly invited to evaluate new curricula proposals as well as the professional training offered in different technical and vocational courses.

However, despite some improvements in education processes, the reforms introduced are yet to produce the desired outcomes. Overall, the quality of graduates produced in all levels remains unsatisfactory.

Teaching methods

As happens in other post-colonial contexts, with a few exceptions, teaching methods in Mozambique follow the traditional format. Despite efforts to change the status quo, overall pedagogy remains teacher-centred and teacher discourse remains authoritarian. In general, lessons are organized in a platform format, the teacher is the one who speaks most of the time, uses question-and-answer techniques and evaluates pupils' contributions. Pupils are expected to listen attentively to teachers' discourse, answer their questions, take notes and follow instructions. In most cases, when pupils raise questions and challenge teachers' authority, they are treated as *indisciplinados*, that is, as unruly students. This classroom interaction pattern is much more pervasive in rural primary schools, where teachers' authority is more pronounced than in urban settings.

The language barrier and teachers' *habitus* (taken-for-granted mind set) are factors that can be used to explain the patterns described above. As a norm, most pupils in rural Mozambique only use and have access to Portuguese in the classroom. They can hardly speak or understand complex academic instructions in this language. Teachers (not pupils) have access to and control over Portuguese as a communicative resource and are also the sole custodians of the knowledge conveyed through that language. This asymmetry of power between teachers and pupils seems to be the factor which conditions the authoritarian nature of teachers' discourse (see Chimbutane, 2011). The recurrent use of discursive strategies such as pupils' repetition after the teacher and pupils' chorusing responses can be regarded as a response to pupils' poor control over the language of instruction. In contrast, in urban settings most pupils tend to have control over Portuguese, have access to information and knowledge outside the school context and they also live in a more liberal context, where it is common to interact in an unconstrained way with parents and other adults as well as challenge their authority. All these factors concur to destabilization of traditional classroom practices, making urban classroom environments less constrained and less authoritarian.

The language barrier argument can be further substantiated when classroom interaction in local languages is taken into consideration. Indeed, as Chimbutane (2011) found from a study on bilingual schools, in classes in African languages, pupils feel at ease, participate in class and are visibly motivated to learn. They not only reply to the questions asked by the teacher, but, when the opportunities arise, also take the initiative to make conversational moves in whole-class exchanges. This learning environment seems to be prompted by the fact that teachers and pupils share a common language and cultural values, which enable pupils to negotiate with and challenge their teachers on both language and cultural issues. In spite of difficulties of a different nature, including lack of learning and teaching resources and trained human resources, mother tongue based bilingual education seems to provide a better learning environment for the majority of Mozambican children than the Portuguese monolingual education.

However, in both types of programmes (monolingual and bilingual), teaching techniques tend to follow the same fundamental patterns. The habitus associated with teachers' trajectories seem to have a bearing on classroom pedagogical practices: teachers tend to teach as they were themselves taught. Studies report that lessons in Mozambican primary schools rely almost entirely on memory and oral recitation, even when books are available (Crouch, 2011). These patterns add to the teacher-centred pedagogies and the authoritarian discursive environment described above. Since teachers were also taught based on these same pedagogical and interactional strategies, they also tend to follow suit. They use those strategies, in part, because they are usually not acquainted with alternative teaching methods, such as task-based and communicative methods.

Assessment and quality of education

There is an ongoing debate in Mozambique around the level of education quality. The general public perception is that schooling quality has been dropping. In fact, empirical data also shows that learning outcomes and quality are on decline. In 2011, the pupil-teacher ratio was 63:1 for lower primary level (Grades I–V). About 16.8 per cent of primary school teachers are unqualified (MINED, 2011b). Most primary schools accommodate two shifts a day.[4] The quality of educational facilities is often poor, especially in rural areas. Although textbooks are provided to pupils free of charge, they are often not enough for every child. All these concerns constrain pupils' learning opportunities hence affecting school outputs and outcomes.

The MoE has been implementing some policy and practical initiatives in order to improve the quality of education. However, the sector still lacks a comprehensive system to monitor education quality over time. Indeed, a recent study commissioned by the United States Aid Agency (USAID) concluded that the Mozambican education system 'has no ability to measure, track, and react to quality. The system does not really have the right indicators yet, or does not use them, to set, monitor, and enforce quality-oriented policies' (Crouch, 2011: 11). Among other things, this conclusion is based on the observation that: (i) the system does not have enough information tracked about school processes, which would be analysed at district, provincial and national levels and generate input to schools; (ii) there are not agile mechanisms for using learning outcomes information to provide feedback to teachers on instructional activities; and (iii) some of the assessments conducted raise questions over validity and reliability.

In the absence of a nationwide, comprehensive monitoring system in Mozambique, education quality can only be appraised based on results from national examinations and from small-scale assessments conducted occasionally. Data on learning achievement, based on national examinations for Grades V, VII, X and XII, has been regularly collected by the National Council for Examinations, Certifications and Equivalence. It should be noted that all school examinations up to Grade X are marked at the school level, in most cases by the same teachers who taught the pupils sitting for exams. As pointed out in some studies, this set up raises questions about the validity and reliability of these data and therefore of its utility (Crouch, 2011)

Data from national examinations has been the most visible barometer of school outcomes in the country, being used to fuel the ongoing lively debate over the quality of schooling. For example, the results from 2011 secondary school final examinations showed an alarming 30 per cent pass rate, indicating that the majority of secondary school pupils are far from fulfilling the expected grade level requirements.

A few learning assessments on national representative samples have been conducted by INDE, as part of their own assessment programme or in partnership with regional initiatives such as SACMEQ. There are also independent assessments conducted on small samples of schools by national or international organizations, as part of their project objectives. The SACMEQ results are regarded as the most objective and rigorous indicators of national education quality available in Mozambique (see Crouch, 2011).

The SACMEQ results from the last two out of three assessment rounds conducted so far suggest that learning outcomes have on average come down. Table 5.1 shows that reading and mathematics scores dropped significantly both within each gender group and on average.

A study conducted in 2010 by the USAID-funded EQUIP2 project teamed with the Aga Khan Foundation on pupil's reading ability in the northern province of Cabo Delgado also showed that 59 per cent of a sample of Grade III children could not read a single Portuguese word out of simple passages and reading lists (Adelman et al., 2011).

A number of studies (e.g. Bartholomey et al., 2010; RM, 2010; Adelman et al., 2011; Chimbutane, 2011; Passos et al., in preparation) point to a set of different reasons why pupils are learning poorly in Mozambique, which include: (i) the language barrier, as the majority of primary school pupils do not have control over Portuguese, the de jure language of instruction, (ii) the employment of ineffective teaching methods, (iii) the scarcity of (quality) teaching and learning materials, (iv) the lack of systematic monitoring of education processes,

Table 5.1 Reading and mathematics SACMEQ scores in 2000 and 2007

Pupil gender	Reading		Mathematics	
	2000	**2007**	**2000**	**2007**
Boys	518.4	478.4	537.0	488.2
Girls	514.1	473.2	519.5	478.2
Average (Mozambique)	516.7	476.0	530.0	483.8
Change	−40.7		−46.2	

Source: Passos et al. (in preparation)

associated with the lack of the culture of using results from monitoring processes and learning outcomes information to improve instructional activities, (v) the accommodation of multi-shifting and poor time management, which result in a shortened school day for students and very low time on task[5] and (vi) parents' poor involvement in their children's schooling, either because they claim to be very busy or because they are illiterate and cannot help the children with their learning activities at home.

Poor quality in public schools has led better-off families, especially in urban areas, to enrol their children in private schools or even abroad. Although this is not always the case, private schools are perceived to offer higher quality education than public schools. In general, these schools are well resourced (they have libraries, learning and teaching aids, availability of computers, motivated staff, good infrastructures, etc.) and are better managed than public schools. As a consequence, children from families of higher socio-economic status have better learning opportunities than those from low income families, which may further contribute to increase socio-economic disparities in the country.

The indicators considered in this section suggest that if quality of education is to be achieved in Mozambique much more needs to be done at the implementation level of policy. Policy changes are not enough, there is also a need to monitor and ensure the implementation of those policies as well as evaluate their implications on education quality.

Teacher education

There are two types of teacher education in Mozambique: pre-service training for student-teachers in teacher education colleges and in-service training for teachers already teaching in schools. Pre-service training is provided by public colleges, known as *Institutos de Formação de Professores* (IFPs), and also by a few national and international organizations.[6] In-service training is mostly provided by IFPs and INDE, but also by NGOs, predominantly within their project areas. There is also a distance education course for lower primary in-service teachers who have been recruited without any pedagogical training. This course is provided by the *Instituto de Ensino à Distância Aberto/* Open Institute for Distance Learning (IEDA), a public institution under the responsibility of the MoE.

The entrance requirements to teacher education institutes and the duration of training have been changing over the years, mainly based on teachers' demand and on the goals set up for the education sector. Indeed, when the goal of education was mainly to increase access to basic education and, hence, the numbers of teachers needed were high, candidates were admitted with five and seven years of education. They were then trained for one to two years, in what is known as 5+1/5+2[7] or 7+1/7+2 training models. It was within this context that the distance 7+3 teacher education course provided by IEDA (former *Instituto de Aperfeiçoamento de Professores* – IAP) was launched in 1996.

When the supply of trained teachers seemed to meet the demand but the quality of schooling started to be a matter of concern, the entrance bar was raised to 10 years of schooling, irrespective of individual performance marks. If initially the system adopted the 10+2 model, this was later changed to the 10+1 model. The need for additional trained teachers in the rapidly expanding primary level and a Word Bank imposition to contain the salary bill (10+1 teachers earn less than their 10+2 colleagues) were the major reasons for this policy change. As a matter of fact, the output of graduates from teacher training colleges has increased dramatically and, as a consequence, the recruitment of untrained teachers reduced significantly. In the present situation more than 90 per cent of the new teachers entering the profession are trained, but not necessarily qualified to do the job. In fact, the general perception has been that the increase in output of graduated teachers was achieved at the expenses of quality.

Now that government goals focus more on education quality, which it is assumed can be achieved though the raising of teaching standards, since 2011 the admission requirements have been raised from ten years of education with a ten out of 20 performance marks to ten years of education with a minimum of 12 out of 20 performance marks. Teacher education policy is now back to the 10+2 model, and includes one year of distance learning as part of certification requirements, in addition to two years of pre-service training (making it a 10+2+1 model).

The need to improve teaching standards has also led to successive teacher training curriculum reforms, with the last two devised in 2006 and 2011. The 2011 reform, which was introduced in 2012, follows what is called a critical-reflexive paradigm (INDE/MINED, 2011). Within this paradigm, teacher trainees should be prepared to be creative and flexible agents, ones who should be able to adjust the school curriculum to changing needs. The new curriculum stresses the use of teaching pedagogies centred on teacher trainees and the adoption of skills-based teaching/learning methods. The rationale underlying these philosophical changes has been that when these IFP graduates are deployed to schools, they will be able to use the same teaching techniques used to teach them during their pre-service training (e.g. participative teaching/ learning and skills based teaching/learning).

Teachers targeted by in-service training interventions include those who have certifications from teacher colleges and those who have not received any pre-service training. These interventions offer teachers opportunities to learn pedagogical methods and update their teaching practices. Given the inefficiency of pre-service training and the fact that there are many primary school teachers without proper pedagogical training, in-service training emerges as one of the interventions that could help counteract these deficiencies and improve teaching quality. However, the practice indicates that despite being well planned, in most cases in-service training initiatives are not implemented chiefly due to financial and organizational constraints. In fact, even when these initiatives are implemented, their content is questionable, mainly because they do not draw on teaching practice, but rather based on theoretical considerations and targeting an idealized teacher, which has nothing to do with the one in the field.

Despite efforts to improve the quality of education through initiatives focusing on teacher training (e.g. improvement of selection criteria of student-teachers, lengthening of the duration of pre-service training and curriculum reforms), there is no evidence that these measures have any direct impact on teaching quality and student learning. In fact the system lacks a mechanism to monitor and assess teaching quality and student learning, as well as linking these with the quality of training provided to teachers in pre-service and in-service training initiatives. The general perception has been that the overall teaching quality in Mozambican primary schools is poor: teachers use ineffective pedagogical methods (e.g. teacher centred classes, reliance on reading and writing activities, almost an absence of active and interaction-based learning, reliance on repetition and recitation modes of teaching, etc.); teachers absenteeism; teachers' poor management of instructional time (teachers arriving late to classrooms, time wasted copying materials from the pupils' books to blackboards, even when books are available to every pupil). It is true that some of these ethical and pedagogical issues cannot be exclusively resolved through pre-service and in-service training, but most of them could be, at least, minimized especially if these training initiatives were linked with teaching practice. For example, data from monitoring activities of teachers' performance could be used to inform teacher training policy and practice, since these could draw on pervasive experience-based ethical and pedagogical issues which undermine teaching quality.

Although comprehensive studies of teacher education processes and outcomes still need to be conducted, there is some evidence leading to the conclusion that 'teaching quality and pedagogical methods used to teach student-teachers in IFPs are poor, which then transfer to children's learning in classrooms when these IFP graduates are deployed to schools' (Crouch, 2011: 35). This conclusion is further substantiated by a case study of a teachers' training college, which showed that this institution was not adequately preparing teacher trainees to meet the specific changes envisaged by the new curriculum for basic education, such as transforming teacher-centred pedagogies to learner-centred teaching styles, introducing interdisciplinary approaches to teaching and learning, and changing teaching practices and pedagogies (Guro & Webber, 2010). These authors found that the lecturers themselves did not understand the meaning of interdisciplinarity and, although they could articulate the meaning of learner-centredness, their own lectures were teacher-centred.

Closing remarks

This chapter shows how in education planning and practice in Mozambique there have been attempts to bind quantitative and qualitative goals. In addition to ensuring access to primary and post-primary schooling, the government and the civil society have also been seeking to improve the quality of education offered to students. Despite the effort, the country is still struggling with low education quality without a clear short-term indication of recovery. The study also shows that education priorities in Mozambique are influenced by domestic and international economic and sociopolitical transformations as well as by government commitments to international agendas, including the EFA efforts and the MDGs.

Mozambique has demonstrated significant achievements in terms of progress towards EFA goals, although there are still several challenges ahead. As shown throughout the chapter, there are increasingly more children attending school and also more children staying in schools. Gender disparities at the lower primary level are gradually narrowing, a trend that extends to the upper primary level, though it is less pronounced at this level and beyond. Primary school completion rates are also significantly improving over the years. All these indicators suggest that the government target of providing seven years of primary education to every Mozambican child by 2015 is within reach, though there is still a need to reduce gender and regional disparities.

Although quantitative goals seem to be promising, the same cannot be said about qualitative goals. Indeed, as illustrated, despite government and civil society efforts, quality indicators remain poor, which shows that Mozambican students are not learning sufficiently. The analysis offered in the chapter suggests that there is a set of measures that need to be taken if quality is to be improved in Mozambican schools, these include: (i) increase of instructional time, which can be achieved through improvements in pupils' and teachers' attendance, increase of school days per year, review of the multi-shifting system, improvement of time management in the classroom; (ii) reduction of teacher-pupil ratio, which can be achieved through construction of more schools and deployment of more teachers; (iii) provision of good quality textbooks to all pupils; (iv) improvement of teaching techniques, which can be achieved through improvements in pre- and in-service teacher education; (v) establishment of systems that can gather and analyse information on teaching and learning processes and outcomes with the view of feeding and improving education practice.

Poor quality in public schools has led higher socio-economic status families to send their children to private schools, which are perceived as offering better quality education. As argued, this may contribute to increase in socio-economic disparities in the country, since poor children are denied good learning opportunities making then poorly prepared to compete in an increasingly demanding labour market.

Education policy and planning have been taking the above challenges into consideration, which is a promising development. However, as argued, changes in education policy or improvements in curricula design are not sufficient to improve education quality. There is also a need to monitor how these policy and curriculum innovations are implemented and work out how they can be continuously adjusted to circumstantial contingencies.

Notes

1   Depending on the point in history, two names have been used to refer to the ministry in charge of education in Mozambique: *Ministério da Educação* (Ministry of Education) or *Ministério da Educação e Cultura* (Ministry of Education and Culture). The acronyms MINED and MEC, used in this chapter, stand for the first and the second designation, respectively.

2   In the other grades there are no examinations and pupils are automatically promoted, unless teachers and parents agree that a given pupil did not perform well and therefore should be failed.

3   The Southern Africa Consortium for Monitoring Educational Quality (SACMEQ) is a consortium of Ministries of Education from the Southern Africa sub-region.

Three assessment rounds of Grade VI pupils' achievement in mathematics and reading have already been conducted in the country. These are known as SACMEQ I, II and III.

4 Some schools in urban areas accommodate up to three shifts a day, which, as mentioned so far, shortens school time for pupils and hinders their opportunities to learn.

5 The national average instructional time in Mozambican primary schools is estimated at 600 hours per year. In response, the third strategic plan for education (2012–16) has set to increase this time to 900 hours per year.

6 These include the very active ADPP Teacher Training Colleges, which offer a special programme for education of teachers for rural primary schools. ADPP stands for *Ajuda de Desenvolvimento de Povo para Povo*/Development Aid from People to People.

7 In the teacher education context, 5+1 and 5+2 stand for five years of education plus one or two years of teacher training. The same reading applies, mutatis mutandis, to 7+1, 7+2, 10+1 and 10+2.

References

Adelman, E., Moore, A. M. S. and Manji, S. (2011). 'Using Opportunity to Learn and Early Grade Reading Fluency to Measure School Effectiveness in Mozambique', A study commissioned by the Academy for Educational Development (AED) through the Educational Quality Improvement Program 2 (EQUIP2) www.equip123.net/docs/E2-SE_Mozambique_Case_Study.pdf. [Accessed on April 10, 2012].

Bartholomey, A., Takala, T. and Ahmed, Z. (2010). *Mid-term Evaluation of the EFA First Track Initiative: Mozambique Country Case Study* (Cambridge, UK: Cambridge Education, Mokoro and Oxford Policy Managment).

Chimbutane, F. (2011). *Rethinking Bilingual Education in Postcolonial Contexts* (Bristol, UK: Multilingual Matters).

Comissão Nacional do Plano (1985). *Informação Estatística: 1975–1985* (Maputo: Direcção Nacional de Estatística).

Crouch, L. (2011). 'Education Information and Education Policy and Planning in Mozambique', A study Commissioned by AUSAID to RTI International. https://www.eddataglobal.org/.../ED_DATA_II_MOZ_Final_Report. [Accessed on March 3, 2012].

Guro, M. and Weber, E. (2010). 'From Policy to Practice: Education in Mozambique and Marrere Teachers' Training College', *South African Journal of Education* 30, pp. 245–59.

Human Development Report (HDR) (2011). *Sustainability and Equity: A Better Future for All* (New York: United Nations Development Programme).

Instituto Nacional de Estatística (INE) (2010). *Dados do Recenseamento Geral da População de 2007* (Maputo: INE).

Instituto Nacional de Saúde (INS), Instituto Nacional de Estatística (INE) and ICF Macro (2010). *Inquérito Nacional de Prevalência, Riscos Comportamentais e Informação sobre o HIV e SIDA em Moçambique 2009* (Calverton, MD: INS, INE and ICF Macro).

Instituto Nacional do Desenvolvimento da Educação/Ministério da Educação (INDE/MINED) (2011). *Plano Curricular para Formação de Professores do Ensino Primário* (Maputo: INDE/MINED).

International Monetary Fund (IMF) (2007). 'Republic of Mozambique: Fifth Review under the Three-year Arrangement under the Poverty Reduction and Growth Facility and Financing Assurances Review', IMF country report Nr 07/36 (Washington, DC: IMF).

Ministério de Educação e Cultura (MEC) (1999). *Plano Estratégico de Educação e Cultura 1999–2005* (Maputo: MEC).

— (2006). *Plano Estratégico de Educação e Cultura 2006–2010/11* (Maputo: MEC).

Ministério de Educação (2011a). *Estatística da Educação: Levantamento escolar – 2011* (Maputo: Ministério da Educação).

— (2011b). *Estatística da Educação: Aproveitamento escolar – 2010* (Maputo: Ministério da Educação).

— (2012). *Plano Estratégico de Educação 2012–2016* (Maputo: MINED).

Newitt, M. (1995). *A History of Mozambique* (London: Hurst & Company).

Passos, A., Nahara, T., Magaia, F. and Lauchande, C. (in preparation). 'The SACMEQ III Project in Mozambique: A Study of the Conditions of Schooling and the Quality of Education', Working report (Harare: SACMEQ).

República de Moçambique (RM) (1990). *Constituição da República* (Maputo: Imprensa Nacional de Moçambique).

— (1992). Sistema Nacional de Educação. *Boletim da República*, I Série, No 12, 23 de Março (Maputo: Imprensa Nacional).

— (2004). *Constituição da República (actualizada)* (Maputo: Imprensa Nacional de Moçambique).

— (2010). *Report on the Millenium Development Goals* (Maputo: Republic of Mozambique).

World Bank (2007). 'Beating the Odds: Sustaining Inclusion in a Growing Economy – A Mozambique Poverty, Gender and Social Assessment', Report Nr 40048-MZ.

6

Namibia: An Overview of System Reform

Gilbert Likando
University of Namibia

and

Charl Wolhuter
Potchefstroom Campus, North-West University

Introduction

With the advent of independence very recently (Namibia was the last country in southern Africa to attain independence), in 1990, the government of the independent state embarked upon an ambitious educational expansion and reform project. This chapter portrays the contextual and historical background and details of that exercise, as also the caveats and promises.

Contextual background

Geography

Namibia covers 824.269 square kilometres (National Planning Commission, 2008) – a large swathe of land located in Southern Africa between 17° south and 28° south latitude and 13° and 20° east meridian. It is bordered by the Atlantic Ocean in the west, Botswana in the east, South Africa in the south and Angola and Zambia in the north. The country has four major regions: a desert (Namib desert) in the west, a semi-arid high plateau in the middle, a semi-desert in the east (Kalahari) and a savannah in the north. Only two major roads, the Trans-Caprivi and Trans-Kalahari highways and two railway lines cross the territory: from South Africa in the south through Windhoek (capital) to Grootfontein, with an extension from Tsumeb to Oshikango on the Namibia Angolan border in the north, and from Walvis Bay (the main port) in the west through Windhoek and Gobabis to Botswana in the east.

Demography

The territory was populated by a succession of immigration waves. The first waves were the Khoi and San people. A wide variety of rock paintings and rock engravings dating from c. 29,000 to 1,500 years ago are the most persistent evidence of early human habitation in the area (Namibia Government, 2006). In later centuries, people known in Anthropological nomenclature as Bantu or Negroid settled in the territory. There is some agreement that the first traces of Bantu-speaking communities appear in the north between 2,000 and 1,500 years ago (Namibia Government, 2006). Then in the eighteenth and nineteenth century people of mixed-race descent came from the south (what is today South Africa). The biggest of these groups were the Namas. In 1885 the territory, thence called German South West Africa, became a German protectorate. A number of Germans settled in the protectorate. The administration was taken over by South Africa in 1915, and since 1915 numbers of White South Africans moved into South West Africa, as it was called from 1915. 93 per cent of the population is Black (i.e. of African descent), 5 per cent are White (i.e. of European descent) and 2 per cent mixed-race descent (Johnson & Devlin-Foltz, as quoted by Dahlström et al., 1999: 149).

The total population of the country is estimated at 2.13 million (UNESCO, 2011: 272). The annual growth rate of the population has slowed down from 3.1 per cent in 1991 (World Bank, 2004: 257) to the current 1.9 per cent (UNESCO, 2011: 272). The latest National Planning Commission's preliminary report of the 2011 National Housing and Population Census puts Namibia's population at 2.1 million, with 1.5 per cent average annual growth rate (Smit, 2012). The biggest concentration of people is found in the northern Savannah, followed by the central plateau. The two deserts are extremely sparsely populated.

Based on the latest preliminary 2011 census report 42 per cent of the population live in urban centres, chief of which are in Windhoek (340,900) in the Khomas region (Smit, 2012). According to Anon (2005: 5) in the previous sensus Walvis Bay was the second most populated town with 50,000 inhabitants, followed by Oshakati (37,000) and Ondangwa (33,000). In the 2011 Population and Housing Census Rundu was the second most populated town in Namibia (61 900) after Windhoek with 322 500 inhabitants (National Planning Commission, 201: 57). Because of the rural-urban drift, Windhoek is currently experiencing a rapid 4.45 per cent annual population growth rate (Anon, 2005: 5).

The population has a fairly youthful profile. Almost a quarter of the population is aged 14 years and under, 52.3 per cent is aged 15–59 years, while only 6.7 per cent is aged 60 years and older (Likando & Scott, 2011: 72). It is worth noting that in terms of gender distribution 51 per cent are female while the remaining 49 per cent are male (Smit, 2012).

Socio-economic situation

The annual per capita gross national income is $4,200 (2008) (up from $2,030 in 1998) (UNESCO, 2011: 273) which places Namibia in the World Bank category of upper middle income economies (per capita gross national income between $3,036 and $9,385 per annum) (World Bank, 2011). The Gini-index of inequality stands at 70.7 – the highest in the world (World Bank, 2004: 259). This means Namibia is a highly stratified society. The ratio of per capita income between the top 5 per cent and the bottom 50 per cent of the country is about 50:1 (Makuwa, 2005). What makes the situation even more volatile is the fact that the border line between the affluent and the poor socio economic strata is to a great extent coterminous with the racial divide. The population of European descent is more affluent than the population of African descent. 55 per cent of the population lives on less than $2 per day (UNESCO, 2003: 303). Poverty is therefore widespread. The current unemployment rate stands at 51 per cent (Republic of Namibia, Ministry of Labour and Social Welfare, 2008: 39). 22.5 per cent of the population in the age group 15–49 years are infected with Human Immunodeficiency Virus (HIV)/Acquired Immunodeficiency Syndrome (AIDS) (UNESCO, 2003: 302). Although life expectancy is low, and dropping – for example, the life expectancy for males dropped from 59 years in 1981 to 48 years in 2001 and the life expectancy of females from 63 years in 1991 to 50 years in 2001 (Central Bureau of Statistics, Namibia, n.d.) to 45 years in 2003 (UNESCO, 2003: 302) – the 2011 Human Development Report reports a significant improvement as it puts the average life expectancy at 62.5 per cent (UNDP, 2011).

Agriculture accounts for 10.0 per cent of GDP, industry for 34.2 per cent and services for 55.8 per cent (Turner, 2004: 1,178). The Namibian economy is heavily dependent on mining (especially uranium, diamonds, silver and zinc) and fisheries. Although the country is dependent upon mining – the mining sector accounts for 50 per cent of exports – the majority of the population is employed in agriculture.

As could be expected from the socio-economic situation, the country is technologically underdeveloped, although developing rapidly amid the present economic upsurge. The following statistics are illustrative: 32 per cent of households have electricity for lighting (2001 figure, up from 24% in 1991) and 80 per cent of households have access to radio (2001 figure, up from 59% in 1991) (Central Bureau of Statistics, Namibia, n.d.).

Language

The 2001 census gave the main languages spoken at home, as follows: Oshiwambo: 48 per cent of households; Nama/Damara: 11 per cent of households; Afrikaans: 11 per cent of households; Kavango: 10 per cent of households; and Otjiherero: 8 per cent of households (Central Bureau of Statistics, Namibia, n.d.). People commonly speak two or three or even more languages. Due to the country's history Afrikaans – the language of the previous South African administration – is still widely spoken and functions as the *lingua franca* in Namibia (Namibia Government, 2006). After independence English was made the language of the civil administration. Article 3(1) of the Constitution of Namibia states that the official language of Namibia shall be English.

Politics

Namibia became independent on 21 March 1990. It is a constitutional republic. Namibia is a multiparty republic, with an independent judiciary and an executive president. The president is elected by popular vote, for a five year term. In the most recent presidential election, held on 27–9 November 2009, the incumbent and South West Africa People's Organisation (SWAPO) candidate, Hifikepunye Pohamba polled 76 per cent of the votes and became the second president.

The bicameral legislature consists of a National Assembly and a National Council. The National Assembly has 78 members, 72 of which are elected by popular vote for a five year term by means of proportional representation, and 6 appointed by the president by virtue of their position of expertise. After the most recent elections, the ruling SWAPO party has 54 seats in the 78 member National Assembly and the two biggest opposition parties, the Rally for Democracy and Progress and the Democratic Turnhalle Alliance, have 8 and 2 respectively.

The upper house, the 26-seat National Council, consists of two members elected by each of the 13 Regional Councils (second tier governments) for a term of five years consistent with the members of parliament in the national Assembly.

According to the World Bank report Namibia is an over-governed, 'bureaucracy-swollen' country which is clear from the following: in Namibia it takes 85 days to start a new business (world average: 50.8; in Canada it takes 3 days) (World Bank, 2004: 249).

The Namibian Constitution guarantees the fundamental rights of all its citizens, including the right to freedom of education – Article 20 states '. . . all persons have the right to education' (Republic of Namibia, 1990).

Religion and philosophical outlook

As enshrined in the Namibian Constitution, *Article 21* guarantees the right to fundamental freedom and, among others, the freedom to practice any religion (Republic of Namibia, 1990). Although the majority of the Namibians belong to Lutheran and the Roman Catholic churches there are a number of Pentecostal churches the majority of their membership being blacks. In spite of the fact that the majority of the Namibians are considered Christians a significant number still combine cultural practices (belief in ancestors) and Christianity. It is interesting to note that since independence the spread of Islam in Namibia has been visible through the building of mosques in the central, north and northeastern part of Namibia, but, comparatively speaking, followers of this religion are still in minority.

On a secular plane, the modern Western liberal, individualistic and materialistic philosophy, with its attendant value system, has taken root in the country among all population groups, existing side by side with:

- traditional cultures and philosophical systems;
- religious groups with their philosophical systems;
- political groups with their philosophical overtones.

Education system

Objectives of education

Direction-giving documents in the structuring of Namibia's post-independence education system have been:

- the Constitution of Namibia (1990);
- the Ministry of Education's 1990 document titled *Education in Transition: Nurturing our Future*, in which the broad goals of Namibia's education system are outlined;
- the Ministry of Education's 1993 policy document *Towards Education for All – A Development Brief for Education, Culture and Training*;
- the *Namibian Qualifications Authority Act*, Act 9 of 1998; and
- the 2001 *Education Act* – Act 12 of 2001.

In the run-up to independence, SWAPO made the expansion of educational opportunities a central issue in the quest for independence (see Republic of Namibia, Ministry of Education and Culture, 1993:2–3). Educational opportunities were assessed as inadequate. For example, in the former Ovamboland, where the majority of Namibians live, 70 per cent of pupils who made it to the final year of primary education in 1984 did not proceed to secondary school (Amukugo, 1993: 193). A particular grievance was the inequalities between the education for White pupils and for Black pupils in the pre-1990 segregated education system. For example, in 1986/87 average per pupil expenditure in White schools was R3,213 and in Ovambo (Black) schools R329 (1987: $1:R3.67) (Coombe, 1993). There was also the view that the pre-1990 education system was tailored to suit the purpose of the South African administration, and that it did not respond to the needs of Namibia – economically, socially or culturally (Craelius et al., 1995: 684; Mwetulundila, 2000: 11).

The major policy documents mentioned above put it that the major goals of Namibian education will be access, equity, quality and democracy.

- *Access*: (see Voigts, 1998: 4). Article 20(1) of the Constitution states that all persons shall have the right to education (Legal Assistance Centre, n.d.: 14);
- *Equity*: given the historical legacy of 1990, an important goal has been to provide equal educational opportunities and chances to all (see Republic of Namibia, Ministry of Education and Culture, 1993: 34–7);

- *Quality:* this includes a high level of teacher training and competence, good physical facilities and high achievement levels of pupils (see Republic of Namibia, Ministry of Education and Culture, 1993: 37–40);
- *Democracy:* pupils should learn how democratic societies operate and about the obligations and rights of their citizens. Furthermore, the education system should be organized democratically, that is, around broad participation in decision-making and the clear accountability of those who are the leaders (Republic of Namibia, Ministry of Education and Culture, 1993: 41–3).

The education ministry has also set itself the goal of lifelong learning (Voigts, 1998: 1). Furthermore, education has been given the task of bringing about reconciliation and nation-building (see Coombe, 1993).

Finally, education should be an instrument of national development, and supply a trained human resource pool for the country. The SWAPO government recognized that an educated population is *the* crucial requirement for Namibian development (Gonzales, 1999: 105). Namibia's post-independence policies have prioritized a rapid build-up of the educated and skilled human resources required to support economic growth and equitable social development (Republic of Namibia, Department of Education and Culture, Namibia, 2005: 7).

Organization and administration

Central level

Upon independence an effort was made to create an organizational structure which was flexible, interactive, unified and decentralized (Craelius et al., 1995: 688). The first task was the amalgamation of the 11 ethnically and racially based education administrations which had existed until 1990, into one unified national structure.

At central executive level were two ministries: the Ministry of Education and the Ministry of Higher Education, Training and Employment Creation. Currently only one Ministry of Education exists. The Ministry of Education has the task of determining national policy on basic education. The Ministry of Education is divided into the Department of Formal Education Programmes and Department of Culture and Life-long Learning (adult and non-formal education). The objective of the Department of Formal Education Programmes is to co-ordinate, implement and monitor all formal education activities. This department is made up of the following directorates: National Examination and Assessment, Programme Implementation, Inspectorate and Advisory Services and Special Education Programmes. The objective of the Department of Culture and Life-long learning is made up of the following directorates: Adult Basic Education, Arts and Culture and Library and Archives.

A Natural Advisory Council exists to advise the minister on educational matters. The Council consists of 24 members appointed by the minister who must select two staff members, as well as one person from each of: institutions of education higher than basic education, each Regional Education Forum, non-governmental organizations, national employers' organizations, unions of teachers, representative bodies of learners and students, representative bodies of churches, the Council of Traditional Leaders and natural organizations for persons with disabilities.

Of the N\$ 8.3 Billion of the total public budget for the 2004/5 financial year, 22.01 per cent was earmarked for education (Anon, 2011). Personnel expenditure is a large and growing part of the education budget. It rose from 60.6 per cent of the education budget in 1990/91 to 86.81 per cent in 1998/9 (Republic of Namibia, Ministry of Education, 2005b).

Regional level

The administration of education in Namibia is divided into 13 educational regions, which corresponds to the political regions that have been created, namely: Caprivi, Kavango, Kunene, Oshana, Ohangwena, Omusati, Oshikoto, Khomas, Hardap, Erongo, Omaheke, Otjozondjupa and Karas.

Each region has a Regional Education Forum. The functions of a forum is to advise the minister, the regional council (second tier political structures) and local authority councils in that region on matters regarding education, to advise school boards on educational matters and to initiate and facilitate educational development in the region.

A Regional Forum consists of the regional director of education, who is an ex officio member and has no right to vote, and 20 members appointed by the minister on the grounds of special knowledge, skills and expertise in educational matters from the persons nominated. The minister must invite the following bodies to nominate the specified number of persons: three persons representing the regional council and local authority councils (i.e. the second and third tier political structures) in the region, three persons representing the school boards in the region, three persons representing the unions of teachers in the region, three persons representing the bodies of learners in the regions, two persons representing the private schools in the region, two persons representing the Council of Traditional Leaders and two persons representing the national organization for persons with disabilities. The numbers adding up to 18 are the minimum to be nominated in each category, the other 2 (to come to a total of 20) are left to the discretion of the Minister.

Institutional level

The *Education Act* makes provision for a School Board for every state school. The School Board administers the affairs of the school and promotes the development of the school and its students. The purposes and functions of the School Board are: to develop the mission, goals and objectives of the school, to advise the school's management on the extramural curriculum of the school, to advise the regional director of education on the educational needs and the curriculum of the school, to recommend the appointment of teachers and other staff members at the school and to allow the reasonable use of the school facilities for community purposes. A School Board is constituted by not less than five and not more than 13 members, who must be parents, teachers, the principal and, in the case of a secondary school, learners nominated by the Learners' Representative Council.

On private schools, Section 41 of the *Education Act* states that a person has the right to establish and to maintain a private school at such a person's own expense, but is required to register such a school with the Minister. The Minister must register a private school if he is satisfied that the school is suitable and adequate in accordance with the prescribed minimum requirements applicable to state schools. The Minister may grant financial aid to a private school (Republic of Namibia, 2001).

Institutional fabric

At independence, Namibia had inherited the South African qualification structure of standards (being a former British colony, South Africa had the Scottish system). After independence, Namibia opted for the American system, that is, Grades I to XII. The 12 year school structure consist of a seven year primary school (which, in turn, is made up of Lower Primary: Grades I to IV and Upper Primary: Grades V to VII) followed by a five year secondary school cycle (Junior Secondary: Grades VIII to X and Senior Secondary: Grades XI to XII) (Tjipueja, 2001: 25). Section 53(1) of the *Education Act* stipulates that schooling is compulsory for every child from the beginning of the year in which the child attains the age of seven years to the last day of the year in which the child completes primary school before the age of 16 years, or the last day of the year in which the child reaches the age of 16 years.

The higher education sector consists of the University of Namibia, the Polytechnic of Namibia and four Colleges of Education, incorporated into the University of Namibia too as from 2011 through cabinet Resolution no. 18/29.09/011.

The *Namibian Qualifications Authority Act* (Act 29 of 1998) established the Namibian Qualifications Framework. The aims of the Namibian Qualifications Framework are to

- provide a coherent base upon which to develop, publicize and determine the correspondence of qualifications;
- represent a unified system of qualifications and associated learning pathways; and
- encompass rigorous transparent quality assurance against clear standards and criteria (Karmu, 2005).

The Namibian Qualifications Framework consists of ten levels, defined by level description in terms of increasing complexity of the outcome of learning (Kaimu, 2005). Level 10 is doctoral level, Level 9 Masters, Level 8 Honours/Professional Bachelors level and Level 7 Bachelors level.

Curriculum

The curricula inherited at independence were considered somewhat irrelevant to the needs of independent Namibia, and in many ways outdated (Craelius et al., 1995: 689). Textbooks have also constituted a problem as they were mostly produced in South Africa and reflected the South African situation (Craelius et al., 1995: 690). The new system of assessment (to be discussed in following sections) too necessitated new curricula.

In 1996 a new prescribed curriculum was introduced. In 1998, new curriculum panels and subject committees began their work. By 2006 32 syllabuses in a range of subjects were already completed (Republic of Namibia, Ministry of Education, 2006).

The National Institute for Educational Development (NIED) has recently developed a National Curriculum for Basic Education, and Special Needs Education which builds on the experience and achievements of the first cycle of Namibian curricula and syllabuses that were introduced in the 1990s (NIED/ MoE, 2009). Imperative to note is that this new curriculum is a continuation of the foundation that was laid in *The Constitution of The Republic of Namibia* (1990), *Towards Education for All: A Development Brief* (1993), and draws mainly upon the *Report of the Presidential Commission on Education, Culture and Training* (1999), *The Education Act* (2001), *The Language Policy for Schools in Namibia* (1996), *The Language Policy for Schools in Namibia Discussion Document* (2003), *ICT Policy for Education* (2005), *Learner-Centred Education in the Namibian Context: A Conceptual Framework* (2003), *the Special Education Policy* (2005), *Namibia Human Capital and Knowledge Development for Economic Growth with Equity* (2005) as well as the curriculum syllabus reviews undertaken in the education sector since 2002 (NIED/MoE, 2009: 1).

The Basic Education Curriculum reflects the following *core skills* grouped into seven areas: Learning to learn, Personal skills, Social skills, Cognitive skills, Communication skills, Numeracy skills and Information and Communication Technology skills. The *key learning* areas are: Languages, Mathematics, Natural Sciences, Social Sciences, Technology, Commerce, Arts and Physical Education (NIED/MoE, 2009: 3). In terms of school phases the following subjects are prescribed for the various school phases:

- *Pre-primary Phase* (Grade 0): Development of communication skills, motor and social skills and concept formation.
- *Lower Primary Phase* (Grades I–IV): Literacy, Numeracy, Environmental Studies, Religious & Moral Education; Arts and Physical Education.
- *Upper Primary Phase* (Grades V–VII): Languages; Mathematics; Natural Sciences and Health Education; Life Skills; Social Studies; Agriculture; Design & Technology; Home Ecology; Arts; Physical Education; Basic Information Studies.
- *Junior Secondary Phase* (Grades VIII–X): Languages; Mathematics; Life Sciences; Physical Science; Life Skills; Design & Technology; History & Geography; Economic and Management Sciences; Religious & Moral Education; Agriculture; Needlework & Clothing; Home Economics; Computer Studies; Physical Education; Basic Information Studies; and Arts and Culture.
- *Senior Secondary Phase* (Grades XI–XII): Languages; Mathematics; Physical Science; Design & Technology; History; Geography; Economic and

Management Sciences; Biology; Development Studies; Agriculture; Fashion & Fabrics; Home Economics; Computer Studies; and Arts and Design.

Given the central role early childhood development and pre-primary education plays in the overall development of a child and their chances of future successes in school, the Education and Training Sector Improvement Plan (ETSIP) proposed that these programmes be integrated into the mainstream education (Republic of Namibia, Ministry of Education, 2005a). As result of ETSIP's proposal a three year pre-primary education programme was introduced in 2008, which has been extended to 2013.

Teachers

Namibia has 14,000 primary school teachers (2008) and 7,000 secondary school teachers (2008) (UNESCO, 2011: 332–3). High absenteeism rates among teachers (see Voigts, 1998: 59, 60) suggests, similar to that among pupils, a deficient culture of teaching on the part of the teachers. Another cause of concern is the high levels of stress among teachers (see Möwes, 2004). According to Möwes (2004) the main causes of high stress levels among teachers are, in order of importance, serious learner discipline problems, large classes, lack of support from parents, low salaries for teachers and low pupil achievement.

Learners

At independence in 1990, Namibia's gross primary and secondary school enrolment ratios were 129 per cent and 44 per cent (UNESCO, 1999: 11–282). The corresponding figures for 2000 were 128 per cent and 61.7 per cent (UNESCO, 2003: 335, 351) and for 2008, 112 per cent and 66 per cent (UNESCO, 2011: 308, 325). Learner absenteeism being a major problem (see Voigts, 1998: 59, 60) suggests the lack of a proper learning culture among learners. Several studies indicate severe gender-disparities in Namibian education (e.g. Kasanda & Shaimenanya, 1997; Mwetulundila, 2000). For example, in the 1991 final secondary school examination results, in the rural areas of Namibia only half as many girls as boys were successful (Mwetulundila, 2000: 24). Mwetulundila (2000: 26–35) identifies four barriers to girls successfully participating in education: the hidden curriculum, stereotyped attitudes about girls, lack of female role models and socio-economic factors coupled with teenage pregnancy.

Teaching methods

Prior to independence in 1990 the teaching methods operating in schools were described as tending to foster memorization and rote learning (Republic of Namibia, Ministry of Education and Culture, 1993). Teaching in most of the schools was the traditional talk and chalk involving learners to memorize large chunks of material for the sake of passing examinations. In Gonzales' words, '. . . colonial education alienated children from the educational process by allowing students little-to-no input in classroom decision-making' (1999: 111). The experiential teaching that is required for learners to get real hands-on knowledge was rarely practiced due to pressure to complete the syllabus and to prepare the learners for the examinations. Thus, the dominant form of teaching had a negative impact on the acquisition of skills for the majority of Namibian school-going children. With the introduction of the new curriculum in 1993 it was decided that the teaching approach would be learner-centred where the classroom practice would reflect and reinforce both values and practices of democracy (Republic of Namibia, Ministry of Education and Culture, 1993). Vision 2030 states that the envisioned knowledge-based society requires a learner-centred approach to teaching and learning. Therefore, the education provided in schools should be inclusive to prepare the society envisaged in Namibia Vision 2030. Consequently, learners with special educational needs and other individual needs were to be included in the mainstream schools and their needs given particular attention through differentiation of methods and materials as needed (Republic of Namibia, Ministry of Education and Culture, 1993). The new National Curriculum for Basic Education sets out some didactic considerations in learner-centred education. It argues in this document that the successful implementation of competence-based education requires a variety of repertoire teaching roles and teaching techniques (NIED/MoE, 2009).

Language of learning and teaching

Prior to independence teaching was through the medium of the mother tongue in the first four years of schooling; after that it was either through English or through Afrikaans. After independence Afrikaans-medium after the fourth school year was discarded, and all teaching as from the fourth school year now takes place through the medium of English. This is cause for concern for a variety of reasons. Many children do not have the level of proficiency in English required by schooling through that medium as research as shown (Republic of Namibia, Ministry of Education and Culture, 1994: 37). English language competence is low in the general population and even in professional groups (Indabawa, 1999: 110). Especially in rural areas teachers are not proficient in English (Naudé, 1995: 11). Research, such as that of Garrouste (2011), has shown the detrimental effect on learner achievement of the language of learning and teaching not being the same as the home language. Many educationists therefore make a case for the development of the indigenous languages to become media of instruction (e.g. Harlech-Jones, 1998; Mutumba, 1999).

Assessment

In Basic Education, teachers and learners monitor progress against certain minimum competencies. The Junior Secondary Certificate is written at the end of Grade X. Concerning the final secondary school examination (end of Grade XII), after independence the Cambridge system, that is, the International General Certificate of Secondary Education (IGCSE) replaced the South African matriculation examination (see Hoveka, 1999). Results are not good – for example, in 2002 21.9 per cent of Biology candidates could not obtain as much as 20 per cent in the examination. For mathematics and geography respectively, 24.8 per cent and 27.4 per cent of candidates could not obtain even 20 per cent (Republic of Namibia, Education Management Information System, Ministry of Basic Education, Sport and Culture, 2005: 64).

In order to provide relevant education that takes into consideration leaners' context the Ministry of Education decided to localize the curriculum and examination system. In providing the context for this change Prime Minister Nahas Angula, the then Minister of Education and Culture, commented:

> IGCSE is specifically tailored for foreign countries while GCSE is the version in the use in Great Britain. Overall it would seem to me that IGCSE is specifically tailored export model as against GCSE which is the real thing. This requires that we build up our own capabilities – our own examination system, and our own assessment mechanisms . . . (van der Merwe, 1995: 181)

It should be emphasized that the prime minister's sentiments concretized the need for localization. Thus, in 2006 the Namibian Senior Secondary Certificate (NSSC) Ordinary and Higher level syllabi and examinations were implemented in Grade XI. These syllabi are mostly based on the CIE's International General Certificate of Education (IGCSE). The realization of this initiative was hailed as another achievement of the education and political systems of the country as it was for the first time ever the country would have its own examination system.

Given this, the Ministry of Education took trouble and care in developing the new syllabi and examinations insisting that it should be of 'a high quality in order meet the international recognition and that the standard should at least be equivalent to or higher than that of IGCSE and HIGCSE' (Ministry of Education, 2007: 2).

Teacher education

With the four teacher training colleges being incorporated into the University of Namibia as from 2011, the University of Namibia is now the sole teacher education institution in the country. Teachers are trained by means of a four year programme which is offered in three areas, namely: Early Childhood Development (ECD) and Pre-primary; Primary and Secondary education degree. At present secondary education is only offered at the main UNAM campus in Windhoek, while other former colleges offer a degree in ECD and pre-primary as well as primary education.

The emphasis of expanding teacher training in pre-primary in Namibia was prompted by the fear that the quality of education in the country was on the decline since independence. Amukugo et al., 2010: 107) citing the World Bank Report (2005) candidly stated:

> General education in particular is ineffective, mainly because of inadequacies in a range of education quality enhancing inputs. Due to lack of access to early childhood development (ECD), and to pre-primary education programmes, 80 percent of children enter the first grade of primary education without the required level of learning readiness. Invariably, these children are exposed to ineffective teaching.

The emphasis therefore, in ECD and pre-primary after incorporation of the colleges of education to UNAM was to improve the quality and effectiveness of early childhood development and general education.

Namibia vision 2030 and ETSIP

Namibia's policy framework for long-term national development (Vision 2030) is committed to the principle of sustainable development, as advocated by the United Nations Agenda 21 Principles (Amukugo et al., 2010). Education in this regard has been identified as a driving force to achieve Vision 2030. In Amukugo et al.'s (2010) observation, Vision 2030 provides the Namibian government's firm commitment to improvement of quality of life of all people. Thus, the provision of quality education is the precondition to the balanced supply of human resources responsive to the demands of the labour market in the country.

Within this context ETSIP was established to enhance the education sector's contribution to the attainment of strategic national development goals; and to facilitate the transition to a Knowledge-based Economy (KBE) as required by Vision 2030 (Republic of Namibia, 2004). Based on the 2011 ETSIP Midterm review, progress has been made in the area of pre-primary, primary and secondary education in terms of achieving access, equity, quality and efficiency (Republic of Namibia, 2011a). Although progress has been made in some areas of the education system, critical aspects such as inclusive education, introduction of free primary education (recently in 2013 the namibian government have partially implemented free education from Grade 1–7), training of ECD care-givers, funding and management of ECD centres need careful attention. At policy level the review puts emphasis on the finalization of the draft policy on inclusive education and the conceptual framework for primary education that is considered weak at present. With regards to teacher development, pre-service and in-service training need careful consideration as the development of teacher education programmes have to address the student-teacher's level of English proficiency, in order to meet the National Professional Standards for Teachers. In addition, pre-service and in-service programmes need to provide capacity building opportunities for the roll-out of inclusive education practices (Republic of Namibia, 2011a).

In the area of vocational education the review points out the three major issues that still need to be addressed; these are: (i) the introduction of the levy system to enable the Namibia Training Authority (NTA) to diversify funding for Vocational Education and Training (VET) in Namibia, (ii) improving external efficiency and (iii) standardizing VET training qualifications and ensuring bridging possibilities.

Finally, in the area of higher education the review has put emphasis on the strengthening of Continuous Professional Development (CPD), strengthening of institutional capacity and the development of postgraduate programmes and research. Quality assurance in higher education institutions is also another area that needs attention. Here the National Council of Higher Education (NCHE) has to play a crucial role in ensuring that mechanisms are put in place by higher education institutions and maintained through the development and delivery of quality programmes.

Conclusion

While Namibia has made impressive progress since independence with the increase in (especially secondary school) enrolment ratios and the reform of the curriculum and (at least as far as policy formulation is concerned) with the reform of education methods, formidable challenges remain in bringing it in line with modern world trends and ideas on learning and teaching. These include the problem of the language of learning and teaching not being the same as the first language of teachers and learners alike, inequities in educational achievement and poor achievement levels, especially in key subjects.

The conclusion of the ETSIP mid-term review provides a concise but lucid summary of the challenges in the education sector that need to be addressed urgently:

> There are still inadequacies and inefficiencies in the sector performance. Although the legal and policy frameworks have been established . . . some policy flaws persist with sometimes weak conceptual framework like for primary education – delays in approving acts and regulations (Higher Education, Knowledge and Innovation), and lack of sector coherence (Early Childhood Development). While robust systems have been set up notably in terms of quality objectives (assessment of learners' achievements, continuous professional development), they are lagging behind in terms of equity objectives. (Republic of Namibia, 2011a: 28)

Worth noting is that these challenges if not adequately addressed have the potential to undermine the achievement of quality, equity and efficiency which are the cornerstone for a well functioning education system.

References

Amukugo, E. M. (1993). *Education and Politics in Namibia: Past Trends and Future Prospects* (Windhoek: Gamsberg Macmillan).

Amukugo, E. M., Likando, G. and Mushaandja, J. (2010). 'Access and Quality Dilemma in Education: Implication for Namibia Vision 2030', *RIHE Journal* 7, pp. 101–11. http://en.rihe.hiroshima-u.ac.jp/. Accessed, 10 April 2012.

Anon (2005). 'Rural-urban Drift "Suffocating" Windhoek', *The Namibian*, 24 July 2005, p. 5.

— (2011). 'Namibia 2011/12 Government Budget', *The Namibian*, 10 March 2011. www.namibian.com.na/index.php?id=28&tx_ttnews%5Btt_news%5D=79024&no_cache=1. Accessed 20 December 2011.

Central Bureau of Statistics, Namibia (n.d.). Namibia. 2001 Population and Housing Census (Windhoek: Central Bureau of Statistics).

Coombe, T. (1993). 'The New System of Higher Education in Namibia', *Journal of Southern African Studies*, 19, 1. In EBSCO Host:Academic Search elite, Full Display: www.sa.ebgsco.com. Accessed 31 July 2002.

Craelius, M. H., Kano, U. and Mukendwa, M. J. (1995). 'Namibia', in T. N. Postlethwaite (ed.), *International Encyclopedia of National Systems of education* (2nd edition) (Oxford: Pergamon), pp. 683–5.

Dahlström, L., Swarts, P. and Zeichner, K. (1999). 'Reconstructive Education and the Road to Social Justice: The Case of Post-Colonial Teacher Education in Namibia', *International Journal of Leadership in education: Theory and Practice*, 2, 3, pp. 149–64.

Garrouste, C. (2011). 'Explaining Learning Gaps in Namibia: The Role of Language Proficiency', *International Journal of Educational Development*, 31, pp. 223–33.

Gonzales, M. C. (1999). 'Re-educating Namibia: The Early Years of Radical Education Reform, 1990–1995', *Africa Today* 5, 3, pp. 105–24.

Harlech-Jones, B. (1998). 'Viva English! Or is it Time to Review Language Policy in Education?' *Reform Forum*, February, pp. 9–15.

Hoveka, U. (1999). 'Cambridge Revisited', *Namibia Review*, February/March, pp. 14–16.

Indabawa, S. A. (1999). 'On the diversity of non-formal education provision in Namibia', in K. Legese, P. K. Wainaina, R. K. Auala, A. Scott and M. Bumus (eds), *Seminar Papers* (Windhoek: Faculty of Education and National Institute For Educational Development (NIED)).

Kaimu, H. I. (2005). 'The NQF Journey in Namibia', Paper presented at the 5th Q-Africa Conference, Gallagher Estates, South Africa, 17 November 2005.

Kasanda, C. D. and Shaimenanya, C. (1997). 'Factors Hindering the Provision of Quality Education for Girls in Namibia', Paper presented at BOLESWA, Botswana, Lesotho and Swaziland Education Society, Conference University of Swaziland Kwaluseru Campus, Swaziland, 28 July–1 August 1997.

Legal Assistance Centre (n.d.). *The Constitution of Namibia* (Windhoek: Out of Africa Publishers).

Likando, G. and Scott, A. (2011). 'The Education System of Namibia', in G. Likando, C. C. Wolhuter, K. Matengu and J. Mushaandja (eds), *Comparative Education: An introduction* (Noordbrug: Keurkopie), pp. 69–80.

Makuwa, D. (2005). *The SACMEQ II Project in Namibia: A Study of the Conditions of Schooling and the Quality of Education* (Harare: SACMEQ Educational Policy Research Series).

Möwes, A. (2004). 'The Levels and Specific Causes of Stress Perceived by Primary and Secondary School Teachers in the Windhoek Region', *NERA Journal* (ISSN 1609–2716), 2004, pp. 83–102.

Mutumba, J. (1999). 'Mass Participation Limited by English as Sole Medium', *Reform Forum* April, pp. 23–26.

Mwetulundila, P. N. (2000). 'Why Girls aren't Fully Participating in Science and Mathematics in Namibia', *Research Forum* 11, pp. 23–35.

Namibia Government (2006). 'Namibia in a Nutshell: Population'. www.grnnet.gov.na/. Nam_Nutshell/Population/Languages.htm. Accessed 26 February 2006.

National Institute for Educational Development/Ministry of Education (2009). *The National Curriculum For Basic Education* (Okahandja: NIED).

National Planning Commission (2011). *Namibia 2011 Population and Housing Census Preliminary Results*. Windhoek: National Planning Commission.

Naudé, C. (1995), 'Matriekslaagsyfer val skerp ná kitsveranderings in Namibië', *Beeld*, 31 Maart, p. 11.

Republic of Namibia (1990). *The Namibian Constitution* (Windhoek: Ministry of Information and Broadcasting).

— (2004). *Namibia Vision 2030: Policy Framework for Long Term national Development* (Windhoek: Office of the President).

— (2011a). *ETSIP 2011 Annual Sector Review* (Draft) (Windhoek: Ministry of Education).

— (2011b). 'Merger of the Colleges of Education with Faculty of Education, University of Namibia', *Cabinet Resolution no. 18/29.09/011* (Windhoek: Government Press).

Republic of Namibia, Education Management Information System, Ministry of Basic Education, Sport and Culture (2005). *Education Statistics 2002* (Windhoek: Education Management Information System, Ministry of Basic Education, Sport and Culture).

Republic of Namibia, Ministry of Education (2005a). *Education and Training Sector Improvement Programme (ETSIP)* (Windhoek: Government Press).

— (2005b). Ministry of Education. www.op.gov.na(Decade_peaceb_Edu.htm. Accessed 26 February 2006.

— (2007). 'Replacement of the IGCSE/HIGCSE Curriculum and Qualifications of Cambridge International Examinations with the Namibia Senior Secondary Certificate Curriculum and Qualifications', *Press Statement*, 21 September 2007.

Republic of Namibia, Ministry of Education and Culture (1993). *Toward Education for All: A Development Brief for Education, Culture and Training* (Windhoek: Gamsberg Macmillan).

— (1994). *How much do Namibia's Children Learn in School? Findings from the 1992 National Learner Baseline Assessment* (Windhoek: Ministry of Education and Culture).

Republic of Namibia, Ministry of Labour and Social Welfare (2008). *Labour Force Survey 2008: Report Analysis* (Windhoek: Directorate of Labour Market Services).

Smit, N. (2012). Namibia's Population Hits 2.1 Million. *The Namibian*. 12 April 2012. www.namibian.com.na/index.php?id=28&tx_ttnews[tt_news]=95806&no_cache=1. Accessed 13 April 2012.

Tjipueja, G. E. (2001). 'Provision of Equal Access to Boys and Girls in Formal Schooling in Namibia', *Reform Forum: Journal For Educational Reform in Namibia* 14, pp. 24–32.

Turner, B. (ed.) (2004). *The Stateman's Yearbook 2005* (Houndmills: Palgrave Macmillan).

UNDP (2011). Human Development Report. http://hdrstats.undp.org/en/countries/profiles/NAM.html. Accessed 05 May 2012.

UNESCO (1999). *UNESCO Statistical Yearbook 1999* (Paris: UNESCO).

— (2003). *Gender and Education for All: The Leap to Equality* (Paris: UNESCO).

— (2011). *EFA Global Monitoring Report 2011. The Hidden Crisis: Armed Conflict and Education* (Paris: UNESCO).

Van der Merwe, C. I. F. (1995). 'Cooperation with UCLES and the Localization of the IGCSE and HIGCSE Examinations in Namibia', in C. Kasanda and F. Phiri (eds), *Proceedings of the (H) IGCSE Colloquium on Teacher Education* (Windhoek: John Merneit Publishers), pp. 1–65.

Voigts, F. G. G. (1998). 'Some Policy Suggestions for Primary Education Based on a National Survey of Schools at Grade Six', in C. W. Snyder and F. G. G. Voigts (eds), *Inside Reform: Policy and Programming Considerations in Namibia's Basic education Reform* (Windhoek: Gamsberg Macmillan), pp. 1–65.

World Bank (2004). *World Development Report 2005: A Better Investment Climate for Everyone* (Washington, DC: The World Bank).

— (2011). *2011 World Bank Development Report* (Washington, DC: The World Bank).

7

South Africa: Educational Reform – Curriculum, Governance and Teacher Education

Vusi S. Mncube and Nomanesi Madikizela-Madiya
University of South Africa

Historical and political background of education in South Africa

Formal education in South Africa, which commenced when Jan van Riebeeck arrived at the Cape in 1652, was for many decades clouded by racial inequalities and segregation, with schools being organized according to different' racial groups and uneven educational provision being the order of the day (Kallaway, 1984; Christie, 1992; NEPI, 1992; Kgobe, 2000). In this colonial set-up of education there were separate schools for black and white children. The Dutch East Indian Company founded schools for White children while formal schools for Black children, on the other hand, were provided by missionaries (Wolhuter, 2010). The apartheid system further separated schools according to blacks, whites, Indians and coloureds, with unequal provision of educational resources in these schools. For example, towards the end of apartheid in 1988–9 the per capita government expenditure for different races was 2,882 South African Rand per white pupil, 2,067 South African Rand per Indian pupil, 1,221 South African Rand per coloured pupil and 656 South African Rand per black African pupil (Christie, 1991). So, the government spent much more money on white education, with R4 spent for every white pupil while only R1 was spent on the education of the black pupil. This was regardless of the fact that whites made up only 20 per cent of the population (Christie, 1992). The statistics for 1987 are shown in Table 7.1.

Table 7.1 Comparative statistics 1987

	White	Indian	Coloured	African
Population size (1,000s)	4,911	913	3,069	33,580
Population %	11.6	2.1	7.2	79.1
Per capita expenditure	R2508	R1904	R1021	R476
Per capita ratio	5.3	4	2.1	1
Pupil-teacher ratio	16:1	21:1	25:1	41:1
Standard X pass rate (%)	95	93	69	56

Adapted from Christie, 1992 and (Hofmeyr, 1989: 21), South African Institute of Race Relations

Harber (2001: 7) summarizes the political and educational history of South Africa based on Kallaway (1984), Nkomo (1990) and Christie (1991) as follows:

> A white minority dominated a black majority in a context of stark social, political and economic differentiation . . . While the apartheid state used force to maintain this system, formal education was also used to make the basic tenets of apartheid 'normal' and 'acceptable' in the minds of South Africans. From the apartheid government's point of view, the role of education was to help to perpetuate and reproduce a racist system to encourage obedience and conformity to that system. It is not therefore surprising that in 1970s and 1980s education also became a key site in the struggle against apartheid.

In addition to inequalities in educational resource distribution, there were also massive racial disparities in relation to access and quality of education. The enormous variations in relation to the per capita expenditure for different races had an impact on the quality of education provided for the different race groups. This led to differences in the rates of progression of learners of different races. Kgobe (2000: 2) comments:

> The rates of progression for blacks and whites differed tremendously, with white schools achieving good pass rates and progressing through the system fairly rapidly. Black schools on the other hand produced poor results and . . . high dropout and repetition rates. The Education Renewal Strategy suggests that only 51 to 52% of African children reached standard 6 in 12 years. In contrast, 96% of white learners reached this grade in 8 years.. . .

Until the National Party (NP) came into power in 1948, there was state-provided education for whites only. However, in 1953 a Ministry of Black Education was created to administer education for blacks and the NP undertook a policy of centralized control and decentralized administration (NEPI, 1992). In the black community there was strong opposition to the system of segregated education and to the policy of black education in particular. Black education was:

- seen as a deliberate attempt to train Blacks for lower graded and lower paid jobs in a racially stratified economy;
- condemned as being too content-centred and too examination-oriented; students were expected to spend all their time with rote-memorization, rather than with the cultivation of comprehension and critical-thinking;
- regarded as extremely authoritarian;
- criticized as being too Europe-centred, excluding the cultural heritage and achievements of the rest of humanity; especially neglecting the African heritage (Mphahlele & Mmninele, 1997; Nkabinde, 1997; Wolhuter, 2010).

Education in South Africa during the apartheid-era was based on a racist political ideology. In 1954, the Minister of Native Affairs, Dr Verwoed, as cited by Carter et al. said:

> The Bantu must be guided to serve his own community in all aspects. There is no place for him in the European community above the level of certain forms of labour . . . For that reason it is of no avail for him to receive a training which has its aim absorption in the European community, where, he cannot be absorbed. (2003: 4)

However, apartheid education did not go unchallenged. As Marxist theorists contend, conflict and change are two sides of the same coin (Fagerlind & Saha, 1989), and this implies that for change to occur, conflict is often necessary. A significant manifestation of the conflict was the 1976 Soweto Uprisings where youth, in particular, rejected the apartheid education system. During these boycotts and demonstrations students attacked anything that was in their way, starting from school principals who were not democratic and those who were seen to be nurturing the existing *status quo* of apartheid. During these boycotts the most popular slogans were '*Liberation Now, Education Later*', or '*Liberation Before Education*'. These slogans were powerful, although sometimes confusing to students, as to whether they should continue boycotting schools or return to classes. The 1976 Soweto uprisings, the 1980 Cape schools boycotts and the 1984 protests were all part of the broader protests against the apartheid system (Christie, 1992).

In response to these boycotts, the state attempted some limited reforms and where they failed, repressive measures were used in order to gain support (Christie, 1992; Harber 2001). These reforms were: increased spending in the restructured Department of Education and Training (DET), the expansion of secondary and technical school provision, the appointment of the De Lange Commission, which was a major commission of inquiry into education, and the introduction of a new National Policy for General Education Affairs Act (NPGEAA) in 1984 (Christie, 1992). However, these reforms were meaningless in the eyes of students as was evident from the continued resistance in black schools and townships.

Highlighting the legitimacy of students' demands and the magnitude of the boycotts, Christie notes:

> The national student organisation, the Congress of South African Students (COSAS), continued to press for improved conditions in schools, the establishment of the democratically elected student representative councils (SRCs), the release of detainees, the removal of the army from black townships, and the lifting of (the state of) emergency regulations. On all these issues, the state remained unresponsive, and relied instead on coercive measures to contain student opposition. This is well evidenced by the numerous clashes between students and police, by the banning of organisations, and by the detentions, deaths [and disappearances] and exile of thousands of students during this period. (1992: 46)

As a result of these boycotts, and with the hope of curbing violence, those opposed to apartheid formed different committees. One such major committee was the National Education Crisis Committee (NECC), later called the National Education Coordinating Committee (NECC). One reason for the formation of the NECC in 1986 was to try to restore the collapsed relationship between students, parents and teachers, and to create conditions that would enable students to return to schools. So, together with the African National Congress (ANC), the NECC campaigned for students to return to school (Christie, 1992). The slogan '*People's Education for People's Power*' replaced the slogan '*Liberation Before Education*'. This was an attempt to create an atmosphere conducive to learning, to get students back to schools and in classes and to give education a positive context as opposed to apartheid education. As a strategy, People's Education purported to provide an alternative education governance system, one opposed to that of apartheid. It is here that the establishment of the Parent-Teacher-Student-Associations (PTSAs) began (Sithole, 1994). The reasons for the formation of the PTSAs was to transfer or shift power from the then inactive school committees to the stakeholders of the schools, namely, parents, teachers, students and their organizations. From the formation of NECC there was a shift from violence to negotiations. This change of atmosphere occurred in the early 1990s after the removal of the ban on the African National Congress and other organizations advocating democracy. It was clear that the struggle to determine the future of South Africa had taken another form and shape and there was also a change in political language.

The apartheid system of education left South Africa with some key challenges which the new South Africa has had to face, namely inequitable access shaped by race, class and gender, and the effect these had on progression and skills development among the population. As a result, the issue of educational transformation has been at the top of agenda since 1994 when South Africa became a democratic state, and a range of policies have been developed and adopted with the aim of transforming education (Kgobe, 2000).

The main goals and priorities for education post-1994

The first task of the post-1994 government was to create a single education system for all South Africans. The 19 departments of education that existed prior to 1994 were collapsed into one Department of Education after 1994 and the South African government introduced the National Qualifications Framework (NQF), providing for a network of lifelong learning for all South Africans. The NQF is designed as follows (Republic of South Africa, 1996):

- Level 1: The General Education and Training (From Grade I to Grade IX – the compulsory schooling age).
- Levels 2–4: From Grade X to Grade XII.
- Levels 5–10: Higher Education Diplomas and Degrees.

The South African NQF is tabulated in Table 7.2.

However, the post-apartheid education system has also been aimed at developing the entire population and to promote various societal goals. These goals, the *extrinsic* goals of education, include:

- Economic goals: the eradication of poverty and the promotion of the country's economic productivity and development;
- Political goals: empowering citizens to take part in the processes of a democratic society, nation building: building a communal value system for a society characterized by democracy, equality, freedom, peace, justice, tolerance and stability;

- Social goals: building a society free of racial, gender and other forms of unfair discrimination, creating a socially-mobile society and the removal of artificial hierarchies and abstractions in the way of progress;
- Cultural goals: empowering people so that they can participate in the process of cultural expression (Wolhuter, 2010).

Table 7.2 The South African NQF

Level	Band	Types of Qualifications		Location of Learning for Qualifications
10	Higher Education and Training Band	Doctorates		Universities
6		Higher Degrees (Masters) Professional Qualifications		Universities
5		First Degrees (Bachelor and Honours Degrees)		Universities
4		Diplomas/Certificates		Universities, Colleges, private/pro
3	Further Education and training band	Secondary school: Grade XII	School/Training College/NGO certificates	Schools, work place training, community programmes, non-governmental organizations (NGO's) programmes, Labour Market Schemes
2		Secondary school: Grade XI		
1		Secondary school: Grade X		
1	General Education and Training Band	Senior Phase School Grade VI–IX Intermediate phase school Grades IV–V Foundation phase schools Grades I–III Pre-primary school	Adults Basic Education and Training Level 4 Adult Basic Education and Training Level 3 Adult Basic Education and Training Level 2 Adult Basic Education and Training Level 1	Schools, work place training, community programmes, NGO programmes, Labour Market Schemes

Source: The South African National Qualification Framework, 1997

The first white paper on education and training set out the key goals of the new education system (Department of Education, 1995). First, there was considerable emphasis on education as human capital as a meritocratic attempt to move away from unequal social and economic reproduction of apartheid to more equal opportunities for all. An integrated approach to education and training was key to human resource development as the old academic/applied or 'head and hand' distinctions were seen as having helped to reproduce occupational and class distinctions. There was a need for a form of education that provided the skills and predispositions for continual learning, moving flexibly between occupations and taking responsibility for personal performance as a contribution towards developing a successful economy (Department of Education, 1995; Harber & Mncube, 2012). This emphasis on the role of education in providing the skills necessary for economic competition in the global market place has continued (McGrath & Akoojee, 2007) and was reflected in the Revised National Curriculum (NCS) of 2001 where two key developmental outcomes for schooling that are relevant to the economic role of education, for example, are to explore education and career opportunities, and develop entrepreneurial capacities (Department of Education, 2001; Harber & Mncube, 2012).

Second, there is an emphasis in the original white paper on creating a 'modern' society through education by means of an efficient, professional and well-managed education system (Department of Education, 2001). Some of the attributes of a modern person are spelt out in the revised national curriculum where the kind of learner envisaged will, for example, display a developed spirit of curiosity to enable creative and scientific discovery and display an awareness of health promotion, use effectively a variety of problem-solving techniques that reflect different ways of thinking and make informed decisions and accept accountability as responsible citizens in an increasingly complex and technological society (Department of Education, 2001: 13).

Third, post-apartheid education policy has had an overwhelming emphasis on the role of education in helping to create a more democratic and peaceful society. The White Paper on Education and Training clearly articulates the need to move towards democratic school governance and this is clearly articulated in the following statements:

> In adopting a Constitution based on democracy, equal citizenship, and the protection of fundamental human rights and freedoms, South Africans have created a completely new basis for state policy towards the provision of schooling in the future. Unavoidably, because inequality is so deep-rooted in our educational history and dominates the present provision of schooling, a new policy for school provision must be a policy for . . . creating democratic governance. (Department of Education, 1995: 82)

The realization of democracy, liberty, equality, justice and peace are necessarily conditions for the full pursuit and enjoyment of lifelong learning. It should be a goal of education and training policy to enable a democratic, free, equal, just and peaceful society to take root and prosper in our land, on the basis that all South Africans without exception share the same inalienable rights, equal citizenship and common destiny, and that all forms of bias (especially racial, ethnic and gender) are dehumanising. (Department of Education, 1995: 22)

That this new philosophy based on democracy and human rights would mean changing all aspects of the education system was also recognized.

The letter and spirit of these rights and freedoms should inform the intellectual culture in all schools and educational institutions, and professional services in departments of education. This has unavoidable implications for curricula, textbooks, other educational materials and media programmes, teaching methods, teacher education, professional supervision and management culture. (Department of Education, 1995: 43)

Democratic change in South African education

The next two sections of this chapter will focus on the key goal of the extent to which South Africa has achieved democratic reform of its educational system. Certainly, some individual schools operate more democratically. In a study of three schools operating in a more democratic manner at the end of the 1990s (Harber & Muthukrishna, 2000),

. . . the schools were clearly and recognisably carrying out their basic functions as schools in a consistent and reliable way, something which cannot necessarily be taken for granted in South Africa. All three schools exhibited an orderly, purposeful and calm atmosphere with clean premises and businesslike behaviour. Teachers and students were in classrooms when they were supposed to be and learners experienced a full day's planned curriculum each day. However, the schools were also interesting in that they went beyond these possible minimum level indicators of functional effectiveness in their willingness to embrace change and in their commitment to implementing a new educational ideology aimed at fostering a non-violent, non-racist democratic society. (430)

However, this begs the question of the extent to which larger-scale democratic reform has taken place. One aspect of system-wide democratic reform was reform of the curriculum.

In South Africa, the Outcomes-Based curriculum, known as Curriculum 2005 and introduced in 1997, was designed to facilitate more active, participant and democratic forms of learning by focusing more on the desired outcomes of learning than specific content. As argued in one paper:

> The principles which guided the new curriculum are purported to be based on cooperation, critical thinking and social responsibility, thus enabling individuals to participate in all aspects of society. Concomitant with this is the envisaged need for teachers to change their pedagogy from one that is more didactic and teacher controlled to one which encourages more active learner participation. (Scholtz et al., 2008: 22)

The initial version of the curriculum reform was criticized for being over complex and demanding for teachers and was subsequently reviewed and revised in 2000 and replaced by a National Curriculum Statement (NCS), which was written in plainer language, and

> . . . gave more emphasis to basic skills, content knowledge and a logical progression from one grade to the next. It combines a learner-centred curriculum requiring critical thought and emphasising the democratic values embedded in the Constitution, with an appreciation of the importance of content and support for educators. (Motala et al., 2007: 22)

The *National Curriculum Statement Grades R-12: Curriculum and Assessment Policy* emphasizes aspects like teamwork, human rights, inclusivity, active and critical learning (Department of Education, 2011) and is an approach to curriculum which still emphasizes the active participation of learners, thus making teaching and learning more learner-centred.

However, in line with NCS, the Curriculum and Assessment Policy Statement (CAPS) has recently been developed and, through it, it is hoped to improve the quality of teaching and learning. The Curriculum and Assessment Policy clearly advocates 'an active and critical approach to learning, rather than rote and uncritical learning of given truths' (Department of Education, 2011: 3). The CAPS is not a new curriculum but part of NCS. The focus will be on content to be taught per term and the required assessment tasks for each term, although in some subjects there will be more curriculum changes than in others. Under

CAPS every subject in each grade will have a single, comprehensive and concise document. It appears therefore that the CAPS is placing a greater emphasis on content than OBE and is going back to terminology that was used in education in South Africa before OBE was introduced. It is also seemingly aimed avoiding the jargon that was used when OBE was implemented. Liebenberg (2011) describes succinctly the key changes of the CAPS:

- CAPS will mean less group work and more individual work;
- Learning Areas and Learning Programmes will be called Subjects;
- Learning Outcomes and Assessment Standards will be replaced with Topics;
- The CAPS will break down each Subject into teaching weeks and outline the topics that need to be covered per week;
- The number of Subjects in the Intermediate Phase (Grade IV to VI) will be reduced from eight to six;
- The number of projects for learners will be reduced from the year 2010;
- Annual National testing of Grade III, VI and IX will be fully implemented by the end of 2011.

However, despite attempts at curriculum reform and further attempts to make it more teacher-friendly, realities in the classroom have been slow to change in many schools. For example, a study of schooling in rural South Africa found that, while 90 per cent of teachers claimed to be using a variety of active teaching methods, the responses from pupils and the observations of the researchers strongly suggested that the majority of teachers continued to use traditional, teacher-centred methods of monologue and rote learning. Classroom activity was dominated by three modes: reading, writing and correcting (Nelson Mandela Foundation, 2005: ch. 5).

In regard to school governance and decision-making, as indicated above, the struggle against educational injustices by parents and students in the 1980s led to the establishment of the PTSAs. PTSAs were school governance structures that were viewed 'as community structures which gave political voice to the disenfranchised' (Sayed & Soudien, 2003) and were later replaced by School Governing Bodies (SGBs). In 1996 the new democratic state published a White Paper on the organization governance and funding of schools (Republic of South Africa, 1996), from which emanated the *South African Schools Act no 84 of 1996* (SASA). The SASA became operative at the beginning of 1997 and mandated that all public state schools in South Africa must have democratically elected SGBs composed of teachers, non-teaching staff, parents and learners (the latter in secondary schools). Parents are supposed to be the majority in the SGBs and the chair of the school governing body should come from the parent component (Mncube et al., 2011). The SASA mandates that secondary school learners, who are members of the Representative Council for Learners (RCL), should also be part of school governance through participation in school governing bodies. The SASA is regarded as a tool aimed at, inter alia, redressing past exclusions and facilitating the necessary transformation to support the ideals of representation and participation in the schools and the country. By the establishment of the SASA the state aimed at fostering democratic school governance and thereby introducing a school governance structure that involves all educational stakeholder groups in active and responsible roles in order to promote issues of democracy: tolerance, rational discussion and collective decision-making (DoE, 1995: 16).

Crucial to the democratic functioning of schools, including SGB's, is the role of the principal. Naidoo (2012) studied two functioning democratic schools in the Durban area. She found that the principals displayed strikingly similar characteristics, including commitment, openness, integrity, excellent communication and interpersonal skills, being good listeners and having faith in others. However, despite the existence of these democratic principles and practices, Naidoo still found that learners were still insufficiently involved in decision-making in the two schools. Indeed, a number of scholars in South Africa have been critical of the actual practices of SGBs (see, for example, Naidoo, 2005). They have argued that conflicts and dilemmas among the membership of school governing bodies are central to the experience of school governance. Studies of the functioning on the new school governing bodies (Bush & Heystek, 2003; Ministerial Review Committee, 2004; Mncube, 2005; Brown & Duku, 2008) found that members of governing bodies tended to be male, that principals still played a dominant role in meetings and decision-making processes and that teachers tended to participate in meetings more than other stakeholders. Parents, the numerically dominant group under the legislation, were hampered in many areas by a skills capacity deficit and communication and transportation problems. Learner participation was only moderate and concentrated on fundraising, learner discipline and sports activities. So, while the structural dimension of democratic governance had been established, power relations, that is, the dominance of the principal, remained much the same. Moreover, because of existing inequalities in the wider society, by '. . . devolving functions to the governing body, the State may unintentionally be contributing to a perpetuation of inequalities in the school environment' (Karlsson, 2002: 333). Brown and Duku (2008) further contend that school governing bodies are fraught with social tension, rejection, domination and psychological stress which, in turn, leads to the isolation of those parents who are of low socio-economic status and as such their participation is compromised. Further research also suggested that low socio-economic status negatively affects how some parents participate in school governing bodies (Ministerial Review Committee, 2004).

A study conducted by Mncube et al. (2011) looked at effective ways in which parents can participate in SGBs came up with some interesting findings. The context within which a school operates has been found to play a major role in the effective functioning of SGBs. The general opinion of the KwaZulu-Natal SGBs was that such bodies have made a positive contribution to the development of effective schooling, despite some problems and challenges, such as the illiteracy of some parents, having been encountered which have limited the ability of some members of SGBs to make a meaningful contribution in the running of their schools. The general view of most of the SGBs from both the Western Cape and KwaZulu-Natal provinces was found to be that, in the former Model C schools, the functioning of the SGBs had led to the effective functioning of the school, whereas the opposite case was found to have held true in the black schools. The situation in Western Cape schools was found to be markedly different from that prevailing in the KwaZulu-Natal schools, with the participants from SGBs in the latter province expressing a belief that the involvement of parents in such a body had not resulted in the effective functioning of the school, but, rather, that such involvement had exacerbated the situation in schools, due to SGBs being fraught with corruption and having their powers usurped.

The participants in the study proposed certain ways in which parents could be encouraged to participate more fully on SGBs, including the payment of those parents who are SGB members, and the establishment of regulatory mechanisms to discipline lazy or uncooperative members. In addition, the participants expressed a belief that the following would contribute to the effective functioning of the SGBs: the valorization, recognition and appreciation of those parents who are school governors; the co-option of parents with relevant skills; the election of parents with relevant skills, even if such parents do not have children in attendance at the school and the effective training of members of the SGBs. They also affirmed their belief that, once parents are members of the SGBs, they should receive ongoing training on issues pertaining to the functioning of the SGBs (Mncube et al., 2011).

As with parents, learners were also seen to be shortchanged in terms of their participation. The above investigation (Mncube et al., 2011) also explored the role of learners in SGBs in South Africa in relation to issues of democracy and social justice. Despite being afforded a full role in school governance by post-apartheid educational policy, learners do not always play their part in school decision-making. The investigation considered the responses of different groups at schools in two provinces to the issue of involvement of learners in SGBs and whether the introduction of SGBs was perceived to have led to more effective functioning of schools, what barriers exist to filler learner participation, the key issue of training for learner involvement and whether SGBs have contributed to the development of democracy in South African schools. Learner participation in SGBs in South Africa offers considerable potential for both school improvement and making a contribution to the deepening and consolidation of democracy in South Africa but there is much work still to be done.

School organization and disorganization

Democracy needs to be built on an effective, functioning, modern organizational and institutional base (Leftwich, 1996). If schools are to be a key source of 'modern', bureaucratic organizational attitudes and behaviours then young people must experience them through the effective operation of schools as organizations and the professional behaviour of staff. For example, Bloch has argued in relation to South Africa that, 'It is clear that honesty, reliability, determination, leadership ability and willingness to work within the hierarchies of modern life are all characteristics that society rewards. These skills are, in part, formed and nourished by schools' (2009: 19).

There are many effective and well-organized schools in South Africa. Importantly, there are many examples of such schools in areas affected by poverty and poor resources which function effectively and achieve good examination results (Harber, 2001: 66–8). Bloch (2009: ch. 5) provides further positive examples. He cites a Ministerial committee that examined the nature of successful schools in South Africa which found that the key to success was doing the basics well:

> Firstly, all of the schools were focussed on their central tasks of teaching, learning and management with a sense of purpose, responsibility and commitment. Secondly, they had a strong organisational capacity, including leadership and management and professionalism was valued. Thirdly, all of the schools carried out their tasks with competence and confidence; all had organisational cultures or mind-sets that supported hard work, expected achievement and acknowledged

success. And lastly, all had strong accountability systems in place which enabled them to meet the demands of external accountability, particularly in terms of Senior Certificate achievement. (2009: 138)

However, the problem of disorganized schools has also been recognized as a serious issue in post-apartheid South Africa for some time. In 1997 the Deputy Minister of Education said,

> In many of our education departmental offices there is a chronic absenteeism of officials, appointments are not honoured, punctuality is not observed, phones ring without being answered, files and documents are lost, letters are not responded to, senior officials are inaccessible, there is confusion about roles and responsibilities and very little support, advice and assistance is given to schools . . . Many of our parents fear their own children, never check the child's attendance at school, are not interested in the welfare of the school, never attend meetings, give no support to the teacher or principal . . . Many of our teachers are not committed to quality teaching, their behaviour leaves much to be desired, are more interested in their own welfare, are not professional and dedicated, are never at school on time, pursue their studies at the expense of the children, do not prepare for lessons. . . . Many of our children are always absent from school, lack discipline and manners, regularly leave school early, are usually late for school, wear no uniform, have no respect for teachers, drink during school hours, are involved in drugs and gangs, gamble and smoke at school, come to school armed to instil fear in others . . . Many of our principals have no administrative skills, they are the source of conflict between students and teachers, sow divisions among their staff, undermine the development of their colleagues, fail to properly manage the resources of their school, do not involve parents in school matters. (Mkhatshwa, 1997: 14–15)

> A later research report of 2007 noted that educator attendance varies widely between schools but is known to result in significant loss of learner time. Apart from arriving at school late and leaving early, reasons for educator absence include strikes and stay aways, examinations and sporting events and municipal activities. The report also noted that loss of learning time will undoubtedly adversely affect achievement, outcomes and progression. (Motala et al., 2007: 58–9)

In a sustained analysis of what he terms 'dysfunctional' schools, Bloch (2009) relates in some detail evidence of poor educational outcomes in South Africa to poor internal organization. Acknowledging serious problems of infrastructure in schools in relation to the supply of electricity, libraries, laboratories, computers, clean water and suitable toilets, he also notes the enormous difficulty of recruiting competent heads to manage all 27,000 schools in South Africa. As a result:

> Schools are often not well organised, timetabling is poor, institutional process is arbitrary and ineffective. At a teaching level, haphazard planning and time management are often reflected in a poor ability to plan and timetable teaching plans for the curriculum over the year. (2009: 82–3)

The nature of teacher education, teacher recruitment and supply

Like all government sectors in South Africa, teacher education has a history that relates to the former political system of apartheid. Keevy (2006) notes that most white teachers were trained in well-resourced urban universities, while most black teachers started their careers without even having completed their secondary and tertiary education. Tracing back the origins of teacher training in South Africa from as early as the eighteenth century, the Council on Higher Education (CHE) (2010) indicates race has always been an issue. For example, teacher training started in the black communities when local assistants were trained to help with teaching in the mission schools that were in the black community. While this was the case, more advanced teacher training ended up being attained by those that were trained for teaching white children in the years to come. After the formation of the union of South Africa in 1910, teacher education remained for a long time divided along racial lines. For example, the CHE (2010: 8) mentions that teacher training colleges were structured according to race, with, for example, colleges for whites, for coloureds, for Indians and for black African people, and these were administered by different departments by the end of the 1980s. There were also some in the 'homelands', mainly for black South Africans.

By 1994, when South Africa attained democracy, it was realized that challenges facing teacher education needed to be addressed. This led to the Ministry of Education commissioning a National Teacher Education Audit in 1995. It is this audit that highlighted the challenges that included 'the fragmented provision of teacher education, a mismatch between teacher supply and demand, and high number of unqualified and under-qualified teachers' in the country (Department of Education, 2006: 6). Recommendations were then made from this Audit that teacher education needed restructuring due to its poor, inefficient and cost-ineffective state. Such restructuring brought about the rationalization and incorporation of colleges of education into universities and the then technikons. This followed the stipulations of the Education White Paper (Department of Education, 1997: 3) in which the Minister of Education noted the need for a single national co-ordinated higher education system in order to address the problems and the legacy of the past, while creating a learning society with necessary creative and intellectual energies towards meeting the goals of reconstruction and development.

Specifically, the aim of incorporating teacher education colleges into universities and technikons was to achieve efficient use of resources, improve the quality of teaching programmes and research outputs, infuse quality assurance mechanisms into the system and address the gross differences in participation rates between blacks and whites (TESA proposal, 2005). Other changes that affected teacher education included the restructuring of the same universities, in different settings, some of which had incorporated colleges of education through the processes of merger and the development of new university types. This meant, among others things, that some former college teachers were to become university teachers and perform according to university standards as they were preparing teachers for the profession. In addition, the mergers in higher education sector led to a tremendous decrease in the number of institutions that offered initial teacher education, from the former 120 colleges in 1994 to only 20 institutions in 2005.

The other initiatives that followed addressed the challenges facing teacher education during the restructuring period. These were the development of the Norms and Standards for Educators introduced in 2000, the present NQF ACT (67/2008) and the Policy on the Minimum Requirements for Teacher Education Qualifications. This latter policy was meant to set 'the requirements of the Department of Education as an employer in respect of knowledge, skills and values that an educator must acquire to be competent and capable' (Robinson, 2003; Parker & Deacon, 2004: 6). For example, it indicated that by the completion of a training programme, the teacher should display foundational competence, practical teaching competence and reflexive competence, that is, competence at subjects, the practice of teaching and reflecting critically upon their own teaching.

Quality assurance was another aspect that characterized changes in teacher education. According to Robinson (2003) prior to the transformation process teacher education programmes were not nationally registered, and therefore were not open to any national quality assurance process. With the changes in place it meant that teacher education programmes had to be designed such that they met the regulations stipulated in the Norms and Standards for Educators. TESA's proposal (Teacher Education in South Africa, 2005) was still questioning the quality of some professional teacher education programmes laying the blame on the low subsidy and the dispersal of quality assurance functions among a variety of bodies while the quality assurance environment was still unstable. Even the manner in which a single education system was created did not in turn create opportunities for interaction and power sharing among the previously different systems. The result of this, according to TESA proposal, 'is a dispersed system, and a great deal of energy is absorbed in trying to work out the relationships and areas of authority of each part of the system' (2005: 4). In particular, the proposal notes a contest between the Department of Education with its Norms and Standards for Educators, the South African Council for Educators (SACE) with responsibility for the registration of qualified teachers and the South African Qualifications Authority (SAQA) with its educator in schooling qualifications, as well as the Council on Higher Education (CHE) which is responsible for the quality assurance of all higher education through its Higher Education Quality Committee (TESA, 2005: 4). Such contests have been identified even within the same Department where different groups such as the Ministerial Committee, the Deans of Education and the Higher Education branch have different positions about the teacher education qualifications. The Norms and Standards for Educators were themselves regulated by the wider legislation that included the NQF, the General Education and Training (GET), the Further Education and Training (FET and the Higher Education and Training (HET)) (Parker & Deacon, 2004; South African Council for Educators (SACE), 2011).

In addition, a consortium that comprised of the Center for Education Policy Development (CEPD), the University of Pretoria's Center for Evaluation and Assessment (CEA), the Human Sciences Research Council (HSRC) and South Africa Institute for Distance Education (SAIDE), developed a research and development programme in 2005. The overall goal of the programme was to contribute knowledge and information towards the formulation and implementation of new policies related to the organization and practice of initial teacher education (both pre-service and upgrading) in the county. Focus on initial teacher education was informed by the fact that, among others, there was an increasing demand for teachers, especially secondary school teachers, while the government funding policies were not making teaching any more attractive to tertiary education students. According to Welch and Gultig (2002) teacher education got the least funding compared to other faculties in the HEIs, which indicated that it was regarded as a 'stepchild' of higher education. While this was the case TESA (2005: 7) notes that there were 'too few teachers . . . entering the teaching profession, too many teachers . . . leaving the profession and too many teachers . . . inappropriately deployed in the teaching profession to meet the human resources needs of the country'. However, with time the government came up with strategies to encourage both initial teacher training and upgrading of qualifications by the practicing teachers.

Among the strategies was the Funza Lushaka Bursary scheme which is offered to undergraduate students who are studying towards the teaching of mathematics, science and technology in the Foundation phase in rural schools. This led to an increase in the number of first-time enrolments in all teacher education programmes by 37.1 per cent between 2008 and 2009 (Department of Basic Education (DBE) & Department of Higher Education and Training (DHET), 2011). In their Integrated Strategic Planning Framework for Teacher Education and Development in South Africa, 2011–25, these departments also note an increase in the number of Full-Time Equivalents (FTEs) for teacher education programmes such as Bachelor of Education (BEd) and Postgraduate Certificate of Education (PGCE) by 25 per cent from 2008 to 2009, for all phases in the institutions where these programmes were offered. A similar increase was noted for the number of Foundation Phase FTEs for the same programmes by about 24.9 per cent from 2008 to 2009. This was a remarkable improvement considering the fact that the country had been having a shortage of Foundation Phase teachers in the previous years, while learner performance in this phase, in both literacy and numeracy, was unsatisfactory (Green et al., 2011). Also incentives, in the form of bursaries, were given to the under-qualified (Relative Education Qualification Values 11 and 12) practicing teachers to do the National Professional Diploma in Education (NPDE). NPDE's principal rationale was to improve the quality of teaching and learning, not only in schools but also in the FET colleges (CHE, 2006).

The other issue that has been identified as significant while dealing with teacher education challenges in South Africa has been the addressing of teacher development needs. This according to the DBE and DHET (2011) is being addressed through mechanisms such as the Integrated Quality Management System (IQMS) and programmes for continuing professional development. IQMS came about through the integration of two quality management programmes in education: the Development Appraisal System (DAS) and the Performance Measurement System. In other words it combined processes of individual teacher appraisal with the evaluation of teachers for salary progression. According to the DBE and DHET (2011) IQMS was an attempt to make teachers work collaboratively with others in taking control of their own development through self assessment and Personal Growth Plans (PGPs). This system was, however, reported to have a number of shortcomings and not being completely welcome by the teachers and the unions. Among these was the fact that it was 'too time-consuming and 'personnel heavy', with too much bureaucratic control, and it was suggested that there needs to be reduction in the amount of paperwork entailed' (DBE & DHET, 2011: 95). Based on the problems identified about the IQMs the 2011 to 2015 strategic plan by the two Departments of Education has made recommendations such as the separation of teacher development from performance appraisal.

With regards to salaries, the Education Labour Relations Council (ELRC) contracted the CEPD in 2010 to conduct research on the current teacher salary system and to present options for the future. The CEPD (2011) reported that it is generally difficult for teachers to progress in salary terms without seeking a promotion and leaving the classroom. Unlike in the past, however, the CEPD found that the salary system has significantly addressed the issue of racial and gender inequality. This however does not imply that salary levels by race have become equal because they are still affected by the remnants of the past in which white teachers were better qualified than black teachers. With regards to gender the CEPD found that the salary differences were caused by imbalances in promotion posts which, as indicated above, determine salary increases and which has little to do with the salary system.

The CEPD report also addressed the findings of the national audit that was conducted in 2001 by the Department of Education in which it was found that 44 per cent of the Early Childhood Development (ECD) teachers earned less than R500 a month, levels that were very poor when compared to other teaching profession sectors. However, the DBE (2010) reports that, although still not completely satisfactory, salary increases for teachers have been recently considerable, culminating in a real increase of 12 per cent in 2009. It has been crucial that the government considers the issue of salaries for teachers because it was affecting teacher supply. SACE (2010), for example, indicates that the individual's decision on whether or not to enter the teaching profession is affected by both the financial and non-financial factors. Teacher salaries are equal regardless of the school's geographic location and resources. Schools in remote areas are affected more by this issue because, SACE argues,

> . . . those teachers finding themselves in rural school, their derived utility is lower than those who are in schools that are resource endowed or are in areas with amenities . . . [They] . . . will either exit the profession or move to schools that increase their utility by increasing the non-financial part of the utility. . . . some . . . research findings . . . indicate shortages in rural schools because teachers do not supply labour in these areas, more especially science, math and language teachers. The Ministerial Committee on Rural Education (2005) found rural areas were experiencing shortages of competent and qualified teachers. Similarly the HSRC (2004) found that there is a shortage in supply of educators teaching technology, economics and management sciences in rural as compared to urban schools. (2010: 7)

Still arguing the value of salary when individuals make decisions about the teaching profession, SACE further states:

> . . . individuals do not value current salary or non-financial rewards only in their decision matrix, they also value future salary stream. This is the salary flow throughout the lifetime of the teacher in the profession discounted into current values ρ. The discounted salary flow has to be greater than the cost of investing in the development of the specialised human capital κ. . . .

What this implies, according to SACE, is that teachers constantly compare their lifetime earnings with those of other professions and in South Africa research has previously proven teaching salaries to be lower than the alternative profession (Crouch, 2001). This makes more experienced teachers leave the profession. Even though means are tried to counteract this trend by rewarding teachers who stay in the profession by increasing their salary bands, this has not yet been proven to be the best management strategy (SACE, 2010).

Conclusion

This chapter presented a brief history of different aspects of education in South Africa, highlighting how racial segregation impacted not only on education but on the whole economy and society of the country. The discussion indicated that South Africa has been, and is still, in the process of reform and change since the attainment of democracy in 1994. A number of challenges have been encountered with regards to the restructuring of curriculum in a more democratic direction but changes in curriculum have also meant the need for changes in teacher education. The chapter has shown how teacher education programmes had to change after the attainment of democracy in South Africa and also to undergo quality assurance processes. These changes in teacher education were mainly meant to ensure that teachers not display only foundational competence when they complete their training, but also practical teaching competence and reflexive competence. These changes are in line with the broader education reform towards an OBE framework. Not only curriculum and teacher education have and/or are undergoing change in the South African education sector, this chapter has also discussed how school governance has been restructured in pursuit of involving different stakeholders in a more democratic manner and what the obstacles to this are. However, both departments of education (DBE and DHET) continue to work on the process of democratizing the education system so that it meets the intended transformation goals.

References

Bloch, G. (2009). *The Toxic Mix* (Cape Town: Tafelberg).

Brown, B. and Duku, N. (2008). 'Negotiated Identities: Dynamics in Parents' Participation in School Governance in Rural Eastern Cape Schools and Implication for School Leadership', *South African Journal of Education* 28, pp. 431–50.

Bush, T. and Heystek, J. (2003). 'School Governance in the New South Africa', *Compare* 33, 2, pp. 127–38.

Carter, C., Harber, C. and Serf, J. (2003). *Towards Ubuntu: Critical Teacher Education for Democratic Citizenship in South Africa* (Birmingham: Development Education Centre).

Center for Education Policy Development (CEPD) (2011). Revised Salary Structure Proposals: Report Prepared for the Education Labour Relations Council (ELRC). www.elrc.org.za/

Christie, P. (1991). *The Right to Learn* (Johannesburg: SACHED).

— (1992). 'From Crisis to Transformation: Education in Post-apartheid South Africa', *Australian Journal of Education* 36, 1, pp. 38–52.

Council on Higher Education (CHE) (2006). 'Higher Education Quality Committee Criteria and Minimum Standards for the National Professional Diploma in Education'. www.che.ac.za. Accessed 11 May 2012.

— (2010). Report on the National Review of Academic and Professional Programmes in Education (Pretoria: CHE).

Crouch, L. (2001). Turbulence or orderly change? Teacher supply and demand in the age of AIDS. Occasional paper. Department of Education: Pretoria. April.

Department of Basic Education & Department of Higher Education and Training (2011). Integrated strategic planning framework for teacher education and development in South Africa: 2011–2025. www.education.gov.za

Department of Education (1995). *White Paper on Education and Training* (Pretoria: Government Printers).

— (1997). Education White Paper 3: *A Programme for the Transformation of Higher Education* (Pretoria: Department of Education).

— (2001). *Draft Revised National Curriculum Statement* (Pretoria: Government Printers).

— (2006). The National Policy Framework for Teacher Education and Development in South Africa. http://www.info.gov.za. Accessed 14 May 2012.

— (2011). *Curriculum And Assessment Policy Statement (Caps) Mathematics Foundation Phase* (Final Draft) (Pretoria: Government Printers).

Fagerlind, I. and Saha, L. (1989). *Education and National Development* (Oxford: Pergamon).

Green, W., Parker, D., Deacon, R. and Hall, G. (2011). 'Foundation phase teacher provision by public higher education institutions in South Africa', *South African Journal of Childhood Education* 1, 1, pp. 109–22.

Harber, C. (2001). *State of Transition: Post Apartheid Education Reform in South Africa* (United Kingdom: Symposium Books).

Harber, C. and Muthukrishna, N. (2000). 'School Effectiveness and School Improvement in Context: The Case of South Africa', *School Effectiveness and Improvement* 11, 4, pp. 421–34.

Hofmeyr, J. (1989). 'Equalising Educational Opportunities', *South African Journal of Labour Relations* 13, 2, pp. 20–42.

Kallaway, P. (ed.) (1984). *Apartheid and Education* (Johannesburg: Ravan Press).

Karlsson, J. (2002). 'The Role of Democratic Governing Bodies in South African Schools', *Comparative Education* 38, 3, pp. 327–36.

Keevy, J. (2006). 'The Regulation of Teacher Education in South Africa through the Development and Implementation of the National Qualifications Framework (1995 to 2005)', Paper presented at the 'Preparing teachers for a changing context' conference hosted by the Insitute of Education, University o f London, 3–6 May 2006.

Kgobe, M. P. (2000). Transformation of the South African Schooling System: A Report form the First Year of Education 2000 Plus, a Longitudinal Study to Monitor Education Policy Implementation and Change (Braamfontein: CEPD).

Leftwich, A. (ed.) (1996). *Democracy and Development* (Cambridge: Polity Press).

Liebenberg, H. (2011). 'What are the Curriculum and Assessment Policy Statements? DoE', www.education.gov.za. Accessed 11 May 2012.

McGrath, S. and Akoojee, S. (2007). 'Education and Skills for Development in South Africa: Reflections on the Accelerated and Shared Growth Initiative for South Africa', *International Journal of Educational Development* 27, 4, pp. 421–34.

Ministerial Review Committee (2004). Review of School Governance in South African Public Schools: Report of the Ministerial Review Committee on School Governance (Pretoria: Government Press).

Mkhatshwa, S. (1997). 'Speech Delivered at Culture of Learning, Teaching and Service Campaign Consultative Conference', 22–4 August.

Mncube V. S. (2005). 'School Governance in the Democratisation of Education in South Africa: The Interplay between Policy and Practice', Unpublished PhD Thesis, University of Birmingham, Britain.

Mncube,V. S., Harber, C. and Du Plessis, P. (2011). 'Effective School Governing Bodies: Parental Involvement, Training and Issues of School Effectiveness in Two Provinces of South Africa', *Acta Academica* 43, 3, pp. 210–42.

Motala, S., Dieltiens,V., Carrim, N., Kgobe, P., Moyo, G. and Rembe, S. (2007). 'Educational Access in South Africa: Country Analytic Review', Project Report. Consortium for Research on Educational Access, Transitions and Equity (CREATE), Falmer, UK.

Mphahlele, M. C. J. and Mminele, S. P. P. (1997). *Education through the Ages, Part 3* (Pretoria: Kagiso).

Naidoo, P. (2005). *Educational Decentralisation and School Governance in South Africa* (Paris: Institute for Educational Planning).

Naidoo, R. (2012). Experiences and Practices of School Principles in Creating, Leading and Governing Democratic Schools, PhD Thesis, University of KwaZulu Natal.

Nelson Mandela Foundation (2005). *Emerging Voices* (Cape Town: HSRC Press).

NEPI (1992). *Curriculum Report* (Cape Town: Oxford University Press)

Nkabinde, Z. P. (1997). *An Analysis of Educational Challenges in the New South Africa* (Lanham, MD: University Press of America).

Nkomo, M. (ed.) (1990). *Pedagogy of Domination* (Trenton: Africa World Press).

Parker, B. and Deacon, R. (2004). Theory and Practice: South African Teacher Educators on Teacher Education (Centre for Policy Development (CEPD)).

Republic of South Africa (1996). (*SASA*) *South African Schools Act* (Pretoria: Government Printers).

Robinson, M. (2003). 'Teacher Education Policy in South Africa: The Voice of Teacher Educators', *Journal of Education for Teaching* 29, 1, pp. 19 34.

Sayed, Y. and Soudien, C. (2003). '(Re) Training education exclusion and inclusion discourses : Links and Possibilities', in R. Subrananian, Y. Sayed, S. Balagopalan and C. Soudien (eds), *Education Inclusion and Exclusion: Indian and South African Perspectives*, IDS Bulletin 34, 1 January, University of Sussex.

Scholtz, Z., Braund, M., Hodges, M., Koopman, R. and Lubben, F. (2008). 'South African Teachers Ability to Argue: The Emergence of Inclusive Argumentation', *International Journal of Educational Development* 28, 1, pp. 21–34.

Sithole S. (1994). 'Parent-Teacher-Student Associations (PTSAs): Present state and future prospects'. *Education Monitor* 5, 1, pp. 1–8.

South African Council for Educators (SACE) (2010). A review of teacher demand: a research gap and the role of SACE. www.sace.org.za. Accessed 12 May 2012.

— (2011). A Position Paper on the Professional Registration of FET College Educators. www.sace.org.za.

TESA (Teacher Education in South Africa: A Collaborative Programme) (2005). Centre for Education Policy Development (CEPD); Centre for Evaluation and Assessment (CEA); University of Pretoria; Human Sciences Research Council (HSRC); South African Institute for Distance Education (SAIDE).

Welch, T. and Gultig, T. (2002). *Teacher Education: Looking in the Mirror to Plan the Future* (10th anniversary edition) (Johannesburg: SAIDE).

Wolhuter, C. C. (2010). 'South Africa: Worldwide educational reform programme telescoped into an instant time-space', in C. C. Wolhuter and H. D. Herman (eds), *Educational Reform in Southern Africa: Prospects for the New Millennium* (Potchefstroom: C.C.Wolhuter), pp. 1–16.

8

South Africa: Making Post-Apartheid Rights into Realities

Shireen Motala
University of Johannesburg

Introduction

Improving access to education in the developing world has received concerted global attention for the last two decades, with commitments made at the 1990 Education for All Conference in Jomtien, Thailand, being translated into the Millennium Development Goals (MDGs) ten years later. One of these goals is to ensure that, by 2015, children everywhere will be able to complete a full cycle of primary education (World Education Forum, 2000). Getting learners into schools is therefore important and establishes an important basic right.

But evaluating access to education is not simply a technical accounting exercise that matches numbers of children to spaces on school benches. By that calculation, South Africa's apartheid government would be said to have done well, evidenced by its high gross and net enrolments in schooling. But as the 'Bantu Education' policy under apartheid so forcefully demonstrated, physical access does not necessarily translate into meaningful access for individual children, nor does it necessarily promote greater justice in society.

If one is to judge South Africa's progress towards universal basic education then a review of structural access is necessary but inadequate. Physical access is just the first hurdle on the way towards ensuring that children have access to education. It should be expected that their education will provide them with at least a minimal set of skills, knowledge and values that will allow them to function in the economy, in social life and in democratic processes. Curriculum outcomes set a benchmark that all learners must attain. This is what can be described as 'meaningful access', referring to an enriching and rewarding educational experience for all learners which is manifest in the mastery of the set curriculum.

The concept of meaningful access casts a wider than ordinary lens on schooling and the processes involved in becoming educated. The concept encompasses both 'physical' and 'epistemic' access. Meaningful access is not merely about good quality teaching – though that must be present. It must, in the words of Wally Morrow, lead to 'a sense of the significance of systematic learning' (2007: 29). A meaningful education inducts and progressively moves children into the knowledge and skills that allows them to engage in the wider world. Meaningful access must include high attendance rates and progression through grades with little or no repetition (Lewin & Wang, 2011). It also includes issues of equitable access to schooling. In the South African context, equity is inextricably bound to development, and contributes to delivering rights in education.

Using the broadened concept of access, this chapter suggests that despite significant funding shifts, equitable access to quality education has not taken place. It critically considers policy and legislative shifts and implementation of the school funding norms and curriculum reform processes and addresses how far we have come in achieving equity and quality in education. An overarching theme is that of devolution and decentralization and how this has facilitated or hampered access, quality and equity in South African education.

Funding equitable access

The right of access to a basic education is a fundamental human right enshrined in the South African Constitution (1996). South Africa has also ratified various international conventions entrenching the right to education, in terms of which the state is obliged to provide free education: the 1989 United Nations Convention on the Rights of the Child, the African Charter on the Rights and Welfare of the Child, the Millennium Development Goals EFA (Education for All) which includes the provision of education to all children by 2015 and the Dakar Framework for Action, 2000. In terms of these commitments, the government is obliged to provide free basic education to all children. In fulfilling its obligation to remove all possible barriers to educational access, the government introduced two policies that seek to make education more accessible: the Exemption Policy (SASA, 1996) and the 'No Fee' Schools policy (2006).

In 2010, around R61 billion was spent on education, making it the largest category of government expenditure. This comprised 5.3 per cent of the Gross

Domestic Product (GDP) and about 18 per cent of consolidated government expenditure. In comparison to other developing countries, education spending in South Africa as a proportion of GDP is high although it is less than the UNESCO benchmark of 6 per cent. It has been noted that these relatively high levels reflect mainly expenditure on educator salaries with spending on other inputs being below international norms. Education expenditure takes place at both the provincial and national levels. In 2010, 86.5 per cent of education expenditure was on public school education, although it is a declining proportion of GDP (Department of Education, 2010: 28).

The Organisation for Economic Co-operation and Development (OECD) report on South Africa (2008: 143) identifies a number of trends in education spending. These include that real spending has escalated rapidly in recent years and will continue to do so in the medium term; as a positive trend personnel expenditure has declined from over 89 per cent in the late 1990s to below 80 per cent in 2008, there have been improvements in funding equity both between provinces and schools as real funding interacted with pro-poor funding norms. However questions continue about the impact of this funding shift, arguing that the real impact has been less marked in terms of real education opportunities and education quality.

An increasing feature of the government spending patterns is on a constrained and austere fiscus, as it continues to balance meeting economic growth targets with social expenditure. The Financial and Fiscal Commission recommended that education rid itself of inefficiencies if it wanted to release funds for implementing its redistributive aims (Financial & Fiscal Commission, 1998; Fiske & Ladd, 2004). In pursuance of these efficiency aims, and to regulate access, regulations were introduced to reduce under- and over-aged learners in the system. In 1998, the department brought out age grade norms and specified that learners should proceed along with their age cohort (Department of Education, 1998). Learners can repeat only once per phase (i.e. Foundation, Intermediate and Senior Phase), and those over the age of 16 who have never attended school, and those that fail to make similar progress as their peers, are referred to Adult Basic Education Centres (Motala et al., 2007: 16).

Despite South Africa's higher rates of participation as measured through gross enrolment rates (99% in primary and 87% in secondary education), there continue to be numerous barriers to success, evidenced by poor quality outcomes (Van der Berg, 2010). It is also argued that patterns of participation, evidenced by repetition, dropout and over agedness, are an increasingly important predictor of education outcomes (Taylor et al., 2010; Periera, 2011).

The post-apartheid dispensation saw the introduction of a host of policy and institutional reforms aimed at redressing the legacy of the previous era. A key challenge was to eliminate inequities in school funding that had characterized the previous education landscape. Achieving funding equity has thus been a central consideration of the government during this period.

Specific mechanisms were introduced to improve funding equity, specifically the Equitable Share Formula (ESF) and the National Norms and Standards for School Funding (NNSSF) policy. The ESF reflects provincial variables such as the size of the school age population, the number of learners enrolled in public ordinary schools, the distribution of capital needs, the size of the rural population in each province and the size of the population weighted for social security grants and a poverty index. The aim is to ensure that every province whatever its financial standing is able to spend an equitable amount on each learner. The ESF was phased in from 1996 to 2000 in order to allow provinces, particularly the more wealthy ones, to make adjustments in their budgetary allocations, particularly if they have faced a decline in expenditure. Since provinces make their own decisions about how to spend their equitable share across social services, the actual per capita education expenditure differs from province to province.

The NNSSF was the second major policy mechanism to address inequalities in the education financing system (Department of Education, 1998). Much of SAs education reform is based on a decentralized and devolved model, since schooling is a provincial responsibility. The decentralization of education authority is part of the global reform agenda which introduces market-oriented measures such as choice and competition and from a rights perspective, a participatory model of citizen action and control (Sayed & Ahmed, 2011). The devolution of responsibilities to provinces, districts and schools has not been accompanied by administrative efficiency or the empowerment of schools in order to manage their devolved responsibilities. As various commentators have noted, while schools may be ranked on an equitable basis, the uneven capacity among schools and school government bodies has meant that funds are often not spent effectively and efficiently (Simkins, 2002; Lewis & Motala, 2004; Mestry, 2012). Capacitating the different levels of governance, province, district, school and circuit has received much attention, as the poor level of service delivery in the Limpopo and Eastern Cape provinces continues to hamper the provision of quality education (Chisholm, 2011; *Times* 11 June, 2012). Who safeguards the constitutionality of basic rights in terms of provincial delivery on national mandates continues to be unclear.

Central to the reforms introduced post-1994 was the introduction of South African Schools Act (SASA) (1996). The policy provided for the practice of supplementing state resources through school fees. It also made provisional for learners unable to pay, to be exempted following a means test and verification. School governing bodies (SGB) were empowered to take 'all reasonable measures within its means to supplement the resources supplied to the school in order to improve the quality of education provided for all learners at the school' (SASA, Section 21). In practice, this translated into the levying of school fees. This position was justified on the basis of limited state resources to provide free education, as well as the desire to improve school-level accountability by increasing community control over school resources.

Regulating entrance to schools through financial mechanisms has been most visible in the form of the introduction of user fees. Not only do School Governing Bodies (SGBs) have the power to formulate school admission and language policies, they may also determine school fees (with the explicit consent of parents) and raise additional funds to supplement their school's incomes (RSA, 1996). The rationale behind giving SGBs the power to raise fees was that state resources were not sufficient to bring all schools up to the standard enjoyed by former white schools before 1994 (Harber, 2001). Since increasing the education budget was not an option, and given the government's emphasis on fiscal austerity, permitting wealthier schools to charge higher fees while at the same time receiving less public funding would in turn enable poorer schools to charge no or negligible fees but receive more public funding (Harber, 2001; Ndimande, 2006).

User fees enabled schools to employ additional teachers and secure other resources so as to offer quality education, and probably prevented middle-class flight from public to independent schools; nevertheless, they prevented children from poor families from accessing the same quality of education. In an attempt to address this, the Norms and Standards for School Funding provided mechanisms for partial or full exemption from paying fees (Department of Education, 1998). Parents may receive full exemption if their combined annual gross income is less than ten times the annual school fees per learner, and partial exemption if their income is less than 30 times but greater than ten times the fees. Parents have to apply to the SGB for exemption; if they fail to apply and still do not pay the fees, legal action can be taken against them. Despite this, SGBs may not exclude affected learners from schools (Department of Education, 1998). The exemptions policy has its limitations: many parents who might well qualify for exemption fail to apply because the process is complicated and bureaucratic, and many schools have been reluctant to inform parents about the procedures because schools receive no compensation for fees not paid by those who are exempted.

Moreover, 'there have been instances where a school governing body has misused its power to set and enforce (high) school fees in order to restrict admissions, or to exclude learners whose parents are unable to pay' (OECD, 2008: 143). While most parents consider the fees charged by schools to be appropriate, some schools have acted illegally against children who failed to pay, by withholding reports, seating learners on the floor or sending them home (Department of Education, 2008). Overall, given continued high enrolment rates, it is unlikely that the charging of school fees resulted in significant numbers of learners dropping out of school altogether. What is important, however, is that parents can exercise school choice within the constraints of their own private resources, and so there is regulated access. Woolman and Fleisch (2006) note that government policies are creating markets for education where choice behaviour is exercised. Vigorous debates have been ongoing about whether this quasi-privatization of public schooling has increased inequalities, or whether, as government has argued, that school fees charged at better-off schools can be used to effect redress and equity. The consequence of presence of private income in public schools has contributed to inequity because it has been used to fund quality-related inputs such as employing more teachers and reducing learner:educator ratios (Motala & Sayed, 2009). An unintended consequence of the policy is that it continues to 'marginally favour the rich', because better qualified teachers are present in more affluent schools and the deracializing middle class (Motala, 2006; Sayed, 2009).

Ongoing efforts to enhance access through reducing indirect costs include 'regulating the cost of uniforms and books, improving school budgeting systems, taking over school nutrition schemes from the Department of Health, and facilitating better transport facilities so that the poor especially in rural areas have easier access to schools' (Motala et al., 2007: 21). In 2004, the Norms and Standards for School Funding were amended to ensure more effective implementation of the exemptions policy and to improve monitoring; orphans, learners in foster care and children who receive government grants are also exempted from fees (Department of Education, 2008). Parents with more than one learner in a public school receive a discount if school fees range between 35 per cent and 95 per cent of their annual income.

The funding reforms have been lauded as having led to the attainment of a certain measure of progress in terms of access, equity and redress. Particular gains have been registered with regard to inter-provincial equity, for example, although intra-provincial equity remains a challenge.

However, by the end of the first political term (1999), it had become clear that the gains were not being equally realized for all learners in the country. There were also concerns about the extent to which policy had effected a narrowing of the gap between rich and poor schools. As a response to this, a policy and legislative framework was put in place which included an acknowledgement of constitutional and international commitments.

The Norms and Standards for School Funding were initially implemented in 2000, in response to these concerns. The policy required that 60 per cent of the available resources be distributed to the poorest 40 per cent of learners. Provincial education departments were tasked with developing policy instruments for ranking public schools. No financial benchmarks were stipulated except that the allocations to learners in Quintile 5 (least poor) should be seven times smaller than allocations for learners in Quintile 1 (poorest Quintile) (Wildeman, 2008).

The period from 2000 and 2003 was a period in which lessons were learnt from the initial implementation in terms of financial systems and resource allocation. It became clear that the Norms and Standards required revision especially to address the problem of inter-provincial equity. While large differences in per learner funding across provinces provided one reason for the reform to the school funding norms, the policy was also amended as a result of public complaints that school fees were being used as a barrier and that some schools were unfairly discriminating against learners and parents with the inability to pay. These findings led to the legislative amendments and to procedures informing and regulating the governing of schools. Problems with the implementation of the school fees exemption policy also provided part of the reason for introducing the No Fee schools policy.

A number of studies on the implementation and impact of the No Fee policy have already been undertaken (Wildeman, 2008; ACESS, 2009; Giese et al., 2009; Motala and Sayed, 2009; Sayed & Ahmed, 2011 and others). Several challenges have also been highlighted with the policy, most notably the limitations of adequacy benchmark level and the problems with the quintile system.

Some of the positive outcomes of the policy implementation was that it was found to have significant re-distributive effects, with the largest increases in allocation to the poorer schools (Wildeman, 2008). Studies conducted by the alliance for children's entitlement to social security (Giese et al., 2009) concluded that schools were better off even when the loss of fee income was taken into account. Other research (Hall & Giese, 2008) showed that there were significant gains in terms of revenue for no fee schools and also for households, who were relieved of the burden of having to pay fees.

At the same time numerous challenges existed with the implementation of the policy. These included the annual re-ranking of schools and the declaration of no fee status and the speed with which this could happen. Another was the limitations of the adequacy benchmark which continues to be insufficient to cover even the basic cost of schooling inputs (Veriava, 2005; ACES, 2008). Research shows that while there has been considerable aggregate impact, most allocations in 2007 for the three poorest quintiles fell below the nationally set benchmark and poor provinces in particular were unable to meet national targets. This has significant consequences for the quality of education delivery in schools. A related issue is that the levels of inequality between the No Fee and those in the less poor quintiles also continues to rise since not all schools can be accommodated in the No Fee category (Mestry, 2012).

Most significant is that adequacy is only specific for non-personnel re-current expenditure and, as Motala (2006) and Jansen and Amsterdam have noted, the differences in the number and quality of personnel remain a feature of the current schooling landscape. In relation to the school fee exemption policy as Hall and Monson have noted, potential loss of revenue from exempting learners creates a disincentive to parents of this right as the school does not provide compensatory funding for exempted learners.

At the centre of the discussions of the roll-out of the No Fee policy is the concept of adequacy. While there is recognition to include adequacy as a funding principle, in order to give substance and content to the right of access to education, the combination of limited state resources to fund its adequacy approach and a restricted definition of adequacy that excludes personnel costs has resulted in a weak overall approach of adequacy to date. The potential to provide meaningful access, defined as education of sufficient quality, at least in concerns about adequacy, particularly about the need to ensure that minimum learning resources are available for all children and about the relation between providing more resources for poorer children and obtaining better educational outcomes, are being eclipsed in education discourse by discussions of the notion of No Fees.

Devolved authority to schools have not led to the empowerment of parents in order to access decision-making processes, and have not necessarily been associated with democratization and as a space for parental and civic participation (Sayed & Soudien, 2003; Wilson, 2006).

A consideration of pro poor approaches, will be better served by introducing the notions of education rights and justice into our discourse. There continues to be a tension between the provision of education as an unqualified right in our constitution, and the constraint of macro-economic policy. Tomasevski (2006) has powerfully argued that the fiscal restraint runs counter to the realization of education as a human right . This is very evident in our discussion on adequacy and the inability of the Department of Education to firm up what a minimum learning amount should be which provides a scaffolding for quality education. Social justice approaches are particularly important because the relationship of social justice to education is one that is concerned with fairness, rights and equal opportunity with the aim, as noted by Giroux (1997), to make society more democratic, empowering and transformative.

Equity and quality

With only a few years remaining before the 2015 target date for meeting Education for All goals, the issue of education quality remains a key South African development challenge. The new democratic government which came into being in South Africa in 1994 has shown its commitment to Education for All by, in part, producing numerous policy documents intended to ensure equitable access for all to meaningful learning opportunities. To this end, between 1994 and 2007 seven White Papers, three Green Papers, 26 Bills (of which 17 were amendment bills), 35 Acts (of which 22 were amendments to existing laws), 11 regulations, 52 government notices and 26 calls for comments have been published.

Curriculum 2005, which fundamentally shifted the content and pedagogy of the old syllabus-based system and introduced outcomes-based education, has required substantial adaptation on the part of role players, not least for the government officials implementing it and for the teachers teaching it. Concerns were soon raised about its complex terminology, its lack of alignment and its poor implementation support, and these and other issues have required a decade of revision and gradual introduction into all phases of schooling. The new Revised National Curriculum Statements (RNCS) give more emphasis to basic skills, content knowledge and grade progression, and combine a learner-centred curriculum requiring critical thought and emphasizing the democratic values with an appreciation of the importance of content and support for teachers (Motala & Dieltiens, 2011).

Despite these advances, inadequate time is still accorded to teaching and learning. Although formal contact time is limited to a maximum of 27.5 hours per week, only about one half is spent on actual teaching (OECD, 2008: 175). Many teachers have undergone professional development, but there are mixed views on the quality of the support that has been offered to them. The challenge of accessing adequate books and relevant materials, especially in schools in rural areas, remains.

Seventeen years since the first democratic elections, national, regional and international tests reveal that South African learners are far from mastering basic and minimum competencies across the curriculum, and among these learners it is the poorest and the most marginalized who are especially affected by poor quality education. In the Department of Education's systemic evaluation of Grade VI in 2005, learners obtained a national mean score of 38 per cent in the Language of Learning and Teaching, 27 per cent in Mathematics and 41 per cent in Natural Science (Department of Education, 2005). Six years later, the results of the 2011 Annual National Assessments show little improvement. In the latest findings the Annual National Assessments of almost 6 million primary school learners in February 2011, Grade III learners achieved an average of only 35 per cent for Literacy and 28 per cent for Numeracy, while Grade VI learners managed 28 per cent for Languages and 30 per cent for Mathematics (Department of Basic Education, 2011: 20). These results also varied markedly between provinces and among quintiles.

Compared with learners internationally, including many other African countries, South Africans often score lowest (Strauss & Burger, 2000; HSRC, 2005; Van den Berg, 2011). South Africa also has the highest levels of between-school inequality of performance in both Mathematics and reading in comparison with its regional counterparts like Botswana, Lesotho and Swaziland (Van den Berg, 2005). The international tests such as Monitoring Learning and Achievement (MLA) subjected to Grade IV in 1999, the Southern and Eastern African Consortium for Monitoring Education Quality (SAQMEC) written by Grade VI learners in 2005, the Trends in International Mathematics and Science Study (TIMMS) administered to Grade VIII learners in 1999 and 2003 and the Progress in International Reading Literacy Study (PIRLS) conducted with Grade V learners in 2006, suggest that South African schools are among the worst performers in Mathematics and Literacy (Bloch, 2009: 60–8).

The Diagnostic Report (National Planning Commission, 2011) notes that the government has made serious efforts to raise the quality of education of poor children; however, these attempts have largely failed. Apart from a small minority of learners who attend former-white schools and a small minority of schools performing well in largely black areas, the quality of public education still remains poor. Learners in historically white schools perform better, and their scores improve with successive years of schooling. In contrast, in the majority of schools with black learners, the learner scores start off lower, and show little improvement between Grades III and V. Where there has been some improvement as measured by the pass rate of those who sat the 2011 matriculation exam which was 70 per cent, only 23 per cent achieved a university entrance pass (Department of Basic Education in National Planning Commission, 2011). Research conducted in South Africa by van der Berg (2005: 4) revealed that despite narrowing attainment differentials, unprecedented resource transfers to black schools and large inflows of black learners to historically white schools, studies have shown that historically white and Indian schools still far outperform black and coloured schools in the Senior Certificate Examinations (SCE) and performance tests at various levels of the school system. The consequence of low quality education on life chances is dire. Patel and Gustafson (2006) noted that while education equity had improved, social equity has in fact deteriorated, as evidenced by the widening gini co-efficient, a measure of social inequality in a society. Most recently, Servaas van der Berg (2011), in a paper entitled 'Low Quality Education: The Poverty Trap', notes that the education system generally produces outcomes that reinforce patterns of power and privilege instead of challenging them. Unsurprisingly, he found that inequalities in schooling outcomes manifest via labour market incomes, perpetuating current patterns of inequality. This economic marginalization contributes to our youths 'socially embedded exclusion', introducing us to the worrying concept of the NEETS, the youth who are not in education, employment and training, numbering close to three million.

Current research has also focused a much sharper lens on classroom practice. An absence of meaningful learning and an accumulation of cognitive deficits as learners progress haltingly through basic education remain everyday realities for the poor. In the CREATE numeracy tests, learners performed way below the levels expected of them (Pereira, 2010). Prior learning for the majority of learners was poor, that is, they were not on the expected level for their grade, and the specific numeracy outcomes which required deeper analytical skills were poor. There are serious gaps in the pedagogical content knowledge related to many learning areas, including Mathematics, in primary schools.

Other research notes that there is very little actual teaching and learning taking place: lessons often start late, much time is spent maintaining order, teachers do most of the talking and learners are passive and contribute little (Motala & Dieltiens, 2011). This confirms earlier research which found that many teachers come late to school, leave early and spend only some 46 per cent of their time teaching during a 35-hour week, with most of the rest of their time at school spent on administrative tasks (HSRC, 2005: xi; Taylor et al., 2010). Many Foundation Phase (Grades I–III) teachers are unable to adequately teach learners how to read and write (Taylor et al., 2010).

In research conducted in 14 schools in the Eastern Cape and Gauteng, the absence of written work in classrooms was striking, rote learning and chorusing of lessons was common and coverage of the curriculum was very uneven (Dieltiens et al., 2012). The use of workbooks in the Eastern Cape varied widely between schools, and there were significant differences in the breadth of coverage across Learning Outcomes and in how specific content is covered. Findings suggest that more attention needs to be paid to investigating the differences within and between schools in terms of opportunities to learn and how this may play itself out in terms of learner performance (Venkat, 2012).

Inadequate mastery of the language of learning and teaching is a major factor in the abysmally low levels of learner achievement; yet many parents prefer (with their children's concurrence) to have their children taught in the second language of English by teachers who are themselves second-language speakers of English (Lafon, 2009; Alexander, 2010).

Home support for learning reflects the racially divided and class-stratified nature of South African society, with poorer parents lacking in the time and the cultural capital to adequately support their children's education and middle-class parents more likely to encourage learning and to send their children to higher performing schools. Despite their general lack of participation in school affairs and their low levels of involvement in their children's learning, school-going is highly valued by parents, to the extent of making the best of what one has, or keeping one's child in a school one does not like but which is better than no school at all (Luxomo & Motala, 2011).

How is it that South Africa, with such a strong culture of school enrolment, has such poor levels of learner achievement? Is it due to slow progress in overcoming the legacies of apartheid, or due to the poor training and indifferent quality of instruction by overworked teachers, or due to the impact of perpetual and idealistic curriculum and policy transformation? There is a shortage of facilities and a lack of infrastructure, but there is also an ineffective management and utilization of and care for existing resources – human, financial and material. More infrastructure, better facilities and more funding do not translate directly, if at all, into better quality education. While it is true that fiscal resource inputs are not the only means to the desired educational outcomes, they do, however, have an effect on learner performance. According to Van der Berg (2007: 851), equity of educational outcomes requires both well-targeted fiscal expenditure and efficient schools. Fiscal resources do not necessarily translate into scarce real resources (qualified teachers and school management) required to improve school performance, and even where resources are available, their effective utilization is not guaranteed.

Lack of meaningful access also has to do with the large classes, overcrowded classrooms and the consequent lack of individualized attention which are in part corollaries of high enrolments. It has to do with a certain lack of policy realism, and poor policy implementation; with poverty, and with parental expectations, as much as with a lack of parental and community involvement, or their willingness and capacity to be involved and with the stresses of heavy curricular and administrative demands. The transition from the Foundation Phase to the Intermediate Phase – which is also the point at which English usually takes the place of mother-tongue instruction – appears particularly difficult, due to a fuller and more intensive curriculum and much higher expectations.

Lack of meaningful access has to do, too, with poor time management, a misutilization of teachers and a shortage of expertise in specific subjects; with teacher disillusionment and learner demotivation; with a culture of disrespect; and with bullying, sexual harassment and corporal punishment, and perhaps the lack of awareness, or the ineffectiveness, of alternative forms of discipline. Not least, it has to do with a tendency on the part of all stakeholders to blame each other, and to fail to take responsibility for our present educational condition of meaningless access. One of the features of the last two years, however, is the mobilization of significant sectors in society of the recognition of the depth and breadth of the challenge, a focus on civil society action and broad consensus on the overall direction to be taken (Chisholm, 2011).

What about the vexed relationship between quality and equity? Policy documents and the governments vision on education suggests that it has a mandate to achieve both. The evidence shows that the state has succeeded in achieving a degree of equity, and not quality. The achievement of equity has to be qualified since there are limits to the education expenditure, which can be redistributive, since teacher salaries are based on qualifications and experience, and better qualified and more experienced teachers tend to be present in the better-off schools. Sayed and Ahmed (2011), suggest that while for the state, equity/quality is conceptualized in a simple input-output model, it is less clear how these processes converge and diverge at the policy level and whether both were addressed. At the heart of this debate is whether effective pedagogy is achievable in resource-constrained contexts (O'Sullivan, 2006). Access to education is linked to development, the reduction of poverty and leads to long-term improvements in productivity and well-being. The promise of an innovative pedagogy in Curriculum 2005, did not translate into quality learning outcomes, and the effects of school processes are increasingly being posited as important variables in explaining poor performance. Social equity and education equity need to be addressed simultaneously, so that the low quality of education offered in poor communities does not continue to perpetuate their exclusion (Motala et al., in press).

The delivery of quality education has also been affected by the constitutional provision which allows for considerable decision making and diversity of approaches at the provincial and local level. Some provinces have moved ahead in translating national mandates on literacy and numeracy strategies, while others, such as Limpopo and Eastern Cape have faltered, indicating the pervasiveness of rural provincial inequities. Textbook delivery and the failure by mid-year in 2012 to ensure delivery to schools is the subject of a legal court battle in these two provinces with the national Minister of Education, being taken to task (*Times*, 11 June 2012). While decentralization and devolved education reform processes are part of a global reform agenda, in the South African context it has not worked, and as Weber (2002) has noted 'gave legitimacy to organs of government which had no real power'. Highlighting the policy-implementation nexus, Little (2008), suggests that political will is a necessary but not a sufficient ingredient of educational reforms. Policies and constitutional enactments do not ensure education for all on the ground. The non-technical political factors such as adequate finance and human resources, involvement and a sense of ownership, regular monitoring and evaluation and sustained effort are all necessary conditions of the delivery of quality and equity in education.

Concluding comments

Equity in access to education remains a goal yet to be fully achieved in the South African context. Participation and progression remains strongly associated with household income, despite commitments to pro-poor policies and the investment of resources. Inequality manifests itself in many ways, with socio-economic status continuing to be the major determinant of progressing through grades at appropriate ages, reaching levels of achievement necessary to complete schooling successfully, and with subsequent access to labour markets that can provide meaningful life opportunities. Provincial disparities remain striking in South Africa with significant differences in the quality and quantity of schooling. Universal access and completion cannot be achieved without more equitable opportunities to learn. Pedagogy is often the missing ingredient in EFA discussions of quality which foreground indicators and outcomes and ignore processes very relevant in the South African schooling context. Meaningful access requires learning that has utility using effective pedagogies which will result in appropriate age grade achievement and progression, and transition between schooling phases.

Achieving quality, equity and social justice in education remains a global challenge, and the tensions in developing countries between fiscal restraint and investing in social expenditure has resulted in a degree of pragmatism and realism about choices that have to be made. Whether the pro-poor agenda has been achieved in the context of the huge resource divides that continue to persist, suggests that the social justice approach which promotes fairness, rights and equal opportunities must be foregrounded. Only then will rights become realities in South Africa.

References

Alexander, N. (2010). 'Understanding Language Issues in the SA Context', Paper presented at a Royal Netherlands Embassy/Department of Basic Education Workshop, September, Pretoria.

Amsterdam, C. (2006). 'Adequacy in the South African Context: A Concept Analysis', *Perspectives in Education* 24, 2, pp. 25–34.

Bloch, G. (2009). 'The SA Education Road Map. CREATE South Africa Policy Brief No. 3', The Education Policy Unit at the University of the Witwatersrand, South Africa.

Chisholm, L. (2011). *The Challenge of South African Schooling: Dimensions, Targets and Initiatives in Transformation Audit. Institute of Justice and Reconciliation* (University of Cape Town), pp. 50–8.

Department of Basic Education (1996). *South African Schools Act* (Pretoria: Government printers).

Department of Basic Education in National Planning Commission (2011). Government Policies.

Department of Education (1998). *National Norms and Standards for School Funding* (Pretoria: Department of Education).

— (2005). *Department of Education* (Pretoria: Government Printers).

— (2008). *Foundations for Learning Campaign* (Pretoria: Department of Education).

— (2010). *Action Plan to 2014: Towards the Realisation of Schooling 2025 – The Shorter Version* (Pretoria: Department of Education).

Dieltiens, V., Letsatsi, S. and Ngwenya, E. (2012). 'Inside the School Gates: What do Learners have access to', in S. Motala, V. Dieltiens and Y. Sayed (eds), *Finding Place and Keeping Pace* (South Africa: HSRC press), pp. 72–87.

Financial and Fiscal Commission (1998). *Public Expenditure and Basic Social Services in South Africa* (Johannesburg: Kits Kopie).

Fiske, E. B. and Ladd, H. F. (2004). 'Balancing Public and Private Resources for Basic Education: School Fees in Post-Apartheid South Africa', in L. Chisholm (ed.), *Changing Class: Educational and Social Change in Post-apartheid South Africa* (Cape Town: HSRC Press), pp. 267–91.

Giese, S., Zide, H., Koch, R. and Hall, K. (2009). *A Study on the Implementation and Impact of the No-Fee and Exemption Policies* (Cape Town: Alliance for Children's Entitlement to Social Security).

Giroux, H. A. (1997). *Pedagogy and the Politics of Hope: Theory, Culture and Schooling* (Boulder, CO: Westview Press).

Grant Lewis, S. and Motala, S. (2004). 'Education Decentralisation and Quest for Equity, Democracy and Quality', in L. Chisholm (ed.), *Changing Class: Education and Social Change in Post-apartheid South Africa* (Cape Town: Zed Books), pp. 115–42.

Hall, K. and Giese, S. (2008). 'Addressing Quality through School Fees and School Funding', in S. Pendlebury, L. Lake and S. C. Lake (eds), *South African Child Gauge 2008/9* (Cape Town: Children's Institute, University of Cape Town), pp. 25–33.

Harber, C. (2001). *State of Transition: Post-Apartheid Education Reforms in South Africa* (Oxford: Symposium Book).

HSRC (2005). *Educator Workload in South Africa, Report for the Education Labour Relations Council* (Pretoria: Human Sciences Research Council).

Lafon, M. (2009). *The Impact of Language on Educational Access, CREATE Pathways to Access Series* (Brighton: Consortium for Research on Educational Access, Transitions and Equity, University of Sussex).

Lewin, K. M. and Wang, L. (2011). *Education and Change in Rich, Poor and National Minority Areas in China: Two Decades of Transition.* Pathways to Access Research Monographs No: 61 (Brighton: University of Sussex).

Little, A. (2008). *EFA Politics, policies and progress.* Create Pathways to Access Research Monographs no 13 (London: Institute of Education).

Luxomo, G. (2011). Parental Participation and Meaningful Access in South African Schools CREATE, Policy Brief 4, Centre for International Education, University of Sussex, Britain.

Mestry, R. (2012). A Critical Analysis of the National Norm and Standards for School Funding Policy: Implication for Social Justice and Equities Professorial Inauguration, University of Johannesburg, 12 June 2012.

Morrow, W. (2007). *Learning to Teach in South Africa* (Cape Town: HSRC Press).

Motala, S. (2006) 'Education Resourcing in Post-apartheid South Africa: The Impact of Finance Equity Reforms in Public Schooling', *Perspectives in Education* 24, 2, pp. 79–94.

Motala, S. and Dieltiens, V. (2011). 'Educational Access in South Africa', Country brief, 2008, Johannesburg/Brighton/University of Sussex.

Motala, S. and Sayed, Y. (2009). '"No Fee" Schools in South Africa', Policy Brief Number 7 August 2009. CREATE, Centre for International Education, University of Sussex, Brighton.

Motala, S., Dieltiens, V. and Sayed, Y. (2006). 'Finding Place and Keeping Pace: Exploring Meaningful and Equitable Learning in South African Schools', *Quarterly Review of Education and Training in South Africa* 13, 2, pp. 1–38.

Motala, S., Dieltiens, V. and Sayed, Y. (eds) (in press). *Finding Place and Keeping Pace* (HSRC Press: South Africa).

Motala, S., Dieltiens, V., Carrim, N., Kgobe, P., Moyo, G. and Rembe, S. (2007). Educational Access in South Africa', Country Analytic Review. www.create-rpc.org

National Planning Commission (2011). *Diagnostic Report* (Pretoria: Government Printers).

Ndimande, B. (2006). 'Parental Choice: The Liberty Principle in Education Finance', *Perspectives in Education* 24, 2, pp. 143–56.

O'Sullivan, M. (2006). 'Lesson Observation and Quality in Primary Education as Contextual Teaching and Learning Processes', *International Journal of Education Development* 26, pp. 246–60.

OECD (2008). *Reviews of National Policies for Education: South Africa* (Paris: OECD).

Patel, F. and Gustaffson, M. (2006). 'Undoing Apartheids Legacy: Pro Poor Shifts in South African Public Schooling', *Perspectives in Education* 24, 2, pp. 45–55.

Pereira, C. (2010). 'Access to Learning –Mathematics Performance in Schools in Gauteng and Eastern Cape', CREATE South Africa Policy Brief No.3, Johannesburg/ Brighton: University of Witwatersrand EPU/ University of Sussex.

RSA (1996). *South African Schools Act, Act no.84 of 1996* (Pretoria: Republic of South Africa).

Sayed, Y. and Ahmed, R. (2011). 'Education Quality in Post-apartheid South Africa Policy: Balancing Equity, Diversity, Rights and Participation', *Comparative Education* 47, 1, pp. 103–18.

Sayed, Y. and Soudien, C. (2003). '(Re) framing Education Exclusion and Inclusion Discourses: Limits and Possibilities', *Bulletin* 34, pp. 9–19.

Strauss, J. and Burger, M. (2000). *Monitoring Learning Achievement Project* (Pretoria: Department of Education).

Taylor, N., Mabogoane, T., Shindler, J. and Akoobhai, B. (2010). Seeds of the Struggle: The fealing of underage and overage enrolment amongst Grade 4 learners in South Africa. Create Pathways to Access. Research monograph no.47.

Tomasevski, K. (2006). 'The State of the Right to Education Worldwide: Free or Fee', 2006 Global Report. www.katarinatomasevski.com. Accessed 23 January 2008.

Van der Berg, S. (2005). 'How Effective are Poor Schools? Poverty and Educational Outcomes in South Africa', Paper delivered at SACMEQ International Invitational Research Conference, Paris, September 2005.

— (2007). 'Apartheid's Enduring Legacy: Inequalities in Education', *Journal of African Economies* 16, 5, pp. 849–80.

— (2011). 'Low Quality Education as a Poverty Trap', March 2011. Stellenbosch University, Programme to Support Proper Development. EU /Presidency.

Venkat, H. (2012). 'Reading between the Lines: Examining "Opportunity to Learn" in a Sample of Eastern Cape Workbooks', in S. Motala, V. Dieltiens and Y. Sayed (eds), *Finding Place and Keeping Pace* (HSRC Press: South Africa).

Veriava, F. (2005). 'Free to Learn: A Discussion Paper on the School Fee Exemption Policy', in A. Leatt and S. Rosa (eds), *Targeting Poverty Alleviation to Make Children's Rights Real* (Cape Town: Children's Institute), pp. 267–91.

Weber (2002). 'An Ambiguous, Centred Terrain: Government Models in a New South African Society', *International Journal of Education Development* 22, 2, pp. 617–28.

Wildeman, R. A. (2008). 'Reviewing Eight Years of the Implementation of the School Funding Norms, 2000–2008', Research Paper. Economic Governance Programme. Pretoria: Idasa.

Wilson, S. (2006). 'Taming the Constitution: Rights and Reform in the South African Education System', *South African Journal on Human Rights* 20, 3, pp. 418–47; www.law.wits.ac.za

Woolman, S. and Fleisch, B. (2006). 'South Africa's Education Legislation, Quasi-markets and De Facto School Choice', *Perspectives in Education* 24, 2, pp. 1–24.

World Education Forum (2000). 'Presentation of the "World Declaration on Education for All" and the "Dakar Framework for Action – Education for All: Meeting our Collective Commitments"', Dakar.

9

Swaziland: Access, Quality and Relevance

Edmund Zizwe Mazibuko
University of Swaziland

Introduction

In order to appreciate the developments in education in Swaziland, it is important to appreciate the history and political developments in the country prior to independence. The kingdom of Swaziland is a small, landlocked country in the southeastern part of southern Africa. It is surrounded by South Africa on the north, west and southeast and by the Republic of Mozambique on the east. Swaziland is about 17,000 square kilometres in size, stretching for approximately 193 kilometres from the north to south and about 145 kilometres from east to west. According to the latest figures, the country's population is estimated to be about 1.1 million.

Political background

According to tradition, the people of present-day Swaziland migrated south before the sixteenth century to what is now Mozambique. Following a series of conflicts with people living in the area of modern Maputo, the Swazis settled in northern Zululand in about 1750. Unable to match the growing strength of the Zulus, the Swazis moved northwards in the 1800s and established themselves in the area of modern or present-day Swaziland.

The Swazis consolidated their power under several able leaders. The most important of these leaders was Mswati II from whom the Swazi nation derives its name. Under the leadership of Mswati in the 1840s, the Swazi expanded their territory to the northwest and stabilized the southern frontier with the Zulus.

Contact with the British came early in Mswati's reign when he asked British authorities in South Africa for protection against the Zulu raids into Swaziland. It was also during Mswati's reign that the first whites settled in the country. Following Mswati's death, the Swazis reached agreements with the British and South African authorities over a range of issues, including independence, claims over resources by Europeans, administrative authority and security. The country was under the control of South Africa between 1894 and 1902. After the Anglo Boer war of 1899–1902, Britain assumed control of Swaziland.

Swaziland became a British protectorate under the High Commissioner based in South Africa. In 1921 after more than 20 years of rule by Queen Regent Lobatsibeni, Sobhuza II became the Ngwenyama or head of the Swazi nation. In the same year, a legislative body or advisory council of elected Europeans were appointed to advise the British High Commissioner on non-Swazi affairs. In 1944 the High Commissioner conceded that the council had no official status.

In the early years of colonial rule, the British thought that Swaziland would eventually be incorporated into South Africa. After World War II, however, South Africa's intensification of racial discrimination induced the British to prepare Swaziland for independence. The Swazis also did not want to be under South Africa because they were aware of how Africans were treated in that country. Political activity intensified in Swaziland in the 1960s which saw several political parties formed and all pushing for independence and economic development.

The traditional leaders including the King and his inner council formed the Imbokodvo National Movement, a group that capitalized on a closer identification with the Swazi way of life. Four other parties were formed and these largely urban parties had few ties with rural areas where the majority of Swazis lived. The Imbokodvo National Movement won the elections in 1964 of the first Legislative Council in which the Swazi would participate. In 1966 Britain agreed to discuss a new constitution for Swaziland which agreed on a constitutional monarch for Swaziland with self government to follow parliamentary elections in 1967. Swaziland became independent on 6 September 1968.

The development of formal education

Like most other African countries, the country had its own traditional type of education long before Europeans introduced formal Western education. Education in Africa had been purely indigenous and this is what is known as

African traditional education (Fafunwa, 1974). In a later discussion this is also referred to as community participation in education (Fafunwa, 1993).

However, this section discusses the development of modern formal education in Swaziland. Cazziol (2002) argues that the history of education in Swaziland was characterized by three distinct periods, namely, the missionary period, the pre-independence period and the post-independence period. The missionary period is the period when Christian missions came to Swaziland and brought with them Western culture in the form of religion and the introduction of formal education with its focus on the development of reading and writing skills of the people so that they could provide the civil service required by the colonial administration. In Swaziland, the period during which missionaries were active in the development of education began in 1844 when Rev. James Allison of the Methodist Church tried to establish a school in Mahamba. However, this was not successful, because of the conflict between King Mswati II and his half-brothers, forcing the missionaries to leave the country. The missionaries returned in 1880 and settled in Mahamba in southern Swaziland where they established a school, marking the beginning period of the missionary era in Swaziland. This saw the arrival of a number of different mission denominations in Swaziland to establish schools and churches. The Lutheran missionaries arrived in 1887 and established themselves in Mbabane in the Hhohho region and Mbekelweni in the Manzini region where they built churches and schools. These missionaries were later followed by other missionary groups who established mission stations in different parts of the country, such as the African Methodist Episcopal Church (AMEC) and the Church of the Nazarene in 1904, the Norway Free Evangelical Mission in 1910, the Pilgrim Holiness Church in 1911 and the Roman Catholic Church in 1914. Though European education was initially regarded with suspicion by the Swazi, it later became extremely popular because it provided a pool of educated and literate personnel.

The pre-independence period spans the years between 1946 and 1966. What is of note is the initial reluctance of the colonial administration to involve itself in the development of education during this era as there was active involvement by missionaries in the development of education. It was only in 1946 that the colonial administration built a trade school for practical training. The missions expanded their work through assistance from government funding. They built schools in the mission stations, expanding the primary schools they had initially built in the mission centres. In addition, in some mission stations clinics and health centres were built, expanding the work of the missions beyond evangelizing. The expansion of education resulted in a shortage of teachers and the colonial administration realized the need for building a teacher training college at William Pitcher College to train both primary and secondary school teachers.

Current basic structures of education

The structure of the education system in Swaziland includes pre-primary, primary, secondary, non-formal and adult education and tertiary education.

Pre-primary

The policy of the Ministry of Education and Training has moved away from pre-school education that caters for children from three to six years to a stage that incorporates children from zero to three years. However, the Ministry of Education and Training has no formal control over the early level of education because it has not yet been fully integrated into the formal school system. Pre-schools in Swaziland are run by private interests and the curriculum is not uniform. Most preschools are run as businesses. Table 9.1 shows the number of pre-school inspections by the Ministry of Education in 2010.

Basic education

The concept of basic education is in most policy documents equated to primary education. However, in one education document it was stated that in the future it is the aim of the government to extend basic education to nine years of schooling (MoE, 1996: 16). This shift has now been realized and Swaziland has adopted a ten year basic education programme as part of the Southern Africa Development Community (SADC) Protocol on education. The official age of

Table 9.1 Number of pre-school inspections by Ministry of Education in 2010

Region	More than once	Never visited	Once a term	Once a year	Grand total
Hhohho	31	76	20	64	191
Lubombo	14	51	6	27	98
Manzini	3	61	3	37	104
Shiselweni	1	19	6	15	41
Total	49	207	35	143	434

Source: Ministry of Education, 2011

starting school is six years old. Siswati is the medium of instruction in the first three years, after which English becomes the medium of instruction throughout the school system. At the end of the seven years of primary school, learners sit for the Swaziland Primary Certificate. Students who pass the Swaziland Primary Certificate (SPC) examination proceed to Junior Secondary School. The public is now questioning the need for retaining this examination at this level. The Ministry of Education and Training is currently looking at options that could be implemented to replace this examination.

In 2007, there were 556 formally recognized primary schools enrolling 232,572 learners of whom 48 per cent were females; some 43 junior secondary schools enrolled 60,002 learners of whom 47 per cent were female and 157 senior secondary schools enrolled 22,838 students of whom 48 per cent were females, and due to unmet demands for secondary education an additional 3,084 students were enrolled in illegal private schools since they were not registered with the Ministry of Education and Training (World Bank, 2010: 25). These latter schools are not monitored by the Ministry of Education and Training and they are not recognized as examination centres. They are run as businesses. However, in 2011 the government made an effort to close all schools that were not formally recognized and required them to register with the Ministry of Education. Those that failed to register or were denied registration because they did not meet the requirements have since been closed.

Free primary school education is provided up to Grade IV in 2012. Some of the challenges facing the government at this level include, among others: not enough classrooms to cater to the increase in enrolment resulting from the introduction of free primary education; overcrowding is some classes, particularly in Grades I to IV; not enough primary school teachers to match the increase in enrolment and inadequate teaching and learning resources. These raise questions regarding the quality of education provided in the context of free primary education.

Secondary education

The seven year primary cycle is followed by a five year secondary cycle, of which the first three years constitute Junior Secondary and the last two years High School. As in a number of countries in sub-Saharan Africa, the Swaziland school system allows only a small proportion of students to access secondary school. A large number of the students drop out at the end of primary school. The government is exploring ways that will ensure that graduates at this level possess the knowledge and skills required to participate fully in their country's development. This has led to the introduction of pre-vocational education in 16 schools as a pilot project aiming at skilling secondary school pupils with practical and entrepreneurial skills. However, this programme has not been rolled out to more schools. Even in the pilot schools we have seen a decrease in the number of students taking pre-vocational subjects (Examinations Council Swaziland, 2012).

At the end of the first three years of Junior Secondary education students take the Junior Certificate Examination, which is used for selection purposes for the last two years of senior secondary education. In the 1980s, the Junior Certificate examination certificate was also used for admission to the Swaziland College of Technology for vocational and technical training. The certificate was also used for admission to a primary teacher training programme in the three teacher training colleges (TTCs) namely William Pitcher College, Ngwane Teacher Training College and Nazarene Teacher Training College, and also training in the College of Nursing. However, with the increase in the number of learners completing high school, the entry qualifications to these institutions have since been raised to passes in the school leaving examinations.

For many years Swaziland followed the GCE 'O' Level curriculum. In 2007, the country introduced the Cambridge International General Certificate of Secondary Education (IGCSE) curriculum to replace the GCE 'O' Level, in a programme that saw the IGCSE localized into the Swaziland General Certificate of Secondary Education (SGCSE). The SGCSE curriculum was introduced in the country's schools in 2007. Based on the examination results from the SGCSE, students may enter the universities in the country for degree programmes, the Swaziland College of Technology for diploma programmes or the teacher training colleges for diploma programmes. Students also use this certificate for entry into universities in South Africa. However, some universities in South Africa require students holding the SGCSE to complete a bridging programme before being admitted to degree programmes because this qualification is perceived to be lower than the South African National Senior Certificate, formerly the Matric certificate. Swaziland is now embarking on a process of introducing a higher school leaving qualification to put the Swaziland qualification on a par with other qualifications in the region. There has been a steady increase in the number of candidates sitting for the SGCSE public examination. However, the pass rate of candidates who manage to get at least four credits including English Language has not increased significantly as shown in Table 9.2. On average, only 13 per cent of school graduates meet the entry requirements for tertiary education each year. However, these students do not necessarily get admitted

Table 9.2 Credit pass and overall pass attainment trends 2007–11

Year	Key	Total credits	Total entries	Per cent credits
2007	#	1,073	9,850	10.88
	Ω	7,921	9,860	80.33
2008	#	1,222	9,241	13.22
	Ω	7,200	9,241	77.91
2009	#	1,365	9,863	13.84
	Ω	8,644	9,863	87.64
2010	#	1,395	10,142	13.75
	Ω	8,813	10,142	86.90
2011	#	1,430	10,270	13.92
	Ω	8,968	10,270	87.32

Key: # – Candidates who attained grade C or above including English Language
Ω- Candidates who attained grade G or better including English language
Source: Examinations Council of Swaziland, 2012

in the local tertiary institutions because of the limited number taken each year because of space constraints and also because the government does not have the finances to pay the students tertiary scholarships. On average about 07 per cent of students who graduate from high school do not qualify for tertiary education and these are the students who end up joining the ranks of the unemployed.

Non-formal education

Non-formal education is currently in the hands of non-governmental organizations (NGOs) and other bodies. They mainly address the needs for adult literacy and numeracy programmes. The Sebenta National Institute is responsible for organizing literacy classes for adults who have not had a chance to go to school. Today the institute also has classes for children who have not benefited from the formal school system. Table 9.3 shows a steady increase in the number of students who are taking advantage of the programmes offered by the Institute. With free primary education in place in the public schools, there has also been an increase in the number of students in the Non-formal Upper Primary Education (NUPE) programme.

Students who have failed to pass their Junior Certificate and O Levels can study on a part-time basis and attend upgrading classes at the Emlalatini Development Centre. Students can study any subject and sit for the relevant public examination at the centre. Table 9.4 shows the enrolment at the centre over a period of seven years.

Table 9.3 Sebenta Enrolment

Programmes/ levels	2004	2005	2006	2007	2008	2009	2010	2011
Basic	1,305	2,055	2,264	2,408	2,648	2,674	2,687	2,907
Post Basic	584	326	315	388	426	447	469	472
NUPE	35	404	440	480	528	554	582	603

Source: Sebenta National Institute Strategic Plan

Table 9.4 Enrolment by level and year

Year	JC	O'Level	Total
2010	365	650	1,015
2009	350	410	760
2008	320	380	700
2007	310	230	540
2006	211	340	551
2005	252	371	623
2004	240	350	590

Source: MoE (2011: 13) Annual Report of the Ministry of Education

Management of schools

There are three types of school that are found in the education system in Swaziland. These are government schools, government aided schools and private schools. The main differences between the types of school are the level of government support and the method of control. The government pays all expenses in government schools, pays the salaries of teachers in aided schools and does not financially support private schools. The overall control of education in Swaziland lies with the government, whether it concerns government schools, aided schools or privately financed schools. In government schools, this control is exercised through the principal working in collaboration with the school committee. In aided schools the control is through the Grantee or School Manager working closely with the principal. In private schools the control is through the chairman of the school board. As a matter of policy, the government encourages self-help programmes, such as community-based schools where both governmental and parental participation are common. Most of the aided schools are affiliated to missions and churches. The popular churches that own schools in Swaziland are the Roman Catholic Church, the Church of the Nazarene, the

Anglican Church, The Methodist Church and the Wesleyan Church. These churches contribute significantly to the provision of education in Swaziland as they have numerous primary and secondary schools that offer good education to the Swazi population.

The education system in Swaziland is centralized, with all the power and authority located at the national level. The Director of Education is in charge of the professional aspect and working closely with him/her are the Chief Inspector Primary, Chief Inspector Secondary and the Chief Inspector Colleges. There is minimal delegation of power at the regional level with the Regional Education Officers who report directly to the Chief Inspector Primary. However the main task of the Regional Education Officers is to ensure that national policies are implemented in schools. The Ministry of Education and Training manages the curriculum through the National Curriculum Centre, assessment procedures through schools and the Examinations Council of Swaziland, and the recruitment of teachers through the Teaching Service Commission. The financial operations of the Ministry of Education are decided and monitored elsewhere. Financial planning is not controlled in the Ministry of Education but is controlled by the Ministry of Finance. This situation offers many challenges for the Ministry of Education.

Tertiary education

Up until 1975 the University College of Swaziland (UCS) formed part of the University of Botswana, Lesotho and Swaziland (UBLS), formerly known as the University of Basutoland, Bechuanaland and Swaziland (UBBS), which had its headquarters in Lesotho between 1954 and 1975. The University of Swaziland developed from the UBLS. The UBBS had developed from the Pius XII Catholic University College at Roma, itself the product of a long-held desire for an institution of higher learning for Africans among the Catholic hierarchy in Southern Africa. Pius XII was a college of the University of South Africa (UNISA) and was originally intended to prepare students for the Bachelor of Arts degree. In 1954, a special agreement was reached with UNISA that allowed Pius XII to teach other courses leading to the degrees of Bachelor of Commerce, Bachelor of Science and Post-graduate Diploma in Education.

In the 1950s the college experienced problems affecting its future, such as finance and deteriorating ties with UNISA including restrictions on the college's policy for the admission of students (UNISWA, 2012). By 1963, there were 180 students at the college. In the same year, negotiations were completed between the High Commission Territories and the Roman Catholic Church responsible for the college and as a result of these negotiations a university was established. UBLS conferred its first degrees in Arts, Sciences and Humanities in 1967 after a transitional period in which former Pius XII students continued to take the University of South Africa degrees (UNISWA, 2012). From a total of 188 students in 1964, the student enrolment in the university grew to 402 students in 1970 of which 145 came from Lesotho and the other students came from Botswana, Rhodesia, South Africa and elsewhere.

Comparatively UBLS had little presence in Botswana and Swaziland during its first phase of its existence spanning from 1964 to 1970, although it was equally funded by the three governments of Botswana, Lesotho and Swaziland. In Swaziland the presence of the university was limited to the Faculty of Agriculture in Luyengo and in Botswana it was limited to the Division of Extra Mural Services. The second phase of the development of the university spanned the period from 1971 to 1976. This phase saw the introduction of new campuses in Gaborone in Botswana and Kwaluseni in Swaziland. These campuses were developed through funding from the United States, Britain, Canada, Denmark, the Netherlands, the Anglo-American Corporation and the governments of Botswana, Lesotho and Swaziland. In 1974, some programmes were devolved to the campuses in Botswana and Swaziland.

Following student unrest at Roma, and strained relations between the central UBLS administration and the Lesotho Government over implementation of agreed development plans, the Roma campus was withdrawn from UBLS and constituted as the National University of Lesotho (NUL) on 20 October 1975. In 1976 following recommendations of the Hunter Report, negotiations between the governments of Botswana and Swaziland led to the setting up of the University of Botswana and Swaziland, with two constituent university colleges in Botswana and Swaziland. The two countries realized that in the long term the two university colleges would develop into independent national universities. A development plan for 1975–85 was agreed, with student numbers rising so as to justify independent institutions after the 1981/2 academic year. The agreement was effected as scheduled in 1982 when the University of Swaziland was established with two campuses in Kwaluseni and Luyengo. Today the university has a third campus in Mbabane for the Faculty of Health Sciences. Kwaluseni is the main campus and the administrative centre of the university and has the following departments: Education, Science, Social Science, Commerce, Humanities and the Institute of Distance Education. His Majesty King Mswati III is the Chancellor of the University. Four members of the University Council are appointed by the King. Currently the Chairman of the Council is Prince Phinda who has been in this position for more than a decade. Table 9.5 shows the degrees conferred by the university in the last ten years.

There has been a steady increase in the number of graduates during this period. The Institute of Distance Education is contributing significantly since it admits most of the students who cannot be admitted on a full-time basis. In the last two years the largest number of graduates came from the Institute of Distance Education. The biggest challenge facing graduates is that the job opportunities in the country are limited and a large number of these graduates are unemployed or pursuing careers that are not related to their training. For example, a large number of the graduates from the Faculty of Agriculture end up taking teaching appointments in schools and teaching mathematics and science because of the shortage of teachers in these subjects. Some graduates from the Faculty of Social Science also end up teaching in schools as there is a shortage of teachers, particularly in primary schools and the sciences in secondary schools.

For a long time the University of Swaziland was the only university in the country. This resulted in many qualifying students failing to get admitted because of limited space. Today the government is encouraging more universities to be established. The first such university to be established is Limkokwing University from Malaysia with a campus in Mbabane and offering associate degree programmes in the technical fields. In 2010 the Church of the Nazarene upgraded its Nursing College in Manzini, teacher training college in Manzini

Table 9.5 Degrees conferred by year and faculty, 2002–11

Programmes	2002	2003	2004	2005	2006	2007	2008	2009	2010	2011
Agriculture	49	75	82	83	100	129	134	156	327	163
Commerce	94	81	112	126	84	97	72	94	173	187
Education	38	38	6	9	13	24	18	25	232	189
Health	34	39	65	56	60	62	56	69	171	168
Humanities	113	119	122	112	115	129	117	102	87	52
Law	33	53	8	3	18	—	5	—	—	—
LLB	26	19	26	58	42	61	52	62	76	57
Science	53	47	44	52	72	62	68	56	63	69
Soc. Sc.	67	57	56	69	58	73	64	63	49	48
IDE	28	70	65	107	58	110	156	164	422	449
Post-Grad.	4	11	17	14	18	13	7	13	21	26
Total	539	609	603	691	638	760	749	1,308	1,620	1,406

Source: University of Swaziland Calendar, 2012/2013

and its Bible College in Siteki into the Southern Africa Nazarene University (SANU). The Zimbabwe-based Midland State University (MSU) is also offering programmes in the country in teacher education and business administration. The Swaziland Christian University (SCU) is being built in Mbabane and has started courses in counselling and psychology. There is still a large number of Swazis who are enrolled in tertiary institutions in South Africa.

There are two government teacher training colleges namely the William Pitcher College in Manzini producing primary and secondary teachers at diploma level and Home Economics teachers and the Ngwane Teacher's College in Nhlangano which commenced operations in 1982 and produces only primary school teachers. The Swaziland College of Technology (SCOT) in Mbabane produces technical teachers and commercial education teachers. SCOT was founded in 1946 as a trade school. In 2012 SCOT partnered with Vaal University of Technology to offer degree courses at SCOT. There are plans to develop the college into a technological university in the future. This development will help to produce the required manpower for the technical fields at the degree level as opposed to the diploma level.

Main goals and priorities for education as set out in key government policy documents

The policies that have been developed by the Ministry of Education since independence in 1968 are based on the principles embodied in the Manifesto of the Imbokodvo National Movement – that education is not only an inalienable right for every child but also a key factor in the development of the individual and of the nation (Dlamini, 1972).

These principles were incorporated in the report of the National Education Commission established by King Sobhuza in 1972 to investigate the organization and future development of education in Swaziland. The report of the Commission was presented to the Cabinet in 1975 and the initial education policy of the government emerged from this document.

The third post-independence National Development Plan (1978/1979–83/1984) committed the Ministry of Education to a policy based on two principles;

• Social demand for education as the guiding principle for the provision of education at the lower levels of the system;

- Manpower requirements determining enrolment and courses at the higher levels.

In order to achieve the principles, the Ministry of Education identified major target areas such as:

- The implementation of Universal Primary Education;
- to be extended to a ten year course of basic education;
- restricting enrolment in high school by manpower requirements; and
- expansion and improvement of teacher training facilities.

The focus then was that educational development at all levels would be directed towards:

- The maintenance and improvement of the quality of education;
- The diversification of the curriculum towards the extension and strengthening of the teaching of practical subjects;
- The production of more school leavers with appropriate skills for employment and self employment not only in the modern sector but more importantly in the area of rural development.

In subsequent years, the Ministry of Education pursued a policy of expansion aimed at the enlargement and equitable distribution of educational opportunities in the country and the development of curricula geared to the needs of national development. The three decades after independence saw the expansion of schools and enrolments responding to the high social demand for education. Enrolment at primary school level almost doubled from 69,055 in 1970 to 112,019 in 1980. Secondary education increased by nearly 200 per cent in the ten year period ending 1980 (Gathu & Mazibuko, 2010). The expansion of schools also necessitated the need to increase the number of trained teachers. The government made efforts to build more teacher training institutions. In the 1970s, the government put more resources into a programme of training teachers through in-service teacher training to meet the increasing need for teachers for the increasing primary school enrolment. The next decades saw the government focus more ensuring that the quality of education was of a high standard.

The diversification of the curriculum

The increasing unemployment in the country has necessitated the need to diversify the school curriculum. The major problem facing the country is that the academic bias of the system has fed the traditional desire for white collar, especially civil service, employment. This concern has been there since independence and has not been addressed effectively by the education system even at this present time. The education system has been producing a rapidly growing number of school leavers who either cannot or will not participate productively in their own country. The wishes of the Imbokodvo National Movement have not been achieved as it urged that the education system should be given a bias in the interests of the nation. It stated then that,

> The present bias inherited from our colonial past will have to be uprooted branch, stem and root. Today most children at school aspire to be clerks, teachers, nurses, etc., very few thinking of farming, the trades, and handicraft. The Imbokodvo National Movement believes this is wrong. (Dlamini, 1972: 24)

Based on this objective, the government has made efforts to diversify the school curriculum by putting emphasis on practical and vocational subjects. The government recognized the need to provide the kind and quality of education for motivating and preparing students for employment opportunities that can be generated by the economy, to provide more relevant education to enhance the productivity of the labour force and to change attitudes so that farming or working on land is not rejected as a means of livelihood. The secondary school curriculum has been adapted to include practical subjects such as agriculture, home economics and design and technology. However, there is still very little interest in these subjects as very few students take these subjects as compared to the academic-oriented subjects. This shows governmental failure in achieving its push to get young people interested in agriculture and other practical-oriented subjects.

In recent years subjects like information and communication technology have been introduced in the secondary school curriculum. Many schools have computer laboratories through an initiative of the Computer Education Trust, a brainchild of Natie Kirsh one of the country's leading entrepreneurs. However, one of the biggest challenges facing the teaching of ICT in Swaziland is the shortage of experienced ICT teachers, particularly those who have done a teaching qualification. Most of the teachers do not have a teaching qualification. Another problem is that even though many schools benefited from the Computer Education Trust in terms of getting the computers, most of these computers become a problem as they get old and there is no plan on how to service them or replace them when they get old. In a number of schools, most of the computers are not functioning and the learners are not benefiting from them. In some schools in the country, parents pay a small fee to buy computers and make sure that the computers are replaced when they get old.

According to a study by Issacs (2007) on ICT in education in Swaziland, ICT infrastructure indicators in Swaziland showed that in 2004, there were 46.2 per 1,000 persons fixed line subscribers; 113 per 1,000 mobile subscribers; 19 per 1,000 dial up subscribers; 36 per 1,000 internet users

With the appointment of a Senior Inspector, ICT, one hopes that the teaching of ICT in schools in Swaziland will improve. The performance of candidates in the IGCSE ICT examination is not good compared to candidates taking the examination from other countries (CIE, 2011). This points to the fact that there is a need to look at the way the subject is taught in schools and empower teachers with the appropriate skills to teach the subject effectively.

Swaziland localized the senior secondary curriculum from the content-based GCE Ordinary Level to the International General Certificate of Secondary Education (IGCSE). The localized Swaziland General Certificate of Secondary Education (SGCSE) was based on the skills-based IGCSE. Teacher-centred teaching approaches characterized the old curriculum where teaching methods used were lectures, note giving, handouts and all those techniques that focused on predicting examination questions and focusing on those areas that were likely to come up in the examination. The interest on how schools are performing in public examinations and the role of the media in ranking schools is also putting a lot of pressure on teachers as early as primary school to teach for the test rather than to teach learners for conceptual understanding. Studies conducted since the introduction of the IGCSE and subsequently the SGCSE indicate that though the new curriculum puts emphasis on the development of skills, the teaching methods used by teachers do not reflect this focus as teachers continue to use teaching methods that are not aligned to the assessment objectives in the syllabus (Zondo, 2009; Msibi, 2010). This has resulted in students performing badly in public examinations. The situation is made more serious by the fact that there are no professional development opportunities for teachers in the different subject areas.

Equity issues

Gender equality has been a major issue of concern in many countries because of its close link to health and nutrition, economic development, safety and security, etc. The importance of gender equality in education has been the goal for

Education for All Goals (UNESCO, 2000) and the Millenium Development Goals (MDG) (United Nations, 2006). According to UNESCO (2003) the concept of gender equality in education refers to the notion of boys and girls experiencing the same advantages or disadvantages in attending school, receiving teaching methods, curricula, and academic orientation and producing equal learning achievements and subsequent life opportunities.

The Ministry of Education and Training (MOET) is committed in ensuring that children have access to school irrespective of their gender. In addition, the MOET is committed to ensuring that children are safe and protected all the time. There are a number of initiatives in place for the protection of children. These include setting up a National Children Coordinating Unit (NCCU) within the MOET and establishing a 'call-in line' for children to report cases of abuse. A Southern African Development Community (SADC) initiative called Schools as Centres of Care and Support (SCCS) is being implemented in schools to ensure that children are safe, healthy and secure in schools. The education sector faces many challenges and multiple threats including poverty, HIV/AIDS, drought and food insecurity. Schools are therefore challenged in providing the care and support required by most of the vulnerable children, particularly girls, orphans and the disabled. These groups are experiencing problems related to limited access, increasing costs, large numbers of children out of school, deteriorating nutritional status of children attending school and violence against children in and around school. In addition, there are also initiatives that are in place that encourage girls' participation in school and in following programmes in mathematics and science.

In terms of enrolment at the primary school level, gender is not a serious issue as there were no major differences in the enrolments between girls and boys at this level. However, in terms of performance in reading and mathematics, girls performed better in reading than boys, and boys did better in mathematics than girls in two SACMEQ studies. This implied that the Ministry of Education and Training had not been successful in dealing with the issue of gender inequality in these subjects at primary school level (Shabalala, 2011). However, at secondary school level the issue of gender stereotypes has been observed in the choice of subjects and in the performance of girls in public examinations. In the pre-vocational subjects boys are performing better than girls. This is also true of the sciences. Another issue of great concern at this level is that there is a high number of girls dropping out of school as a result of teenage pregnancies.

The Ministry of Education provides free textbooks to all pupils at primary school level as an intervention that started in 2002. To make education more accessible, the Ministry of Education intensified its efforts in reducing the cost of education at primary school level by providing free exercise books and stationery to pupils in Grades I to IV in 2006, and finally rolled out the programme to all primary grades in 2007. Plans to provide Braille textbooks and other learning materials for children with special learning needs are underway. The government has also made efforts to make education inclusive with the establishment of a Special Education Unit which is charged with the responsibility of driving the process. The Ministry of Education built a high school for hearing-impaired students and those with special needs in Malindza in the Lubombo region. However, the results of the students in the first Junior Certificate public examination in 2011 were very poor pointing to the problems that still need to be addressed by the Ministry of Education. These include, among others, the provision of adequate resources, the training of teachers in special education and provision of in-service training for the teachers. Students with special needs should not be disadvantaged by their disability in getting an education of good quality as against children who do not have special needs.

In an effort to address the issue of internal efficiency and reduce drop outs and repetition in schools, the government introduced Continuous Assessment (CA) as a form of teaching and learning approach especially at primary school level. Another strategy used by the Ministry of Education to increase access to basic education and enhance the quality of education was the introduction of the Capitation Grant. Through this programme, a school receives a flat rate per child for all learners enrolled in the school and a further grant for orphaned and vulnerable children registered in the school. The government also pays examination fees for orphaned and vulnerable children. The school is required to submit a budget proposal every year before the money is released to the school

The organization and nature of teacher education

Teachers for the education system are trained in the three teacher training colleges and the two universities, namely, the University of Swaziland and the Southern Africa Nazarene University, a university that was established in 2011 from the amalgamation of the Nazarene Teacher Training College, The Nazarene Nursing College and the Nazarene Bible College. At William Pitcher College, students take a three-year Secondary Teacher's Diploma majoring in any two teaching subjects plus professional training in Education. The college also offers a Primary Teacher's Diploma that qualifies candidates to teach in primary schools majoring in Social Studies, Science and Mathematics and Language Arts. The Ngwane Teacher Training College prepares teachers for the Primary Teacher's Diploma as teachers for primary schools. The Swaziland College of Technology trains teachers at Diploma level for secondary schools in technical subjects and business. Training for teachers at degree level is problematic for technical teachers at the moment. Some are able to pursue degree courses at the University of Botswana. The entry requirement to these institutions is now credit passes in at least five subjects including English language. Prior to 1995, the colleges offered certificate courses and candidates were admitted with less credits. However, since the upgrading of the qualification to Diploma level, many teachers have gone back to college to improve their qualifications. These colleges are affiliated to the University of Swaziland. Some of the teachers are studying with the University of Swaziland and tertiary institutions in South Africa. Most of the teachers who go to the teacher training colleges are those who have not made it to the university. A Bachelor of Education Primary degree was introduced at the University of Swaziland in the early 1990s for teachers who wanted to upgrade their qualification from Diploma level. This is a four degree programme in the same areas of specialization as in the diploma programme offered in the colleges.

Secondary school teachers are trained at the University of Swaziland faculties of Education and Agriculture. The university trains degree teachers in the BED programme in Science, Humanities, Social Science subjects and Commerce. This is a four year degree mainly for teachers who are upgrading their diploma qualifications. The Faculty of Education also offers a one year Post Graduate Certificate in Education (PGCE) to degree holders in the teaching subjects who want to become teachers in at least two teaching subjects. Students study a variety of courses in psychology, sociology, curriculum studies, etc. and they are also expected to complete 12 weeks of teaching practice. The Institute of Education (IDE) at the UNISA has also offered the BED degrees and the PGCE on part time basis since 2009. Teachers with Agriculture and Home Economics Teachers degrees are trained in the Faculty of Agriculture in Luyengo under the department of Agricultural Education. The University also trains teachers at Masters level. In recent years there has been an increase of teachers enrolling for Masters degrees. These are school administrators, college lecturers and classroom teachers.

In recent years there have been some universities that have been started in the country for offering training for teachers. The Zimbabwean Midland State University in collaboration with Africa Management Development Institute

(AMADI) are offering diploma and degree courses in Swaziland. A large number of teachers are taking these programmes. MSU also offers the Master in Education (MEd) degree for teachers.

In-service teacher education

There are a number of institutions and organizations that provide in-service teacher education in Swaziland with the aim of improving teaching quality. These are the Inspectorate in the Ministry of Education, the In-service Department at UNISWA focusing on science and mathematics teacher improvement programmes, the subject associations and examination of the subject panels. Putsoa et al. (1999) point out in relation to teacher education that the quality of education is often expressed in terms of two levels, the process level and the product level. The process level focuses on the teaching and learning process. Manyatsi and Kelly (2002) argue that improving the quality at the process level will improve the product level, and it is hoped that student achievement would improve. The different reasons for in-service education in Swaziland can be classified as;

- Extension of knowledge where teachers acquire more refined expertise, more knowledge in a subject area;
- Acquaintance with curriculum developments – where courses are developed to introduce serving teachers to a new curriculum that is being introduced in schools;
- Introduction to new teaching methods and teaching aids which promise better results to pupils, teachers and society;
- Conversion courses – this takes place when the Ministry of Education in a country discovers that there are marked discrepancies in the supply of its educational services.

Current issues and problems

Swaziland is currently faced with a number of challenges that are likely to have an adverse effect on the quality of education. These include, among others:

- Serious financial problems making implementation of the ministry programmes and projects difficult;

- The large number of orphaned and vulnerable children who depend on the government for financial assistance to pay for their education. A large portion of the finances caters for these children;
- Overcrowding in classrooms is common as a result of free primary education;
- The large class sizes in some schools raise quality issues;
- Teacher shortage and the use of unqualified teachers at primary school level;
- The shortage of teachers for critical subjects such as Mathematics, Science and ICT in secondary and high schools;
- The constant teacher strikes affects the quality of education;
- Poor resources in schools affect the quality of teaching and learning;
- Teacher professionalism is at a low level and there is an increase in teacher misconduct seen in the rise in cases of teacher–pupil relationships in schools;
- Increasing abuse of school resources and funds, even examination fees;
- The school leaving qualification does not serve the interests of the public as many parents now send their children to South African schools so that they can have a qualification for entry to universities in that country; hence the need for a higher qualification beyond the current school leaving qualification in Swaziland;
- The curriculum is not meeting the needs of the country. Aligning the world of school to the world of work is still a major challenge. This is seen in the hundreds of school graduates who are unemployed and in the hundreds of tertiary graduates who are also unemployed;
- Concentration of well-trained and experienced teachers in urban areas is a big challenge as teachers refuse to take appointments in some rural schools thus disadvantaging learners in rural schools;
- Since education is not compulsory, there are many children who do not attend school because there is no law that requires all school-going children to be in school;
- The CA introduced in primary schools is not popular with teachers who are not committed to teaching (www.ibe.unesco.org).

Conclusion

Though the education system in Swaziland has achieved a lot in terms of putting children in school or in quantitative terms, there is still a major challenge in addressing quality issues in the education system. The problems in dealing with the high number of orphaned and vulnerable children in the system are still a reality to be addressed by the Ministry of Education working closely with other ministries and agencies. The offering of free primary education, though seen as responding to a social need for education, is also facing serious challenges as the government introduced this programme with limited resources. The emerging problems are that classrooms are overcrowded, teachers are not well qualified and resources are not available. This is likely to affect the quality of education in primary schools. Teacher morale and professionalism is also affecting the education system negatively as many teachers are reported to be abusing the children they teach. There is also a huge challenge with regard to the quality of principals managing the schools as most of them lack leadership skills and strategic plans to manage the schools effectively.

References

Cazziol, R. J. (2002). 'The development of education in Swaziland', in B. E. M. Dlamini and R. J. Cazziol (eds), *Theory and Practice of Education* (Manzini: Ruswanda Publishing Bureau), pp. 36–43.

CIE (2011). *Examiners' Report: Information Communication Technology (ICT)* (Cambridge: Cambrigde International Examinations).

Dlamini, M. (1972). *The Aims and Objectives of the Imbokodvo National Movement* (Mbabane: Swaziland Printing and Publishing).

Examinations Council of Swaziland (2012). 'Examinations Report', ECOS Ezulwini.

Fafunwa, A. B. (1974). *History of education in Nigeria* (London: George Allen and Unwin).

— (1993). 'The Changing Patterns of Education in Nigeria', *Education Today* 6, 3, pp. 19–26.

Gathu, K. and Mazibuko, E. (2010) 'Education Reform in Swaziland', in C. C. Wolhuter and H. D. Herman (eds), *Education Reform in Southern Africa: Prospects for the New Millenium* (Potchefstroom: CC Wolhutter), p. 137.

Isaacs, S. (2007). 'ICT in education in Swaziland', Survey of ICT and education in Africa: Swaziland country report. www.infodev.org

Manyatsi, S., Kelly, V. (2002). 'Professional development of secondary teachers through INSET: Experiences in Swaziland', in B. E. M. Dlamini and R. J. Cazziol (eds), *Theory and practice of Education* (Manzini: Ruswanda Publishing Bureau), pp. 107–23.

MoE (1996). 'Our Children First: Education and Training Development Strategy', Prepared by the Education and Training Sector Committee of the National Development Strategy. Mbabane.

— (2011). Annual Report of the Ministry of Education and Training. Mbabane.

Msibi, Z. (2010). 'Teaching and Assessment Practices of Secondary and High School History Teachers', Unpublished MEd thesis, University of Swaziland – Faculty of Education, Kwaluseni.

Putsoa, B., Manyatsi, S. and Dlamini, M. (1999). 'Quality and equity in MST education for secondary education', Unpublished paper presented at the 4th BOLESWA Mathematics, Science ant Technology Education conference held at the Maseru Sun Cabanas Hotel, Lesotho, 8–13 August.

Shabalala, J. (2011). 'Progress in Gender Equality in Education', Swaziland, www.sacmeg.org

Swaziland Government (1978). 'National Development Plan 1978–1983', Mbabane: Government Printer.

Sebenta National Institute (2011). Strategic Plan. Mbabane.

UNESCO (2000). 'The Dakar Framework for Action: Education for All – Meeting our Collective Commitments', World Education Forum, Dakar Senegal, 26–28 April. Paris: UNESCO.

— (2003). Education for All Global Monitoring Report 2003/2004: Gender and Education for All: The Leap to Equality (Paris, UNESCO).

UNISWA (2012). *University of Swaziland Calender 2011/2012* (Kwaluseni: UNISWA).

United Nations (2006). *The Millennium Development Goals Report 2006* (New York, United Nations). www.ibe.unesco.org/international/ICE/natrap/Swaziland.pdf. Accessed 15 September 2009.

World Bank (2010). The Education System in Swaziland. Training and Skills Development for Shared Growth and Competitiveness (Washington, DC: The World Bank), p. 57.

Zondo, Z. (2009). 'Implementing a New History Curriculum in Swaziland: An Exploratory Study of the Perceptions and Professional Roles of Teachers and Students', Unpublished MEd thesis, University of Swaziland, Kwaluseni. Faculty of Education.

10

Zimbabwe: From Education
Reform to Political Instability

Aaron T. Sigauke
University of New England

Introduction

Education in Zimbabwe, as in other developing countries, is regarded as central and critical in the political, economic and social development of the country. Over the years, from the pre- to the post-independence era, the state of the education system has seen major changes following similar changes in the political landscape of the country. This chapter discusses, first, the historical and political background of the country focusing especially on the provision of education during the colonial era in the country. This background is important as it provides a basis for understanding policy changes in education put in place at independence and developments during the first two decades after independence. The rest of the chapter focuses on the current status of the education system resulting from the country's politico-economic developments over the last decade.

Historical and political background of the country as a context for education

Pre-independence education policies

To understand the present state of the education system in Zimbabwe it is necessary that we briefly look at the country's pre-independence political, economic and social conditions that are the context to this discussion. This is important because it influenced decisions on policy changes at and after independence about the nature of the education system in the country. Zimbabwe gained its independence in 1980 after about 90 years of colonialism during which legalized discrimination based on race and colour divided the country's population (Chung & Ngara, 1985). That division was reflected in the economy, education, health and other social service areas at the time. During that period a racially divided education system prepared 'white' young people for economic and political dominance while 'blacks' were politically and economically powerless (Zvobgo, 1997). These discriminatory practices led to a society divided into racial and social classes that included the elite, middle, working, under-employed and the unemployed in urban centres and subsistence peasants in the rural areas.

The education system was divided into two: the European Department of Education which catered for white, Asian and mixed race ('coloured') children on the one hand and the Division of African Education for blacks on the other. This separatist and dual system of education was also reflected in the budget and other resource allocations, types and distribution of schools for the two races, ownership and administration of schools and student completion rates at all levels of the education system. European education was compulsory up to the age of 15, funding for the white child was 20 times more than that allocated to the black child who could just drop out after six or seven years of primary education because of financial constraints and other factors. A number of government instruments were put in place to legalize and justify the system, for example, the Education policy of 1966, Education Act 1979 and others (Dorsey, 1989). As a result of this segregated education system there was very little social contact or interaction between students from the different races and the unequal quality of education was determined by these factors. Further to the racial nature of the whole system, in 1966 the government introduced junior secondary (F2) schools in the African Division of Education with a strong vocational bias alongside the F1 system with an academically-biased curriculum. The F2 schools' students and teachers were stigmatized as inferior by the public since they were associated with 'less able' students who could not be absorbed in the few academically-oriented F1 schools available. F2 schools were seen as a further attempt by the colonial government to deny academic education to the African child and to divide the African population by academic capabilities. However, although the F2 system was discontinued after 1980, the need to ensure that students acquired practical skills during their school career was kept alive as witnessed by the introduction of practical subjects in the secondary school curriculum at and after independence. Every secondary school student after 1980 was expected to study one of these practical subjects. That policy still stands today.

Policy changes at independence and the state of education up to 1990

At independence in 1980 the government carried out a number of reforms in education and training meant to address the above racial imbalances and to meet the country's current and future political, social and economic developmental needs and goals. Reforms were centred on the democratization, and especially the de-racialization, of the education system, that is, making it available to all irrespective of race, gender, class, ethnicity, religion and other differences (Peresuh, 1998; Presidential Commission, 1999). With the adoption of a socialist ideology education was seen as a basic human right to which every citizen had an entitlement, for children to develop mentally, physically and emotionally and therefore changes in education and other areas that had been marginalized during the colonial period were viewed as a must. As a follow up to this and the government's principle of 'Growth with Equity' a number of strategies were implemented. These included free and universal primary education which meant that the highest portion of the national budget allocation went to education to cater to the increased need in the provision of educational infrastructure in areas where schools were inadequate, especially in rural areas where the majority of the previously disadvantaged population lived. It also included the introduction of adult literacy programmes in order to eradicate illiteracy and at the same time promoting self-actualization (Dorsey, 1989), a diversified curriculum, especially in the scientific and technical subjects at the secondary school level and attention to the pre-school education programme. A number of new subjects were introduced in the curriculum including Political Economy, Education with Production (EWP) and Education for Living (EFL) all meant to get students to learn about socialism, the new political ideology (Sigauke, 2011). At the time of its work the Presidential Commission noted that, compared to the pre-independence period:

> There were three times as many children in primary school and twelve times as many in secondary schools. We now have 13 technical and vocational training colleges. About three thousand students graduate each year compared to three hundred who graduated in 1980. (Presidential Commission, 1999: xxv)

There were, however, also negative consequences to these changes: for example, an unprecedented increase in enrolment in schools led to overcrowding, resource shortages (both human and material) and a persistently high demand on budget allocation to education. Quantity does not always match with quality: for the education system in Zimbabwe it was difficulty to maintain a high pass rate in schools facing the above shortages especially in rural areas. The system remained, to some extent, highly differentiated, competitive and stratified.

Education and the economic structural adjustment programme: 1990 to 2000

Problems cited above led to questions about how successful this reform process had been and became an area of focus by researchers on education in post-colonial Zimbabwe. Writing on post-colonial reforms in education in the country Zvobgo (1994, 1996, 1997) points out that there were still glaring contradictions between policy announcements and events on the ground. For instance, there was still evidence of social inequality based on the class structure. A number of elite educational institutions were being established. There was also the problem of the unemployment of educated young people, an indication of the irrelevance of the curriculum to the job needs of learners. During the first decade of independence the school leaver unemployment rate was rising at the annual rate of 200,000 and was predicted to have increased by the year 2000 (Zvobgo, 1994: 95). Perhaps one of the most serious problems was the heavy financial burden faced by government as a result of the socialist ideology adopted at independence, that is, fee-free primary education and health services. As a solution, cost recovery measures in the form of the Economic Structural Adjustment Programme (ESAP) prescribed by the International Monetary Fund (IMF) and the World Bank (WB), were adopted.

Adopting a capitalist solution in the form of ESAP was a humiliating decision for a government that had proclaimed a socialist ideology at independence since this meant a complete reversal of that ideology. It also ushered in high political costs for leaders and social costs for society in general. It generally meant cutting government expenditure through scaling down on the size of the civil service, commercializing or privatization of state enterprises and withdrawing subsidies including fee-free primary education, meaning that parents had to pay school fees (Zhou & Zvoushe, 2012). This had a big toll across all sectors. In the area of education the poor, especially in rural areas, could not afford school fees, therefore many children could not attend school resulting in a decline in enrolments, especially of the girl child. Government per capita spending per child went down and resources became depleted. Outside the education system, many people lost their jobs resulting in widespread unemployment and poverty. Money from the Social Development Fund (SDF), meant for orphans and other disadvantaged groups was not enough for school fees and other needs. The decentralization of financial and other administrative duties meant that poor rural councils could not run schools in the same way as those run by rich councils. This left poor rural schools unable to maintain infrastructure, build new ones or buy resources. The result was that children's performance went down, teachers became demoralized because of low salaries and a de-motivating work environment resulting in some teachers leaving the teaching profession. This state of affairs has culminated in labour and civic group demonstrations which have become common during the last two decades. Up to 1998 there had not been any comprehensive review carried out on the education system. It was during this period that a commission was set up whose mandate was 'to investigate the need for fundamental changes to the current curriculum at all levels' (Presidential Commission, 1999: i).

The current situation in education: 2000 to the present

The current state of, and policies on, the education system follow from recommendations of the Presidential Commission of Inquiry into Education and Training (1999), though some aspects have remained unchanged even well after these recommendations. By 2003 the unemployment figure in Zimbabwe was estimated to be at 60 per cent, made up mostly of young people (Organisation for Economic Cooperation and Development (OECD), 2003). This figure has gone up since then. Other groups in the country, for instance girls, continue to be marginalized. The dichotomy in the quality of education between rural and urban schools is still present. The Ministries of Education, Sport and Culture and Higher and Tertiary Education (2004) also cite problems of infrastructure, manpower and resource shortages, poverty, gender inequality and the irrelevance of the curriculum to job requirements. It appears that education has not been able to provide the needed manpower for the economy, neither has the economy been able to finance reforms in education. Contrary to the often supposed positive link between education and the economy (Fagerlind & Saha, 1983; Carnoy & Samoff, 1990), a mismatch is observed in Zimbabwe. This has led to social problems especially with regard to the unemployment of the educated young people. Writing on problems related to youth unemployment in Zimbabwe Zvobgo notes that:

> Society has tended to write off youth as arrogant and impatient when, in fact, the contrary is often true . . . Driven to desperation the unemployed youth will resort to crime and other socially deviant methods of raising means of livelihood. (1999:192)

Political, economic and other social problems that are consequences of an unstable political environment have been on the increase and have persisted up to 2012. The socio-politico-economic meltdown which rose to a peak in 2008 worsened the situation leading to further demoralization of staff and students in the education sector, a sense of insecurity and 'brain drain' to neighbouring and overseas countries.

Generally the Presidential Commission Report mentioned above has become the basis for current educational policies in Zimbabwe. The following sections present more detailed discussions of current issues concerning the education system in Zimbabwe.

Main goals and priorities for education

The main goals and priorities of education in Zimbabwe announced at independence in 1980 have not changed much in spite of ideological shifts at different points over the years (see section entitled Policy changes at independence and the state of education up to 1990). These are re-stated in a number of subsequent policy documents including the current policy on education. Education is still regarded a basic human right and therefore 'Education for All (EFA)' is a priority for all citizens irrespective 'of race, colour gender, creed, place of origin or any other considerations' (Zimbabwe National Commission for UNESCO, 2001). It is viewed as central to the political, economic and social development of the country. Therefore at all levels attention is directed towards the following objectives: That education has to:

- Contribute to the nation's social and economic development through training in the fields of science and technology, ICT education and entrepreneurial skills;
- Promote values of patriotism and ubuntu philosophy through citizenship education (see Sigauke, 2011);

- Develop a distinctive way of life with a mutual recognition and enrichment of the diverse culture including local languages that had been neglected in the past (see Kanyongo, 2005);
- Teach life skills education, population education, Human Immunodeficiency Virus (HIV)/Acquired Immunodeficiency Syndrome (AIDS) and health education and education for poverty reduction, peace and a sustainable future.

It is believed that by addressing these objectives education would promote the nation's position in a global village. As noted in previous sections a number of negative political and economic factors are making it difficult to achieve these objectives and in some cases have reversed achievements that had been registered after independence.

Basic structures of the education system in the country

Education in Zimbabwe falls under two ministries: the Ministry of Education, Sports and Culture and the Ministry of Higher Education and Technology. The Ministry of Education, Sports and Culture administers the Basic (Early Childhood) Education (ECE) programme, the primary and secondary education sectors. At the head office the permanent secretary heads the ministry assisted by a director and deputy director of education. For this ministry the country is divided into provincial education regions each region being headed by a Regional Director of Education. Further down the region is divided into districts each with a District Education Officer, accountants and other support staff. It is also at the district level that subject officers are housed. These are specialists in specific subject areas, especially for secondary school subjects. Now and again they visit schools in their districts with new ideas about developments in their subject areas and to provide advice to subject teachers at the school level (GoZ, 2008).

Schooling in Zimbabwe starts with the child attending the ECE programme (at between three and six years). Children spend the last one-year of this programme attending a pre-Grade I class (often referred to as 'Grade Zero') which is attached to an existing primary school and in preparation for their Grade I enrolment. Primary schooling is a seven-year cycle from Grade I at about six years of age up to Grade VII at about 12 years of age when they write a national examination. For some students this becomes a terminal stage for a number of reasons, including failure to raise fees for secondary education. Secondary schooling follows after the Grade VII examinations and extends over the next six years. Prior to 2002 the first two years of secondary education were for the Junior Certificate level when students wrote examinations to get a certificate. No such examinations are in place now until after four years when students write Ordinary Level examinations. For those who qualify and can afford the fees the last two years of secondary education are spent on Advanced Level studies. This stage ends with a final examination that qualifies candidates for higher and further education if they do well and if they can afford the fees.

The Ministry of Higher Education and Technology administers all tertiary education activities that include teacher education, technical and vocational education and training and university education. Unlike the Ministry of Education, Sports and Culture distribution of Higher Education institutions in the country is not according to any regional/provincial or district education demarcations noted above. However, deliberate efforts have been made to ensure that each province of the country or its administrative centre has some higher education institutions, either a teacher training college, technical/vocational college or university. There are also a number of private higher education institutions at this level that choose to locate in different areas but have to comply with regulations of the Ministry of Higher Education and Technology. Currently there are 14 teacher training colleges (11 for primary and three for secondary schools), 29 vocational/skills training centres, eight polytechnics/technical colleges, seven universities and two colleges affiliated to the University of Zimbabwe (GoZ, 2008). Universities are administered by university councils and senates.

Entry to the different areas of higher education depends on the candidate's performance at the secondary school level. For university education successful completion of and a good pass at 'A' Level is a requirement depending also on the course to be studied at university level. An 'O' Level pass is the minimum requirement for teacher and vocational/technical education and training.

School management at the local level

The section above has outlined the structure of the Ministry of Education, Sports and Culture from head office down to the district level. At the school level, while all teaching and some administrative staff are government employees private authorities have some influence on the way their schools are run, including resource allocation and salaries for ancillary staff. These include council schools, church schools and schools privately owned by individuals or companies.

Typically, whether private or government owned, primary or secondary school, day or boarding school, the management structure at the school level (administration) is headed by the headmaster/mistress, a deputy head and senior teacher (secondary school) or teacher-in-charge (primary school) (GoZ, 1996). These are involved in the day-to-day management of the school affairs and in most cases the head does not have teaching duties. At the secondary school level subject areas are coordinated by heads of departments who are subject specialists in their departments. Boarding schools also have structures that manage student affairs in the boarding areas. In addition to providing advice on academic matters district education officers also discuss administrative issues with the school administration when they visit schools.

Post-independence policy regulations, especially after the adoption of ESAP, require that local communities should be involved in some way in the running of schools. This has led to the formation of School Development Committees (SDC) made up of members of the School Parents Associations (SPA). SDCs are responsible for infrastructural developments at their schools, for example, buildings, sporting fields and the purchasing of school vehicles, stationary and books. This leads to questions about equity – the level of development in any particular school is thus determined by the economic power of the local authority and the SDC. The decentralization of administrative and financial responsibilities, in some ways perpetuates inequity in education as some disadvantaged, poor areas struggle to improve their infrastructure and purchase of the necessary equipment while rich ones can do so with few financial difficulties. Money for SDCs is sourced through charging levies to parents whose children attend classes at particular schools. Students at rural schools tend to come from peasant family backgrounds; their parents find it difficult to raise the required fees and levies. This negatively impacts on the quality of schooling at these schools and ultimately on student performance in examinations. However, it is not only the social class structure that determines access to and quality of education a child receives but also other equity factors, as discussed in the next section.

Equity issues

Equity in education is about inclusion of individuals and groups of individuals who are disadvantaged because of a number of reasons. These may be excluded from the education system due to their race, colour, social class, gender, health status (HIV/AIDS) or age.

The democratization of the education system in Zimbabwe in 1980 was meant to do away with the unequal access to education that was mainly due to the racial policies of the pre-independence governments. Changes at independence involved the disbanding of the racially divided system that classified schools as A, B and C, expanding access to education by all children through opening opportunities at all levels of education, the diversification of the curriculum and positive discrimination in the allocation of government grants to schools (poor schools getting more than rich ones). However, critics have pointed out that the decentralization of responsibilities to local authorities has resulted in unequal distribution of resources because of differences in class and status between communities (Edwards & Tisdell, 1990). Furthermore, negative attitudes associated with social class differences still exist and are constraints to achieving equity in education. For example, regarding the racially motivated unequal distribution of resources during the pre-independence era it is observed that the former 'whites only' schools (Group A) are still better resourced compared to others. Access to such resources is now being determined by one's class status rather than by race or skin colour. The impact of social class is very much evident in the discrepancies in educational opportunities and school quality between rural areas and urban centres. Opportunities and quality of schooling are still better in the latter than in the rural areas (Edwards & Tisdell, 1990). Again still related to social class, schools and students who can afford foreign currency can pay for and write the 'prestigious' Cambridge Examinations which are internationally recognized other than the local ZIMSEC examinations. This affords them opportunities to study abroad in better-resourced institutions.

While attempts have been, and are being, made to address unequal access to education due to racial, colour and social class differences other factors, for instance gender, still make it difficult for some children to access quality education (Peresuh & Ndawi, 1998). With regards to gender almost every educational policy at various stages after independence mentions gender, especially regarding female participation in education, as an area deserving attention. The neglect of female participation in education in some ways arises from deep-rooted negative attitudes of the male-dominated society towards girls who are regarded as traditionally responsible for the everyday domestic chores and therefore are not expected to leave home. This was worse in the pre-independence era when policies did not even recognize gender inequality in education for the black African girl child. As a result girls received low priority when families considered sending children to school. This is, however, changing with new policies introduced after independence. At independence female participation at all levels of education was given priority (Kanyongo, 2005). Private and non-governmental organizations (NGOs) have also come in to help promote female participation in education through paying school fees, examination fees, levies, encouraging girls to go to school and making society in general aware of the value of sending the girl child to school (ZWRCN, 2012). Currently, compared to the pre-independence period, there has been an increase in the enrolment of girls at all levels of the education system but figures are still low compared to boys (Zimbabwe National Commission for UNESCO, 2001). Poverty resulting from the political and economic crises in the country affects the girl child in education more than it does boys as girls are forced to drop out of school first when fees are difficult to raise. At the higher education level, especially teacher training, policy specifies that 51 per cent of first year enrolments should be female students and 49 per cent males (GoZ, 2005).

Another group that had previously been neglected in education is that of people with disability. During the pre-independence era disabled children were cared for by mission stations and non-governmental organizations. They were segregated in society and therefore given little opportunity in education. Now it is government responsibility to make sure that people with disability receive the same quality of education like their able-bodied counterparts. A Division of School Psychological Services has been established which is responsible for the early identification of affected children and putting in place a Special Needs Education programme. Government has also set up other structures to cater for people with special needs, for example, the National Education Audiological Laboratory and the National Braille Printing Press (Zimbabwe National Commission for UNESCO, 2001).

The HIV/AIDS pandemic has affected a number of children who have had to withdraw from school as they become orphans and cannot raise the finances needed for school fees, examination fees and levies. In terms of gender this has again affected girls more than boys as circumstances force them to remain at home doing most of the domestic duties in a family affected by the disease. However, a social safety network, established in 2001, is in place: the Basic Education Assistance Module (BEAM). This is meant to assist children from poor backgrounds especially orphans affected by HIV/AIDS with their school and examination fees and levies. It is still not enough bearing in mind the large number of children in these circumstances (GoZ, 2005).

Age, that is, the old aged and those regarded as too young to go schools, is mentioned in policy documents and is taken into account in trying to address equity issues in education. For the very young pre-school programmes are available for children from three to six years of age (see section titled Policy changes at independence and the state of education up to 1990). At independence the government established Adult and Non-Formal Education programmes for adult literacy and lifelong learning. Currently Zimbabwe has the highest literacy rate of 92 per cent in sub-Saharan Africa (World Bank, 2011).

Zimbabwean society is made up of a number of ethnic groups, some in a very minority proportion of the population. They have expressed disappointment that they are being marginalized in the education system in that their languages have, for a long time, not been recognized in the curriculum. In response current policies have recognized minority group languages and have now incorporated them in the school curriculum (see also the section on curriculum).

Nature of the curriculum, teaching methods and assessment in schools

Curriculum

Zimbabwe's school curriculum at different levels follows recommendations of the Presidential Commission on Education and Training (1999). The responsibility for designing the curriculum, developing resources and teaching/learning strategies lies with the Curriculum Development Unit (CDU) within the Ministry of Education, Sports and Culture (GoZ, 2008).

English is the official language of instruction at most levels. However, at the primary level rural schools only start using English at Year (Grade) III while for urban schools it is used from Year (Grade) I. Other subjects at the primary level include Mathematics, Shona/Ndebele (local languages) and Content (natural and social sciences). Currently, indigenous languages of some minority ethnic groups who felt marginalized are included in the curriculum (see section on equity issues). In addition to academic subjects primary school children take part in a number of co-curriculum activities (sporting and cultural) sometimes competing with other schools (USAP Global, 2008). At the secondary level subjects fall into three groups:

- Technical, Vocational and Commercial/Business Studies (including ICT);
- Humanities, including HIV/AIDS Education;
- Mathematics and Science.

The Presidential Commission also recommended Citizenship Education which is still to be implemented after facing criticism for being politically biased (see Sigauke, 2011). At the junior secondary school level (Forms 1 and 2) students take eight subjects (academic and practical). Practical subjects are heavily gender biased with girls taking Food and Nutrition and Fashion and Fabrics while boys take Building and Carpentry. Both boys and girls study Agriculture, a key commercial and subsistence activity for the country.

At the middle secondary school level (Ordinary Level: Forms 3 and 4) students carry on with subjects studied at the junior level but may also take up other subjects not offered at the junior level. Subjects offered and subject choice by the student depend on the school attended (rural/urban, private/public) and availability of resources (human and material). For both the student and their parents choice of subjects is done with a view for a future career in the subject area selected. However, in many cases such ambitions are not fulfilled for a number of reasons. A narrowing of the number and type of subject areas selected at 'A' Level, the last two years of the six-year secondary school cycle, is again done with future career prospects in mind. However, very few candidates go for 'A' Level, the majority take up other courses or remain unemployed after their 'O' Level studies. At 'A' Level the student usually takes three subjects either in the sciences, commercial subjects or Arts area plus a compulsory English for Communication course (General Paper before 2004). This specialization also determines the area of study at university if the student decides to proceed to university. As with the primary school curriculum, secondary school students are involved in a number of sporting and cultural activities, competing at the school level and between schools at the district, provincial and national levels (USAP Global, 2008).

Teaching/learning strategies

The CDU is responsible for designing syllabuses, resources and teaching/learning strategies. The unit produces learning kits, tests them before they are sent into schools and evaluates them when they are in schools. Considering that students are from various social and intellectual backgrounds teachers are expected to be sensitive to all students so that each child feels that their work is recognized and worthwhile and that they are getting the attention they deserve (GoZ, 2005). This means that a diversity of innovative teaching/learning methodologies have to be used. These include child-centred and discovery approaches which are motivating to young people so that they desire to be in school. CDU suggests the following approaches: experimentation, group activities, inquiry/discovery methods, collaborative teaching and learning, debates, discussions, role play, interactive drama, value clarification and the use of audio-visual aids such as radios, visual clips, posters and computer assisted learning. However, some of these are only available in well-to-do schools. As previously noted not all schools can afford resources (human and material) to go with the suggested teaching/learning strategies.

Assessment

At all levels, end of primary (Grade VII), 'O' and 'A' Levels, assessment is by both coursework (continuous formative assessment) and final examinations (summative assessment). The local Zimbabwe Schools Examinations Council (ZIMSEC) administers examinations: sets examinations, is responsible for their marking and the release of results. The examination pass rate is regarded as one of the major indicators of quality education in Zimbabwe. Much emphasis is placed on examinations as they provide access to higher education and careers. Provinces, districts and schools are also rated by how well their students pass examinations. At the Grade VII level (end of primary schooling) examinations are important for entry to the secondary school level, Form 1; however, every child is entitled to a place at Form 1 whether or not they pass Grade VII. However, most schools screen students depending on how well they pass at Grade VII, another factor leading to classification of schools into 'good and not so good'. Results for each subject range from Grade I (highest) to Grade X (lowest). Students do not pay fees to write this examination.

At both 'O' and 'A' Levels examination fees are required before a student sits for examinations. 'O' Level results are important for entry to 'A' Level, employment and training (teaching, nursing and others). Pass grades range from A (highest) to C (lowest) with D, E and U as fails. The student is expected to pass at least five subjects including the English language, which is compulsory. Other courses also demand a pass in some specific subject areas, for instance, Mathematics and Science. At 'A' Level a good pass in three subjects guarantees students a place in university or they may be considered appropriate by employers or for training purposes. Pass grades range from A (highest) to E (lowest). Marking of student examination scripts at all levels is done by experienced teachers who are at least holders of a diploma in education. These are trained as markers in their subject areas of specialization. Up to 2002 'O' and 'A' Level examinations were set and marked by the Cambridge Examination Board in the United Kingdom until they were localized when ZIMSEC was formed. However some schools, mostly private, still offer Cambridge examinations which are viewed as internationally recognized and therefore give students opportunities to study outside the country. Taking a Cambridge examination at these schools depends, however, on one's ability to pay the high examination fees often charged in foreign currency.

Organization and nature of teacher education, teacher recruitment and supply and remuneration and professionalism

Teaching is one of the once-highly esteemed professions in the country which has at the moment lost that respect as teachers lead an almost destitute life due to the political and economic crises that has gripped the country in the last ten years, especially since 2008.

Organization and nature of teacher education

The Ministry of Higher Education and Technology administers all tertiary education activities including teacher education. There are 14 teacher-training colleges (11 for primary and three for secondary schools). In addition to teacher training colleges universities also offer postgraduate teacher education diploma training programmes for university graduates who wish to take up teaching as a career, undergraduate degrees in education for teachers who do not hold degrees and master of education programmes for teachers who are already holders of degrees in education (Ministries of Education, Sport and Culture and Higher Education, 2004; GoZ, 2008). The Zimbabwe Government has an agreement with the Government of Cuba for training Zimbabwean secondary school teachers of science and mathematics, a critical area of teacher shortage in the country. Unlike schools with district and provincial administrative structures teacher colleges are centrally administered directly from the head office headed by the secretary of the ministry. At the local level the principal, a deputy principal and a number of department heads make up the college administration. Teacher training colleges are affiliated to the University of Zimbabwe through the Department of Teacher Education at the university responsible for curriculum development, quality control, assessment (coursework and examinations) and student graduation.

Enrolment at teacher colleges depends on a good pass at 'O' Level for a primary school teacher college and at 'A' Level for enrolment at a secondary school teacher college. In some cases in-service programmes are offered to qualified teachers already in the field who wish to upgrade their qualifications. The length of time spent in training and the disciplines studied depend on the level at which the student-teacher will teach after graduation. Training for primary school teaching is usually three years. The student specializes in two subjects but also covers the entire primary school curriculum. This is in addition to the study of professional disciplines such as philosophy, psychology, sociology and pedagogy. At the secondary level teacher training usually takes two years in a specific subject area to be taught at secondary school level in addition to professional disciplines mentioned for primary school teaching. In addition to academic studies at colleges students go into schools for teaching practice sessions varying from one term to five terms; for example, the Zimbabwe Integrated Teacher Education Course (ZINTEC) has a 2–5-2 Model for Teacher Training. This means that, following the three term-sessions per year for schools, student-teachers spent two terms at college, five terms on teaching practice and two terms at college before graduating. This gives them more time training on the job and helps reduce the number of untrained teachers in schools (see GoZ, 2005: 29 for statistics). Assessment at teacher colleges is by coursework, teaching practice and a final written examination.

Teacher recruitment and supply

The majority of teachers in Zimbabwe are civil servants employed by the government whether they are in private or government schools with very few being employed by local authorities. At the end of their training qualified teachers have an option to apply for teaching posts in either privately owned or in government schools. The majority of government schools are in urban areas and attract applications from teachers because of the better conditions in urban areas. However, government policy is that newly qualified teachers have to start from areas of teacher shortages – rural areas. There is still a wide disparity between rural and urban areas in terms of teachers with relevant qualifications and experience. Few want to go to rural areas where schools face problems of accommodation, electricity, water, transport and teaching resources. Currently, even in urban schools, teachers have low morale because of low salaries and unattractive working conditions (Zhou & Zvoushe, 2012).

Remuneration

Perhaps the worst demoralizing factor at the moment is the salary structure which is very low for teachers and lecturers in teacher training colleges. This has resulted in a 'brain drain', especially of the science and mathematics teachers as they leave to neighbouring and overseas countries (Ministries of Education, Sport and Culture and Higher and Tertiary Education (2004)). While government has made promises to review teacher salaries little has been done to address the situation. Over the last few years teacher unions have mobilized members to boycott teaching over issues of low wages and other bad working conditions worsened by the political and economic crises.

Professionalism

Professionalism in the field of education is characterized by, among others, three attributes: professional knowledge, professional practice and professional engagement (Giddens, 1993). Professional knowledge, the first one, is about knowledge of how students learn, that is, the process by which students acquire knowledge, skills and attitudes; about knowledge of how to teach, that is, how best teachers can make students learn what they want them to learn; about knowledge of the subject content that students will learn and about knowledge of learners motivations: what motivates one student differs from what motivates the other. The second attribute, professional practice, is to do with effective planning, effective assessment using appropriate formal and summative assessment methods, creating and maintaining safe and challenging environments that are conducive for learning and using a range of resources to engage students in effective learning. The third and last, professional engagement, is about teacher reflection, evaluation and improvement on professional knowledge and practice and being active members of the teaching profession, that is, belonging to and participating in professional associations.

In the first two decades of independence Zimbabwe's education system was rated as one of the best in sub-Saharan Africa (Presidential Commission, 1999). This was because of the professional level of teacher training, developments in teacher education content, teaching methodologies and regular in-service programmes to upgrade less-qualified teachers. Pre-service programmes were now and again revamped to maintain high quality and professionalism in teacher education (GoZ, 2005). Many teachers also belonged to professional and labour unions that were and are still active in updating members on professional ethics and working conditions. All these activities helped in maintaining high levels of professionalism in education. However, as noted above, the political and economic crises in the country since the beginning of the last decade have undermined the professional integrity of teachers some of whom have been humiliated at political rallies for belonging to and supporting opposition political parties (Shizha & Kariwo, 2011). This has negatively affected the standard of the teaching profession as teachers become demoralized and look for opportunities for careers and professional development elsewhere.

Conclusions, challenges and recommendations

This discussion on the state of education in Zimbabwe has shown that in spite of grand policies made at and progress after independence in 1980 the emergence of an unstable political environment has reversed gains in many areas of society. Policy changes at independence were huge and challenging to the newly independent state but, in a situation of political stability, economic progress and international support, it was possible to establish an education system that became the envy of countries in the region. This involved the allocation of the highest portion of government budget to education, infrastructural developments in areas of need leading to huge school enrolments that resulted in double session classes, innovations in teacher education (ZIMSCI, ZINTEC), equity policies on gender, people with disability, early childhood and adult literacy programmes and innovations in resource and curriculum development that could possibly be a solution to current unemployment problems.

Today the Zimbabwe education system faces many challenges as a result of political instability. Negative events in the political field affect the economy and consequently further trickle down to almost every sphere of society. With particular reference to the education sector almost every aspect of the system is disrupted: basic organizational structures (from the national, provincial, district to the school level) and the demotivation of manpower including teachers and lecturers some of whom consequently fled the country for better places ('brain drain') resulting in acute manpower shortages. This has led to strains on existing manpower leading to weaknesses in the supervision, evaluation and monitoring of activities. At the school level classroom congestion and double sessions in urban schools has led to shortages of resources (textbooks, stationary, furniture) in addition to the deterioration of buildings and other facilities that are in need of repair. An unemployment rate of over 90 per cent (the majority being educated young people) is evidence of some aspects of a curriculum that has become irrelevant to the economic, social and political needs of society. Added to this are problems of school dropouts because of poverty, orphans resulting from the HIV/AIDS pandemic and the persistent inequity issues with regards to gender, disability and adult literacy activities.

There appears, however, to be one possible solution to all these setbacks: a return to the political stability of the 1980s in order to revive and strengthen the economic, educational and other social conditions of the country. Economic growth is necessary for investment in education (increase in government budget allocation to education). Most structures are in place but only need positive conditions of political stability in order to function properly. With regards to HIV/AIDS and poverty there are currently programmes such as the Basic Education Assistance Module (BEAM) scheme, the AIDS levy and the AIDS Education programme providing life skills for both teachers and students. The Inclusive Education programme caters for most groups that were previously left out of the system as result of gender, disability or age. These programmes need a good budget and manpower allocation, strengthening and proper management. The government needs to strengthen its partnership with the private sector, local authorities, NGOs and positive relations with the international community. The curriculum has to be more responsive to the needs of the local communities, for instance, farming in rural areas, craft industries, trade and commerce in urban centres. The unemployment of school and college graduates means that education needs to be relevant to employers and local communities. Linked to this is the need for the electrification of schools in both urban and rural areas if the teaching of ICT is to be a success. Electricity also allows for extended use of school facilities beyond daytime especially in rural areas where adults may only find such time during evenings because of daytime commitments. Improving working conditions, including salaries, will retain and attract qualified staff from within and those who left the country. A large number of highly qualified Zimbabweans are in neighbouring countries and abroad and, like at independence in 1980, would make great contributions not only in the education area of the country but also in other sectors of society if they were to come back. With the formation of the coalition government in 2009 and prospects for a future peaceful political atmosphere, education in Zimbabwe would regain its high status again as was the case in the 1980s.

References

Carnoy, M. and Samoff, J. (1990). *Education and Social Transition in the Third World* (Princeton: Princeton University Press).

Chung, F. and Ngara, E. (1985). *Socialism, Education and Development: A Challenge to Zimbabwe* (Harare: Zimbabwe Publishing House).

Dorsey, B. J. (1989). 'Educational Development and Reform in Zimbabwe', *Comparative Educational Review* 33, 1, pp. 40–58 (Special Issue on Africa).

Edwards, G. and Tisdell, C. (1990). 'Post-independence Trends in Education in Zimbabwe', *South African Journal of Economics* 58, 4, pp. 298–307.

Fagerlind, I. and Saha, L. J. (1983). *Education and National Development: A Comparative Perspective* (Oxford: Pergamon Press).

Giddens, A. (1993). *Sociology* (Cambridge: Polity Press).

Government of Zimbabwe (1996). *Education Act: Chapter 25:04* (Harare: GoZ).

— (2005). *National Action Plan of Zimbabwe: Education for All: Towards 2015* (Harare, Government Printers).

— (2008). 'National Report on the Status of Education: 48th Session of UNESCO International Conference on Education', Geneva, 25–8 November 2008.

Kanyongo, G. Y. (2005). 'Zimbabwe's Public Education System Reforms: Successes and Challenges', *International Education Journal* 6, 1, pp. 65–74.

Ministries of Education, Sport and Culture and Higher and Tertiary Education (2004). 'The national report on the development of education in Zimbabwe', Paper presented at the 47th Session of the International Conference on Education 8–11 September 2004, Geneva, Switzerland.

Organisation for Economic Cooperation and Development (OECD) (2003). *African Economic Outlook 2002/2003 – Country Studies* (Paris: OECD).

Peresuh, M. (1998). 'Post Independence Education in Zimbabwe: Achievements, Constraints and the Way Forward', *Journal of Practice in Education for Development* 3, 3, pp. 129–36.

Peresuh, M. and Ndawi, O. (1998). 'Education for All – The Challenges for a Developing Country: The Zimbabwe Experience', *International Journal of Inclusive Education* 2, 3, pp. 209–24.

Presidential Commission (1999). *Report on the Zimbabwe Presidential Commission of Inquiry into Education and Training* (Harare: Government Printers).

Shizha, E. and Kariwo, M. T. (2011). *Education and Development in Zimbabwe: A Social Political and Economic Analysis* (Rotterdam, The Netherlands, Sense Publishers).

Sigauke, A. T. (2011). 'Citizenship and Citizenship Education: A Critical Discourse Analysis of the Zimbabwe Presidential Commission Report', *Journal of Education, Citizenship and Social Justice* 6, 1, pp. 69–86.

USAP Global (2008). *Education in Zimbabwe.* http://usapglobal.org/zimbabwe/education.htm. Accessed 31 July 2012.

World Bank (2011). *Literacy Rate, Adult Total (% of People Ages 15 and Above).*
www.data.worldbank.org/indicator/SE.ADT.LITR.ZS. Accessed 24 August 2012.

Zhou, G. and Zvoushe, H. (2012). 'Public Policy Making in Zimbabwe: A Three Decade
Perspective', *International Journal of Humanities and Social Sciences* 2, 8, pp. 212–22
(Special Issue).

Zimbabwe National Commission for UNESCO (2001). *The Developments in Education:
The Education System at the End of the 20th Century 1990 – 2000: National Report of
the Republic of Zimbabwe* (Harare, UNESCO International Bureau of Education).

Zimbabwe Women's Resource Centre Network (ZWRCN) (2012). *Gender Budgets
Watch.* March 2004. www.zwrcn.org.zw. Accessed 31 July 2012.

Zvobgo, R. J. (1994). *Colonialism and Education in Zimbabwe* (Harare: SAPES).

— (1996). *Transforming Education: The Zimbabwean Experience* (Harare: College Press).

— (1997). *The State, Ideology and Education* (Gweru: Mambo Press).

— (1999). *The Post Colonial State and Educational Reform: Zimbabwe, Zambia and
Botswana* (Harare: Zimbabwe Publishing House).

Index